R-3076-CHF

Strategies for Controlling Adolescent Drug Use

J. Michael Polich, Phyllis L. Ellickson,
Peter Reuter, James P. Kahan

February 1984

Prepared under a grant from
The Conrad Hilton Foundation

Rand
1700 MAIN STREET
P.O. BOX 2138
SANTA MONICA, CA 90406-2138

PREFACE

This study was sponsored by the Conrad Hilton Foundation as part of an effort to identify the most promising ways in which private initiatives and public policy might reduce the number of adolescents who use drugs.

The study encompasses a broad review of the scientific literature on the nature of drug use and the effectiveness of drug law enforcement, treatment, and prevention programs. It evaluates the prospects for each of the major methods of controlling drug use and suggests an agenda of possible actions. In addition, it identifies the crucial information needed for better articulation of future national efforts to combat drug use.

SUMMARY

At the request of the Conrad Hilton Foundation, The Rand Corporation has undertaken a broad study of measures to control adolescent drug use. The purpose is to evaluate the available evidence on the effectiveness of drug control measures, and to recommend the most promising areas for future private and public programs to reduce the use of drugs by young people.

Illicit drug use is widespread among both adolescents and adults. Programs to control it have employed three principal methods: (1) *enforcement* of drug laws; (2) *treatment* of chronic abusers; and (3) *prevention* of initial drug use. We find that while intensified law enforcement is not likely to reduce adolescent drug use, and the benefits of expanded treatment remain uncertain, prevention programs hold more promise. The most encouraging evidence comes from the success of school-based programs to prevent cigarette smoking, which offer a strategy that may be adaptable to other drugs.

THE SCALE OF DRUG USE

Drug use is a mass phenomenon in the United States. Projections from a 1982 national household survey indicate that 32 million Americans smoke marijuana at least once a year; 20 million smoke it at least once a month. Annual cocaine users number over 12 million. Several million others take hallucinogens, stimulants, sedatives, and tranquilizers without medical supervision. And of course, these figures are dwarfed by the number of people who use legal drugs, including alcoholic beverages (125 million) and tobacco cigarettes (70 million).

Young adults and adolescents are much more likely than older adults to use illegal drugs and to use prescription drugs for nonmedical reasons. Among high school seniors, 29 percent smoke marijuana at least once a month. The other leading psychoactive drugs are alcohol (used by 70 percent of high school seniors) and cigarettes (used by 30 percent). Stimulants are also popular: 11 percent of seniors take amphetamines, and 5 percent use cocaine. These patterns are not concentrated within any particular social or ethnic group or geographic location. Indeed, the wide distribution of drug users distinguishes modern drug use from the patterns of three decades ago.

Drugs are widely available despite legal controls. In a 1982 survey, 88 percent of high school seniors reported that marijuana was easy to get. Even cocaine was rated readily available by 47 percent.

There are many sources for most drugs because it is profitable to produce them. Amphetamines and hallucinogens can be cheaply and easily manufactured in clandestine laboratories. Sedatives such as barbiturates and tranquilizers can be diverted from legitimate pharmaceutical channels, or obtained through forged or improperly written prescriptions. Marijuana grows in all parts of the United States, and domestic production now accounts for an estimated 9 percent of total consumption. For the other 91 percent, foreign sources abound. Among the main illicit drugs, only cocaine is derived from a limited set of sources (a few countries in South America).

Equally important, drugs bring a high price on the U.S. market. Although the raw materials for drugs are cheap, the retail value of every drug is many times its production cost. The value of one kilogram of marijuana, for example, may be only a few dollars on a South American farm, but more than a thousand in a U.S. city. This high mark-up is due to the illegal nature of the business. Drug dealers face many risks: arrest, imprisonment, confiscation of their goods, and theft or violence by others in the market.

These factors make some drugs very expensive. For example, 150 milligrams of 30 percent pure cocaine, enough for a one-hour use session, may cost $25 or more. Because there are so many regular users, the total retail value of illicit drugs is enormous—according to government estimates, at least $53 billion per year. Other estimates suggest the total may be "only" $27 billion, but even so the scale of illicit drug transactions is vast.

RISKS OF DRUG USE

Adolescent drug use is troubling mainly because of the risks in taking psychoactive substances. The principal risks are toxic effects, impairment of function, and the potential for physical or psychic dependence.

The public is justifiably concerned about heroin addiction; however, though heroin is responsible for many serious social problems, it is little used by adolescents, and it accounts for relatively few hospital emergencies or deaths among youth. Moreover, only a small minority of young people use any illicit drug on a daily basis. Most adolescents who take drugs do so occasionally, and only in social situations. Thus, physical dependence or addiction is not the main problem with adolescent drug use.

This is not to say that drugs are harmless for young people. Each class of drugs can have damaging psychological and physical effects. For example, marijuana seldom causes serious toxic reactions, but it does impair memory and motor skills—effects that can be harmful in school or when driving an automobile. Young people may be exposed often to such risks; according to current estimates, 6 percent of high school seniors smoke marijuana every day. There is also some evidence that the compounds in marijuana may contribute to lung disease, immune system disorders, and reproductive dysfunctions.

Stimulants such as cocaine and amphetamines, if taken repeatedly in large doses, can produce temporary but severe disturbances in mental functioning, such as extreme agitation, feelings of persecution, and hallucination. In addition, many heavy users experience profound depression when the drug effect wears off, leading them to take another dose to continue the "high" feeling. This tendency to continue taking a drug, often resulting in frequent use, increased dosage, and psychological dependence on the drug, is a major problem with most psychoactive substances.

The long-term effects of drug-taking raise further concerns. Toxic effects may not appear until long after use has become chronic. It took years of accumulated experience to document the ill effects of cigarette smoking, and the same may be true of marijuana, cocaine, and other drugs. Similarly, the effects of alcohol have only recently been fully documented, and even so the threshold dose for many adverse effects is uncertain. There may be threshold doses for illicit drugs as well, but no one knows what they are.

There are several grounds for special concern about drug use by children and adolescents. First, all psychoactive drugs have acute effects on mood, concentration, and cognitive functioning, including memory, and hence use may interfere with learning and impair school performance.

Second, if a young person will eventually use drugs, it is at least advisable to put off starting as long as possible. Many toxic substances require prolonged exposure to produce an effect, or a long incubation period for the effect to become manifest. Thus, postponing the onset of use reduces the likelihood of adverse effects, and may reduce the chance of becoming a chronic user.

Third, a conservative course of action is especially appropriate when dealing with children and adolescents. In medicine it is generally accepted that a drug should not be administered when it is not known to be safe. When safety is in doubt—for example, during pregnancy or immaturity—special restrictions are often imposed to avoid harm. In the case of illicit drugs, none has been sufficiently studied to warrant a claim of safety.

METHODS OF CONTROLLING DRUG USE

Up to now, the federal government has dominated the nation's drug control effort. In 1982 it spent over $1 billion on drug-related programs. Over 70 percent of that was devoted to law enforcement; most of the remainder went for treatment of adult drug abusers. Only a small part of that effort has been devoted specifically to adolescent drug users, and only a small amount to prevention. Although many communities have drug education curricula and other prevention programs, these approaches have not enjoyed ample funding. Our analysis suggests this emphasis should be reversed. Prevention appears to be more promising than the other two methods of drug control.

Law Enforcement

Law enforcement concentrates almost entirely on the illicit markets for heroin, cocaine, and marijuana. Because few adolescents use heroin, most of our analysis has focused on the latter two drugs. Law enforcement agencies have directed efforts against each of the major market levels: (1) *production,* the cultivation and processing of drug crops such as the cannabis plant, coca leaf, and opium poppy, usually in foreign countries; (2) *import,* the movement of drugs into the United States; (3) *distribution,* the activity of high-level dealers in the domestic drug market; and (4) *retail,* the sale of drugs to consumers. Although these efforts have not eliminated the supply of drugs, they have made drugs more expensive and more difficult to obtain. Nevertheless, further increases in law enforcement activity are not likely to accomplish much more.

We have not attempted to estimate the effects of greatly reduced law enforcement or legalization of drugs. Legalization is most frequently advocated for heroin, as a means of shutting down the illicit market and reducing the crime addicts commit to obtain money for drugs. However, few adolescents use heroin, and few users of other drugs engage in regular criminal activity. Moreover, we have no convincing data on the negative effects legalization might bring. We believe that even under strict regulation, increased availability would stimulate greater drug consumption, which would raise the risks to which the population is exposed. Society would have to weigh these increased risks against any social and economic benefits of the policy. Since we can find no data that suggest the effects of different legal control mechanisms, we have not attempted an analysis of that issue.

The poor prospects for controlling the production level are illustrated by past efforts to reduce opium poppy cultivation in many different countries. These efforts have failed to make a lasting effect on the U.S. market, for reasons that also apply to marijuana and cocaine: (1) Drug crops are more lucrative than most other crops, and hence small farmers have a strong economic incentive to continue production despite government pressure. (2) Governments are often weak in the growing areas, which are typically remote and sometimes controlled by ethnic groups not responsive to the central political power. (3) Many governments are unconcerned about the U.S. drug problem or unsympathetic with U.S. interests. (4) All drugs have several source countries; for marijuana and opium, the number of producers is almost limitless since the crop grows in many climates. When one country's production is curtailed, other producers step in to fill the gap. (5) Because local cultural conditions often allow or encourage a legitimate market in drugs and derivative products, it is difficult to prevent diversion to the illicit market. (6) In many countries, drug cultivation is a traditional economic activity; substitution of other crops is generally not feasible because it would require very costly long-term development to upgrade farmers' skills, provide roads for shipping new crops, and so on. For all these reasons, it would be unrealistic to expect that greater diplomatic or international efforts could significantly constrain the overseas supply of illegal drugs, at least in the foreseeable future.

The prospects for directly affecting the retail market in the U.S. are equally dismal. In the illicit market, each dealer faces many risks and therefore sells to only a few customers to maintain secrecy. This means there is an enormous number of retail dealers—probably over half a million to service the marijuana market alone (which has at least 20 million regular users). Local police make only about 50,000 arrests for marijuana sale each year, and few of those arrests result in imprisonment. We calculate that the probability of imprisonment is probably far less than one percent for a year's dealing in marijuana. Similar conclusions apply to cocaine.

It would be difficult for local police to raise those risks very much. First of all, the available enforcement tactics, such as street patrol and use of informants, do not work well against the cocaine and marijuana trades; traffic in those drugs, unlike heroin, seldom occurs on the street, and most buyers are not involved in other crimes that draw the attention of the police. Second, state and local criminal justice systems already face severe resource constraints and crowded calendars; making more drug cases and imprisoning more dealers would require more prosecution effort, more court time, and more prison space. Finally, the drug traffic is so large that putting far more drug dealers in prison would still cause only a small increase in retail drug prices.

In the face of these problems, the federal government has tried to strike harder at the import level. Interdiction expenditures rose from $83 million in 1977 to $278 million in 1982. Consequently, large quantities of marijuana and cocaine are now seized at the borders and on the seas, perhaps 10 to 30 percent of all drug shipments. The impact on the drug market has not been commensurate, however. For one thing, large quantities of drugs are readily available overseas to replace any shipments that are confiscated. More important, the price structure for all illegal drugs is steeply graduated, with prices rising quickly as a shipment moves through the chain from producer to retailer. A gram of pure cocaine, for instance, is sold for $5 to $10 by a Peruvian refiner and $50 by a U.S. importer "on the beach," but for $625 at retail. Price increases at a high level are passed along to lower-level dealers, but those dealers cannot further raise their prices because of competition among them. Thus, even large price changes at the import level—say, increasing the importer's selling price from $50 to $100— add only a small amount to the ultimate retail cost.

As a result, we find that even doubling the quantity of cocaine seized would raise the price by no more than 4 percent. For marijuana, which is marked up less than cocaine, doubling the seizure rate might increase the retail price by as much as 12 percent; but since a marijuana cigarette sells for about 75 cents at retail, that increase would imply only a 9-cent rise in the price, hardly enough to discourage much consumption.

It has been argued that federal agencies should imprison more couriers who smuggle drugs into the country, but we doubt that doing so would do much to raise retail drug prices. Many South American sailors are willing to engage in smuggling for modest wages. Even if their risks of imprisonment were greatly increased, the additional amount required to compensate them would probably represent less than 1 percent of the drug's retail price.

Finally, federal agencies strive to imprison high-level drug distributors and seize their assets. However, the value of assets seized is trivial in relation to the retail value of drugs. It is true that greater investigative effort could lead to to more incarcerations. Fewer constraints apply here than in the case of local enforcement. The federal government is quite successful in obtaining convictions (nearly 80 percent of drug defendants were convicted in 1982), and federal prisons can hold more drug violators. Nonetheless, investigative techniques that have recently worked well (such as "sting" operations and currency transaction investigations) will probably continue to be effective only against large-scale operations, and only if the dealers remain rather unsophisticated. If the government mounts more such investigations, dealers will presumably take more precautions and shift to smaller-scale transactions.

A large expansion in investigative effort would be costly. We estimate that to increase the price of all drugs by, say, 15 percent, investigative resources would have to be tripled, at least. The cost increase would be perhaps $800 million, a large figure even for the federal government. That amount is, for example, as large as the total budget of the FBI. Such an expansion is unlikely, especially in view of the marginal change it would make in the price of drugs.

For all of these reasons, intensified law enforcement does not appear to be the best recourse. We do not thereby mean to imply that enforcement against drug dealers should be abandoned. Enforcement has certainly made drug dealing more risky, and it may make it more difficult for novice users to find dealers. Its effectiveness might be improved by rearranging priorities; for example, the effects of the current large expenditures on interdiction should be weighed against the possible effects of allocating those resources to other purposes, such as investigating high-level dealers or expanding state prison space for drug offenders. On all of these issues, more complete data are badly needed; at present, basic aspects of the drug market, such as retail prices and dealer network structure, are uncertain simply because the government does not collect and collate the information. With more complete information, adjustments might be made at the margin to obtain more efficiency. Nevertheless, hopes should not be raised too high; it does not seem likely that any reasonable law enforcement measures could wipe out the drug traffic or even raise the price of drugs very much.

Treatment

The treatment of drug abuse is a significant industry in the United States. In 1982 there were more than 3000 treatment facilities, accounting for over $500 million in expenditures. Much of this effort was supported by the federal, state, and local governments (63 percent). Over the past few years, federal support for treatment has apparently declined, but treatment still consumes a significant portion of total drug control expenditures.

Nonetheless, there is little consensus among practitioners about the best methods for treating drug abuse, or even the nature of the problem to be treated. Treatment programs vary widely, depending on whether the patient's drug abuse is ascribed to biological malfunctions, personality disorders, interpersonal relationships, or other factors. There *is* general agreement on one point about adolescents: Most young people entering treatment are not physically dependent, and their heavy drug use often appears to grow out of other underlying conditions, such as peer influence, family problems, or difficulty in school.

The existing treatment system does not seem well structured to deal with adolescent drug abusers. People under age 18 made up only 12 percent of patients entering treatment in 1982, and they were not concentrated in units specifically serving young people. Many adolescents receive treatment in programs designed for heroin addicts, even though marijuana is the principal drug of most adolescents entering treatment. (Marijuana accounts for 62 percent of adolescent treatment admissions; the opiates account for only 1.5 percent.) Thus, young drug abusers often find themselves in programs that are inappropriate for their problems.

Scientific evidence on the effectiveness of drug abuse treatment is limited. Most of the systematic evaluations contain design defects such as inadequate outcome measures, absence of appropriate control groups, or lack of randomized assignment to treatments. Nevertheless, the weight of the available evidence suggests that certain forms of treatment—methadone maintenance, drug-free therapy, and residential "therapeutic communities"—work better than no treatment at all.

"Detoxification-only" treatment, which consists largely of custodial care during withdrawal, appears to achieve little if any effect.

The evaluation literature also indicates that the longer a patient remains in treatment, the better the prognosis. "Graduates" have better outcomes than dropouts. This may indicate that patients benefit from greater amounts of treatment, but we cannot rule out the alternative explanation of a "selection effect": more successful patients may elect to remain in treatment. In any event, dropout rates are high; in 1981, 55 percent of patients in drug-free and methadone maintenance programs dropped out; in therapeutic communities, which typically demand more of their patients, the dropout rate was 67 percent.

Obviously, a critical issue is the relative effectiveness of the various possible treatments for adolescents. Unfortunately, we have found no persuasive evidence on that issue. Many observers advocate "early intervention" with young people, before their drug abuse has become severe, but such intervention has not been empirically evaluated. Another approach, family therapy, treats the family as well as the patient, viewing the family relationships as the cause of the young person's drug abuse. Family therapy has received favorable evaluation as a treatment for other psychiatric disorders, and proved effective in one well-designed randomized trial with adult heroin users. However, it has not been tested with adolescent nonopiate abusers, and its potentially high costs must be weighed against its putative benefits.

Because of the limited evidence available on the effectiveness of treatment programs, we cannot recommend any particular one. We therefore urge the development, testing, and evaluation of specific treatment programs for adolescent drug abusers.

Prevention

Our most optimistic conclusions are related to prevention—not because past drug prevention programs have proven eminently successful, which they have not, but because we believe we know why past approaches have failed: They were grounded in incorrect assumptions about why adolescents begin using psychoactive substances. In contrast, we have found encouraging evidence in the success of new smoking prevention programs, which are based on a more appropriate model of adolescent behavior.

Recent longitudinal studies have tracked the process by which adolescents start using drugs. First, it usually starts in a group setting, among their peers or relatives—*social* influences are the main influences on adolescent drug-taking.

Second, young people have a strong desire to appear "grownup" and independent. If drug use is defined as an adult activity and adolescents see older youth or adults taking drugs, they are more likely to imitate that behavior in an attempt to claim a mature status. Third, young people are present-oriented. They are much more concerned with their life at school, their current social milieu, and their acceptance within the adolescent social group than with the long-term risks of their actions. Thus, warnings about future disease are likely to fall on deaf ears.

Most drug use prevention programs do not focus on social factors. The majority of past "drug education" was based on an information-oriented approach: It provided facts about the pharmacology and effects of drugs, often as a lecture by a teacher, physician, police officer, or former drug user. Such programs assume that children use drugs because they are ignorant of the dangers. Unfortunately, there is a wealth of evidence that mere knowledge of the facts does not often affect behavior directly, particularly if social influences contradict the facts. In addition, many previous education efforts were marred by exaggerations or "scare tactics," which today's sophisticated youth easily detect and discount.

Programs in "affective education" have been the other main approach in the past. These programs, such as values clarification, skill development, and efforts to increase self-esteem, have been popular in the past decade but they have not been shown effective by any scientific evaluation. The model for such programs holds that adolescents start using drugs because they lack some essential trait or ability, such as self-esteem, interpersonal skill, or the capacity to translate values into rational decisions. Such traits are valuable, but we have found no credible evidence that improving them reduces drug use. Indeed, the best-implemented example of such a program, which also contained a well-designed evaluation, showed virtually no effects on drug use.

In contrast, we have found several successful new programs based on a social influence model of adolescent behavior, all aimed at preventing cigarette smoking among junior high school students. These programs begin by identifying the messages and arguments in favor of smoking—messages that come explicitly or implicitly from peers, adults, and the media. They show adolescents how to counter those arguments, thus providing an "inoculation" against future pro-smoking influences. Then they teach students effective but socially acceptable methods of resisting pressure to smoke: how to "say no" gracefully. The reasons for wanting to "say no" are illustrated by the short-term effects of smoking, such as bad breath, discolored teeth, and increased carbon monoxide in the blood, rather than by long-term health effects that seem uncertain and far in the future to most young people. These themes are developed by group discussion in a 7th- or 8th-grade classroom, sometimes led by an older peer such as a high school student. Such programs have been successful in preventing adolescent cigarette smoking, reducing the number of smokers by one-third to two-thirds in a number of independent studies.

Programs based on social influence have not been extensively used in drug prevention, but they could be. The same factors that lead to cigarette smoking lead to drug use. Futhermore, recent surveys show that equal proportions of high school seniors believe that regular marijuana use and regular cigarette use pose great risks of harm, and that nearly 60 percent disapprove of occasional marijuana use. Thus, a healthy base of skepticism already exists among adolescents about the wisdom of using marijuana.

In designing a prevention program, we suggest, first, that it be aimed at all adolescents in a given age group ("primary" prevention), not merely those who are already regular or heavy drug users ("secondary" prevention). Because it reaches young people just before or just as they begin experimenting with drugs (typically in the 7th grade), a primary program may prevent or delay drug use for almost all members of the group. The odds are far less favorable for secondary programs, which intervene only when drug use has become a "problem." It is certainly true in this case that an ounce of prevention is worth a pound of cure.

Second, prevention programs should be aimed at particular drugs rather than at all drugs or at "substance abuse" in general. The substances most often used by adolescents—alcohol, cigarettes, marijuana, and stimulants—differ substantially in their effects, their social patterns of use, and the stage of life at which adolescents begin using them. Generally, an adolescent begins drug use with cigarettes or alcohol. Later, he or she may use marijuana, and still later may go on to other drugs. In effect, each stage appears to be a prerequisite for the others. Therefore, stopping or delaying the onset of marijuana use and cigarette smoking may prevent use of later-stage drugs.

This argument, however, does not apply to alcohol. Regular drinking begins earlier than age 12 for a significant minority of adolescents, and hence a 7th-grade prevention program comes too late to affect them. Because alcohol is so much more commonly used by adolescents and adults, and because its use is so widely accepted, we doubt that the prevention approaches we have identified will work against adolescent drinking. Nonetheless, youthful drinking is a serious problem; further work is needed to develop and test approaches to alcohol prevention.

RECOMMENDATIONS FOR THE FUTURE

Future efforts against adolescent drug use should give greater emphasis to prevention, and not continue to pin hopes largely on law enforcement. Below we outline a number of specific initiatives, explained in more detail in the chapter on conclusions and recommendations.

Drug use and smoking prevention. Top priority should be given to developing and testing drug use prevention programs for junior high school students, based on the peer influence model that has been successfully applied to cigarette smoking. Preferably, such a test should evaluate effects of several curricula oriented to different drugs; we recommend targeting cigarettes, marijuana, and possibly pills, with evaluation of the spillover effects on other substances. The effects of the program should be determined using an experimental design, with follow-up of subjects for several years.

Alcohol prevention. No presently available approach to alcohol prevention appears to warrant major investments. However, youthful drinking remains a prime cause of automobile accidents and other serious problems. We therefore recommend that greater resources be devoted to small-scale experimentation with a variety of alcohol prevention approaches, possibly at the senior high school level and targeted at drinking and driving.

Information programs. The public continues to express a need for information about drugs written in lay language but scientifically accurate. Such information can reach adolescents through the media, schools, parents, and community groups. To satisfy the demand, we recommend greater dissemination of brochures, pamphlets, and print and broadcast announcements aimed at the general public, supplemented by instructional materials for professionals who may influence children. Although the effects of such programs are not certain and may not become apparent for quite some time, the success of antismoking publicity is an encouraging precedent.

Law enforcement data collection. To improve the efficiency of law enforcement, we recommend that the federal government regularly collect and publish much more complete information on drug prices, consumption rates, drug seizures, and other parameters whose accurate estimation is essential for a quantitative assessment of law enforcement effectiveness. Information about the durability and adaptability of dealer organizations should also be gathered. When such data become available, they should be used to evaluate law enforcement policies and programs, develop optimal combinations of strategies, and set priorities among them.

Research and analysis of illicit drug markets. To develop more coherent law enforcement strategy, the government needs better knowledge about drug dealer networks, particularly the relationships among dealers, the prices and conditions of their trade, and their ability to adapt to changing law enforcement pressures. That information would be very useful in predicting dealer response to various enforcement strategies and in analyzing the impact of enforcement policies on drug prices. The information could be gathered from court records and case files, and from interviews with incarcerated drug dealers.

School enforcement. Many observers advocate stricter enforcement of antidrug rules at schools. Drug use during school hours is especially likely to impair learning and cognitive development, and it is likely that a considerable number of drug sales take place on campus. Therefore, several school districts and police departments have carried out well-publicized "crackdowns" on drugs in schools. However, such programs also have their disadvantages, and we have found no systematic evaluation that demonstrates their effects. Therefore we recommmend a detailed study and evaluation of the possible approaches.

Risk assessment. Better data are needed on the risks of psychoactive drugs. For several classes of drugs, including the most popular ones, we lack basic information such as the amount of impairment at a given

xviii

dose and frequency, the risks of short-term versus long-term administration, and the probability of dependence arising from various patterns of use. In addition, the mechanisms of drug action and patterns of metabolism are poorly understood. To identify the seriousness of risks posed by drug use and to help set priorities for efforts against the various substances, research on these issues deserves more support than it now receives.

Treatment of drug abusers. Finally, we urge efforts to improve treatment of adolescent drug abusers. Resources should be invested to encourage scientifically well-designed experiments, randomized if possible, to identify the most effective treatments. Similar evaluation should be done for "early intervention" methods, which attempt to help high-risk adolescent drug users who have not yet developed serious problems. To improve treatment over the long term, we recommend expanding basic research into the etiological factors that cause experimental or beginning drug users to develop serious patterns of drug abuse.

ACKNOWLEDGMENTS

In preparing this report, the authors were fortunate to have advice and assistance from many other people. Most important was the interest and support of Donald Hubbs, President of the Conrad Hilton Foundation, who conceived of this project and initially set it in motion. The keen interest of the Foundation's Trustees also encouraged us to set a broad agenda for the work.

We have benefited from information given by numerous government officials. At the National Institute on Drug Abuse, William Pollin, William Bukoski, Harold Ginzburg, Ann Blanken, Raquel Crider, James Ferguson, and Nicholas Kozel took the time to discuss many of the issues in drug abuse research and helped with interpretation of data on drug use, prevention, and treatment. Richard Lindblad of NIDA supplied important data on program policies and budgets. Carlton Turner of the White House Drug Abuse Policy Office gave us insights into federal strategy on drug abuse.

At the State Department, Rayburn Hess, Mark Steinetz, Clyde Taylor, and Jon Wiant provided helpful discussions of international drug control programs; James Spain also reviewed and commented on our analysis of that matter. Berdj Kenadjian at the Internal Revenue Service made available unpublished data on the frequency of marijuana use among high school seniors. Lowell Jensen, James Stewart, and Mark Kleiman of the Justice Department supplied useful comments on our analysis of law enforcement policy, and John Yoder described the details of various forfeiture programs. The California Bureau of Justice Statistics kindly gave us unpublished data on the disposition of drug arrests.

Assistance from private research groups was also invaluable. Ken Carlson of Abt Associates was very helpful in discussing his ongoing research on the size of illegal drug markets. At the Stanford Heart Disease Prevention Project, Nathan Maccoby, June Flora, and Joel Killen generously shared their work on smoking prevention, as did C. Anderson Johnson, Brian Flay, and William Hansen of the University of Southern California. Denise Kandel of Columbia University provided insights on the antecedents of adolescent drug use, and Ron Roizen and Walter Clark, of the University of California, Berkeley, shared their knowledge of the relevant research. We also received useful advice from Eric Schaps, Molly Hastings, and Thomas Adams of the Pacific Institute for Research and Evaluation in our search for evaluations of drug prevention programs.

Careful reviews of earlier drafts were given by Mansell Pattison, Department of Psychiatry, Medical College of Georgia; Phillip Cook, Institute of Policy Sciences and Public Affairs, Duke University; and Deborah Hensler and Thomas Glennan of Rand. George Tanham, George Goldberg, and Mark Chassin of Rand also gave us advice throughout the course of the study. Alisa Wilson was very helpful in locating and reviewing the literature, and invaluable assistance was given by Lois Haigazian, who expertly managed the typing and word processing for a very large effort.

CONTENTS

FIGURES

TABLES

Chapter 1

INTRODUCTION

For much of this century, attempts to outlaw dangerous drugs, to discourage drug use, and to treat drug abusers have been major issues of public debate and national policy (Musto, 1973). Adult drug users, notably heroin addicts, used to be the main concerns, but since the 1960s the use of illicit drugs has been viewed more as a problem of young people. In response, we have seen a rapid growth in treatment facilities, drug education programs, and federal government action. In the early 1970s, for example, Congress created the National Institute on Drug Abuse, which holds governmental status equivalent to that of the National Cancer Institute and which spent $274 million in 1980 for research and action against drug problems. Law enforcement has also been stepped up, especially at the federal level (Drug Abuse Policy Office, 1982). Nonetheless, drug abuse and drug-related crime still figure in the news almost every day.

This report presents the findings of an 18-month Rand study sponsored by the Conrad Hilton Foundation; its goal was to determine the most promising approaches to controlling adolescent drug use. The report reviews what is known about the nature of drug use and assesses the likely effectiveness of law enforcement, treatment, and prevention programs in dealing with the problem. Our purview includes both private and public programs.

THE CONCERN OVER ADOLESCENT DRUG USE

Public concern about drugs intensified during the campus turmoil of the 1960s, and since then Congressional hearings on drug use have been frequent. At the grass-roots level, local organizations of parents who were worried about adolescent drug use sprang up in a few places in the mid-1970s, and soon mushroomed into a national movement (U.S. House of Representatives, 1982; U.S. Senate, 1982).

That concern is based on the growing numbers of adolescents who take drugs. Figures 1.1 and 1.2 illustrate the upswing among young people during the past eight years as revealed in annual national surveys of high school seniors, who provided confidential reports of their experience with various types of drugs (Johnston, Bachman, and

1

O'Malley, 1982).[1] Figure 1.1 shows the rising percentage of seniors who reported using any illicit drug at any time in the past.

Worse, perhaps, is the occurrence of drug use among the very young. Whereas drug use first became widespread among college students in the 1960s, it rose even among junior high school students in the 1970s. Figure 1.2 demonstrates this change for 8th-graders, with illicit drug experience climbing from 8 percent in 1971 to nearly 20 percent by 1978. Again, the data come from high school seniors' retrospective reports. Despite the possibilities for recall error in such data, the upward trend is clear.[2] Our review shows that virtually all drugs pose certain risks for adolescents, as for older people, so these data suggest there has been a general increase in the level of risk to which new cohorts of young people are exposed.

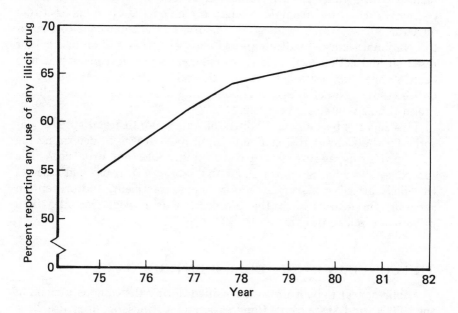

Fig. 1.1—Percent of 12th-grade students with illicit drug experience, by year (from Johnston, Bachman, and O'Malley, 1982)

---

[1]In the survey definition, illicit drug use includes any use of marijuana, cocaine, heroin, or hallucinogens (e.g., LSD and PCP), and nonmedical use of stimulants, sedatives, or tranquilizers. Although sale of alcoholic beverages and cigarettes to minors is prohibited in many localities, the reported results exclude those substances from the category of illicit drugs.

[2]Patterns of *regular* drug use do not necessarily conform with these trends, as shown in Chapter 2.

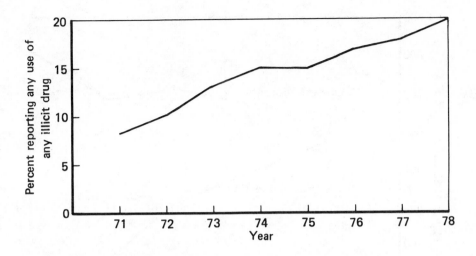

Fig. 1.2—Percent of 8th-grade students with illicit drug experience,
by year (from Johnston, Bachman, and O'Malley, 1982)

A second reason for concern about drug use is the great cost of mounting a national response (see Fig. 1.3). In 1983, the U.S. government spent over $1 billion for its combined efforts in drug law enforcement, treatment, and prevention. That figure does not include expenditures by states and localities, which also support police, courts, prisons, treatment facilities, and school programs aimed at drug-related problems. Though there are no systematic data on the costs of state and local efforts, they are surely substantial: Local police, for instance, made about 500,000 drug arrests in 1981 (FBI, 1981).

Figure 1.3 reveals a recent shift in the emphasis of federal programs. The expenditure figures have been adjusted for each year to reflect the real cost of the federal effort (in 1983 dollars, removing the effects of inflation). That adjustment shows that the value of resources devoted to treatment and prevention has declined from nearly $600 million to about $300 million, while resources for law enforcement have moved upward. However, there has been no systematic study of the effectiveness of these varying methods for controlling drug use. One of our objectives has been to do that: to evaluate how much payoff can be expected from changes in the emphasis given to various methods of drug control.

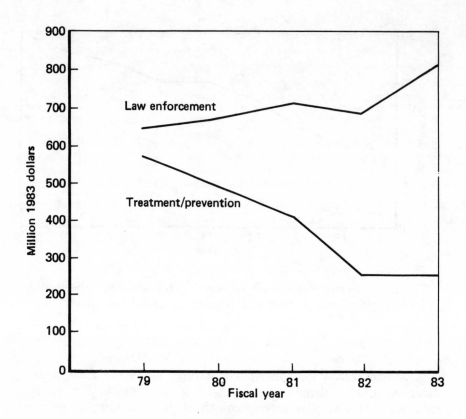

Fig. 1.3— Federal budget trends in drug control
(from Drug Abuse Policy Office, 1982)

STRATEGY OF THE STUDY

This study reviews the current record of scientific data and other evidence about the effectiveness of drug control measures. Where that evidence is incomplete, we have drawn inferences from knowledge in related fields and from our contacts with public officials, scholars, and informed observers.

Chapter 2 presents basic information about availability and consumption of drugs in the United States. Chapters 3, 4, and 5 analyze the three principal methods for controlling drug use. Chapter 6 contains our conclusions, recommendations for future initiatives, and suggestions for the next steps needed to improve programs against drug use.

Our strategy has been to use the evidence on past programs to judge how much more headway can be made by increased efforts using each of the three major control methods:

- Enforcement of laws against drug possession and sale.
- Treatment of chronic drug users.
- Prevention programs to dissuade people from starting use.

We will show that the use of drugs, including illicit drugs, is truly a mass phenomenon in the United States. Users number in the millions, and the market for drugs is vast. We conclude, however, that intensified law enforcement is not likely to be the answer; it will not substantially reduce the supply of drugs, and we doubt that it can raise the price of drugs high enough to reduce sales. We also conclude that increased treatment is not a promising approach for the near future. Evidence about treatment effectiveness is so scant that we cannot knowledgeably choose among treatment modalities, or determine where additional treatment resources might be directed to help adolescent users.

Our most promising findings are for prevention programs. Here, we have found compelling evidence that new approaches are effective for preventing the onset of cigarette smoking among adolescents. We suggest that the same approaches may be transferable to drug abuse prevention.

Chapter 2

AVAILABILITY AND CONSUMPTION OF DRUGS

Adolescent drug use occurs within a context of adult drug-taking, legal controls, beliefs about drug effects, availability of drugs, and other conditions. Knowledge of these conditions is essential to understanding and controlling drug-related behavior. This chapter summarizes some of that knowledge, relying as much as possible on information from published, authoritative sources. We first briefly review the principal psychoactive drugs, outlining the history of each drug, its physical characteristics, how it is administered, and its known effects on the body. We then examine patterns of drug use among both adults and adolescents. Finally, we discuss the availability of drugs, outlining the main sources of drug supplies and the extent of the drug market in this country.

PRINCIPAL PSYCHOACTIVE DRUGS

The main drugs of abuse are *psychoactive* drugs; that is, they affect the mind by changing mood, altering perceptions, and the like. Table 2.1 lists three main groups, defined by their legal status and medical uses. The first group comprises the substances commonly regarded as "illicit drugs." They are rarely if ever dispensed legally to patients for self-administration. The second group includes several classes of prescription drugs with psychoactive properties. Although many of them are now obtained from illicit laboratories instead of by prescription, all of them were introduced to the public through medical practice and some are diverted to the illicit market from medical or pharmaceutical channels. Drugs in the third class are available over the counter, the most prominent being alcoholic beverages, which contain the drug ethanol, and tobacco cigarettes, which contain the drug nicotine. Partly because of the hazards of these substances, their sale is nominally restricted to adults. We include them here to give a perspective on the true extent of drug use in American society, and also because we can learn a great deal about the effectiveness of prevention from experience with these legal drugs.

One of the main problems of psychoactive drugs is their potential for creating *dependence*. As commonly used, "dependence" refers to

Table 2.1

PRINCIPAL PSYCHOACTIVE DRUGS

Drug Group	Examples	Legal Status
Heroin	Heroin, morphine, opium	Heroin illegal, others strictly controlled
Cocaine	Cocaine, coca leaf	Strictly controlled
Marijuana	Marijuana, hashish	Illegal
Hallucinogens	LSD, PCP	Illegal
Stimulants	Amphetamines, methamphetamine	Prescription only
Depressants: sedatives	Barbiturates, methaqualone	Prescription only
Depressants: tranquilizers	Valium, Librium	Prescription only
Alcohol	Beer, wine, liquor	Regulated public sale (adults)
Cigarettes	Commercial brands	Regulated public sale (adults)

several conditions that occasionally, but not always, occur at the same time (Gerald, 1981):

- **Physical dependence,** a condition in which the body has adapted to the presence of the drug and consequently undergoes a *withdrawal syndrome* when use of the drug is interrupted or substantially reduced. Withdrawal symptoms differ widely among drugs, ranging from mild sleep disturbances to gross tremors, convulsions, and life-threatening cardiovascular disturbances depending on drug dosage and history. For example, abrupt discontinuation of heroin use, without therapy using other drugs, leads to a well-known form of withdrawal sickness.
- **Psychic dependence,** a condition of craving or overwhelming compulsion to use the drug. Many psychoactive drugs, notably heroin, cocaine, amphetamines, and cigarettes, produce a strong subjectively perceived "need" to continue taking the drug even if withdrawal sickness does not occur.
- **Tolerance,** a reduction in the body's response to a given dosage of a drug. Tolerance may be due to enhanced capacity to dispose of the drug (e.g., through accelerated metabolism), to changes in sensitivity of cells at the site of drug action (e.g., in the brain), or to alterations in other processes. Tolerance is often recognized by the user as a need to take more of the drug

to "get high" since the usual dose no longer produces the desired response.[1]

In the case of heroin or opium use, these three aspects of dependence are rather quickly developed and prominently displayed. Hence they formed the basic elements of early theories of drug addiction. However, the newer psychoactive drugs do not always exhibit all of these properties. In recognition of that fact, many authorities have moved away from the term "addiction," preferring the less derogatory term "dependence" (WHO, 1952, 1974). Nonetheless, dependent heroin users are almost universally referred to as addicts, and we shall follow that practice as well.

We now turn to each of the drugs in Table 2.2. We begin with heroin and other opium products, because the opiates exhibit most of the principal phenomena of drug abuse and they serve as an implicit standard against which other drugs can be measured.

Heroin and the Opiates

Opium is one of the oldest medicinal substances known to man. Since at least 4000 B.C. it has been extracted from the opium poppy, *Papaver somniferum*, and used to relieve pain and induce sleep (Cox et al., 1983). Opium is the source of several powerful psychoactive drugs, including morphine, heroin, and codeine, which are generally classified as narcotic analgesics or simply *narcotics*.[2] Also included in the opiate class are several synthetic or semisynthetic drugs with similar chemical structures or effects, such as hydromorphone (trade name Dilaudid), meperidine (Demerol), propoxyphene (Darvon), and methadone (Jaffe and Martin, 1980).

History. The opium poppy can be grown in many parts of the globe. It has been widely cultivated and used in China, India, the Middle East, and Africa, and its medical use was recorded in Greece and other ancient cultures. By the 19th century, opium smoking for pleasure had become common in China, and Western trading nations fought a series of Opium Wars for the right to supply the lucrative Chinese market. Later, opium smoking came to public attention in the United States, where newspapers and law enforcement authorities perceived it as a problem among Oriental immigrants (Musto, 1973).

---

[1] In some classifications, tolerance is viewed as a distinct entity from the general dependence syndrome. In fact, tolerance, psychic dependence, and physical dependence can all occur independently (Jaffe, 1980).

[2] The prefix narco- is derived from the Greek word *narke,* meaning numbness or stupor.

Table 2.2

PHARMACOLOGICAL CHARACTERISTICS OF SELECTED PSYCHOACTIVE DRUGS

Drug	Common Form	Route of Administration	Sought-After Effects	Most Common Type of Dependence	Symptoms of Withdrawal Syndrome
Heroin	Powder	Injected, sniffed	Euphoria	Physical	Tremors, cramps, craving
Cocaine	Powder	Sniffed, injected, smoked	Euphoria, energy	Psychic	Depression, craving
Marijuana	Plant material	Smoked	Elation, relaxation	Psychic	Irritability, sleeplessness
LSD	Applied to paper, sugar cube, etc.	Oral	Altered perceptions	Not established	Not established
PCP	Applied to cigarette	Smoked, oral	Altered perceptions	Not established	Not established
Amphetamine	Capsule	Oral	Alertness, euphoria	Psychic	Depression, fatigue
Methaqualone	Tablet	Oral	Relaxation, euphoria	Physical	Anxiety, tremors
Valium (diazepam)	Tablet	Oral	Calming, anxiety reduction	Psychic	Anxiety, tremors
Alcohol	Liquid	Oral	Relaxation, euphoria	Physical	Tremors, craving
Cigarettes	Plant material	Smoked	Stress reduction	Psychic	Irritability, craving, tension

An important discovery was the isolation of morphine, the most potent psychoactive alkaloid in opium, in the early 19th century. Use of morphine in medicine became much more widespread after the invention and perfection of the hypodermic syringe for intravenous injection, which permitted accurate delivery of a precise quantity of the pure drug to the bloodstream. One result was frequent morphine addiction among veterans who had been treated with the drug in the American Civil War and contemporaneous European wars. In 1898 a further complication was introduced by the discovery of heroin (diacetylmorphine), a semisynthetic opiate more potent than morphine. Although originally introduced as a nonaddicting alternative to morphine, heroin turned out to be the preferred euphoriant among many drug users, and its dependence-producing potential was quickly documented.

Nonetheless, until about 1900 narcotic use was not widely perceived as a problem. By that time opium was an ingredient in numerous patent medicines, including "soothing syrups" given to infants. While reliable data on the number of users are impossible to obtain, the number of opiate-dependent persons was substantial enough that many major cities operated narcotic dispensing clinics at the time of the Harrison Act (1914). Shortly thereafter, federal enforcement of the Act made all opium products legally inaccessible to addicts, the clinics were shut down, and private physicians ceased to supply morphine or heroin to addicts (Musto, 1973). Despite vigorous enforcement of laws against possession and sale, the illicit market for heroin seems to have grown throughout the 20th century. At present, manufacture and sale of heroin continues to be banned under the Controlled Substances Act, and use of other opiates is severely restricted; still, the federal government estimates that in 1981 492,000 heroin addicts were active in the United States (NNICC, 1983b).

Production. Production of opium and its derivatives is labor-intensive but technologically undemanding. Workers cut the seed capsule of the poppy before it is ripe and return after a few days to scrape off the sticky brown material exuded from the plant. Pressed into cakes, the raw opium can then be refined to produce its principal alkaloids, morphine and codeine, the latter of which is therapeutically useful as a cough suppressant. Further processing of morphine into heroin is a rather simple chemical process, often carried out in small laboratories or even kitchens. For many years heroin refining was a lucrative business in southern France, drawing on Turkish opium supplies, but after the disruption of this "French connection" in the early 1970s, processing sites appear to have shifted to the producer regions. The U.S. market has been increasingly supplied by poppy fields in Southwest Asia (Pakistan, Afghanistan, Iran), Southeast Asia (Burma, Thailand, Laos), Mexico, and other locations (NNICC, 1982).

Patterns of Use. Heroin appears as a white or brown crystalline powder. Heated and dissolved in water, a dose of as little as 5 milligrams injected intravenously produces psychic effects in nontolerant individuals. Habitual users may require one hundred milligrams or more to achieve an effect. Heroin may also be sniffed (inhaled into the nose and absorbed through the mucous membranes), smoked, or injected under the skin, but most regular users in the U.S. prefer injection.

Effects. Injected heroin brings about an immediate psychic effect, variously described as a "rush," a suffusing warmth, or a "whole-body orgasm" (Jaffe, 1980; Young et al., 1977). Many users then subside into a dream-like reverie ("the nod") characterized by drowsiness, lethargy, indifference to pain, and lack of interest in the outside world. Contrary to a common public image, addicts are anything but prone to violence during intoxication; the problem occurs when the effects subside (8 to 12 hours), at which point a physically dependent individual begins to feel withdrawal symptoms and experiences a strong craving for a new dose. Since a long-term high-dose user may need a "fix" two or more times a day at $20 or more each, he often commits remarkable numbers of burglaries, robberies, and other property crimes (Chaiken and Chaiken, 1982; Ball et al., 1982); hence the strong relation between heroin use and street crime.

Side effects of heroin often include nausea, vomiting, constipation, and constriction of the pupils. Many new users react with dysphoria (mental distress, unpleasant feelings) instead of euphoria. Overdose can cause respiratory depression and death. Although opiates can be used for long periods without substantial organ damage (DuQuesne and Reeves, 1982), ill health is endemic in the addict population. Common conditions are sleep disturbances, hepatitis, endocarditis (inflammation of the heart lining), malnutrition, septicemia (blood poisoning), damaged veins, and skin abscesses. These conditions are linked to the circumstances of heroin use, particularly unsterile injection procedures, adulterants in the drug, and malnutrition due to general self-neglect.

Dependence develops only after repetitive administration of heroin, usually for weeks or longer. Anecdotal reports suggest a substantial population of "chippers," or occasional users who avoid outright physical dependence. The idea that one can be "hooked" after one dose, widely publicized in the past, has not withstood scientific scrutiny. Nevertheless, by all accounts the opiates are highly reinforcing and possess perhaps the greatest liability for physical dependence of any drug class (Cox et al., 1983). With repeated use, tolerance sets in, so regular users must escalate the dose to achieve the desired high, or in some cases just to avoid unpleasant withdrawal symptoms. Withdrawal is accompanied at first by tearing, runny nose, sweats, yawning, and difficulty sleeping; later symptoms may include tremors, "goose flesh" (hence the term "cold turkey"), muscle weakness and spasms, cramps, chills, fever, and diarrhea (Khantzian and McKenna, 1979).

Cocaine

Cocaine has long been incorrectly treated as a "narcotic" by the legal system. In fact, cocaine is pharmacologically a stimulant drug, not an opiate, and it shares very few attributes in common with opiates.

History. Cocaine is derived from leaves of the South American coca bush, *Erythroxylon coca*, which grows at high elevations in Peru and Bolivia. Indians of the Andes mountains chewed coca leaves in ancient times, presumably to ward off fatigue and reduce hunger. Under Spanish government the practice of coca chewing was restricted to the Indian nobility, and in this century it has even been restricted by the level of elevation (allowed in the mountains, but not in the lowlands). The leaf's active ingredient, cocaine, was isolated by European chemists in the 1880s and enthusiastically promoted by Sigmund Freud, among others, as a general tonic and cure for opiate addiction. In 19th century medicine, cocaine proved to be a valuable aid to eye surgery, because it was a local anesthetic and a vasoconstrictor. Today, the drug remains available in medicine as a topical anesthetic but is infrequently used (Gerald, 1981). Classified under the Controlled Substances Act, cocaine possession or sale carries heavy penalties under federal and state laws, a fact which has not prevented a booming market for the drug.

Use of cocaine began to be perceived as a problem in the U.S. during the early 20th century. Especially in the South, newspapers carried lurid accounts of violent acts committed by "drug-crazed" users; frequently these acts were purported attacks by black men against white women. Editorials and Congressional witnesses suggested that cocaine use was a virulent problem in some areas, and racial feelings are thought to have played a significant role in mobilizing public concern about the drug (Musto, 1973). Under the Harrison Act of 1914 and several subsequent laws, cocaine was classifed as a narcotic and users were subjected to extreme penalties. For several decades it seemed to be used by few, but regained enormous popularity in the 1970s.

Production. Coca leaves are processed into coca paste or base by application of solvents, then into cocaine. Typically the plants are grown in Peru or Bolivia, refined into paste, and transported to Colombia. Illicit laboratories in Colombia further process the material into cocaine hydrochloride, a form in which it is easily smuggled via aircraft or ship to the U.S. and Europe, the principal consuming areas outside South America itself (NNICC, 1983b).

In the 1970s it was discovered that cocaine hydrochloride could be reprocessed to pure form (not the salt), and that the resulting "freebase" could be smoked to provide an intense psychic effect. (The salt form cannot be smoked effectively.) The reprocessing requires use of highly volatile and flammable chemicals; reports of injuries have become common since 1977 (Siegel, 1982). Up to now the reprocessing seems to have been done mostly by end-users, not by wholesalers or refiners.

Patterns of Use. Cocaine hydrochloride is usually seen as a fine white powder (hence the term "snow"); other forms are flake and "rock." It is usually sniffed ("snorted") into the nose, often by laying out a thin "line" of the drug and inhaling through a straw or rolled dollar bill. It is rapidly absorbed through the nasal mucous membranes, producing immediate effects. It can also be injected or smoked in the freebase form, methods of administration more likely to lead to strong psychic dependence, dose escalation, and adverse reactions (Young et al., 1977; Post, 1975; DiPalma, 1981).

Effects. Cocaine produces stimulant effects, in sharp contrast to opium derivatives. Users describe intense feelings of energy, well-being, and confidence. Intravenous injection leads to a rush or "flash" of euphoria. Duration of the effect is short, however; within 30 minutes the peak effect is reached or passed, and a new dose is needed to maintain the high. Some users report a psychological "down" feeling as the effects wear off, leading to a craving for readministration (Jaffe, 1980).

Side effects are those common to most of the stimulants: increased heart rate, blood pressure, and excitability, sometimes with anxiety, nausea, and dysphoria. Heavy users who sniff the drug may damage mucous membranes in the nose and even perforate the nasal septum. With high doses or intravenous administration, the user may display short-term psychotic reactions: agitation, feelings of persecution (paranoia), or delusions. For instance, the user may feel small insects or worms ("coke bugs") crawling under the skin and scratch the skin raw to eliminate them (Siegel, 1982).

Psychic dependence has been reported by many individuals, but physical dependence is questionable. Some authorities report an identifiable sequence of symptoms (e.g., irritability) upon withdrawal, but the degree of physical dependence is modest compared with that produced by opiates (Khantzian and McKenna, 1979). Few scientific sources speak of a cocaine "addiction." Nor is there scientific agreement about tolerance to cocaine (DiPalma, 1981; Cox et al., 1983). Many users report a precipitous "crash" at the end of a series of cocaine doses. This can create a strong desire to continue, and since cocaine is very expensive there are common reports of individuals who have spent thousands or tens of thousands of dollars on their habit in a few months.

Unlike heroin, death from cocaine overdose is reported infrequently. Moreover, the social conditions of cocaine use differ radically from heroin. By appearances, cocaine users are generally middle-class people who do not engage in crime to obtain money for drugs, and who feel no strong ill effects if they cannot afford it. Cocaine purchase does not usually require one to enter an underworld atmosphere, and police pressure on cocaine dealers appears to be less intense than for heroin.

Thus far, the high cost of cocaine seems to have limited the cocaine market and held down the incidence of serious effects that might occur if the supply were larger.

Marijuana

Marijuana is the common name used in North America for the leaves of the hemp plant, *Cannabis sativa*. Cannabis is cultivated for hemp fibers, used in rope, and is also a hardy weed that grows wild over a large portion of the earth, including all regions of the U.S., central America, north Africa, the Middle East, and India. Its psychoactive properties come mainly from the resin found on the flowering tops and upper leaves of the plant. The main active ingredient is THC (delta-9-tetrahydrocannabinol). Among the various types of cannabis used as a drug, the most common is "marijuana," a material that usually consists of small leaves mixed with pieces of stems and seeds. Typical marijuana contains 1 to 5 percent THC (Gerald, 1981). A second class of cannabis is hashish, made up of resin scraped from the plant and compressed into brown or black blocks with up to 15 percent THC content. Other variants include hash oil, a very potent liquid processed from hashish, and *sinsemilla*, a new seedless variety of marijuana containing as much as 8 percent THC.

History. Cannabis products have been smoked for their psychic effects throughout history. Use of the drug has been recorded since ancient times in India, north Africa, and China. Carried to southern Europe via north African influence, use of hashish became an intellectual fad in 19th century Paris, where hashish clubs were frequented by famous authors. In the U.S., marijuana appears to have been little used before the 1920s, growing in popularity when alcohol was prohibited, especially among Mexican immigrants in the Southwest.

Marijuana was not prohibited by the 1914 Harrison Act, which outlawed heroin and cocaine. During the late 1920s and early 1930s, however, newspaper reports began to appear linking marijuana smoking with deviant behavior and violent crimes. It appears that a substantial portion of the publicity against marijuana was created by the Federal Bureau of Narcotics, led by Henry Anslinger, a vigorous proponent of legal controls on drugs and punitive measures against drug users. At that time the Bureau encouraged circulation of pamphlets, films, and other materials designed to raise public fear of the drug, claiming that marijuana impaired users' control over their impulses and led to violent, irrational crimes (Musto, 1973). Although these claims were never supported by credible evidence and are now discredited, in 1937 this agitation led to the passage of the Marijuana Tax Act, which gave the government the authority to ban marijuana. All states eventually followed suit, and marijuana was officially classified as a narcotic for many years. Today it is classified along with heroin as a controlled substance.

Despite its prohibition, marijuana use continued in restricted circles (certain ethnic groups, jazz musicians, etc.) and was eventually introduced to college campuses during the turmoil of the 1960s. From there it experienced explosive growth to become by far the most commonly used illicit drug among all social groups. In the 1970s numerous states, representing about one-third of the U.S. population, "decriminalized" possession of small amounts of marijuana, reducing the penalties to citations analogous to a traffic violation. Nevertheless, heavy penalties remain for selling the substance.

Effects. Marijuana is usually smoked in hand-made cigarettes ("joints") or in pipes. The smoke is held in the lungs and absorbed directly into the bloodstream via the same process as absorption of tobacco smoke. It may also be eaten, for instance in baked confections. When smoked, psychic effects are observed within seconds and last 1 to 2 hours. When eaten, effects may take one hour or more to appear and may last for several hours.

Users report the main psychic effects are mild euphoria, changes in perception (heightened appreciation of sounds and colors, for example), and an apparent slowdown in the passage of time. Users may laugh frequently, become hungry and thirsty, or engage in disjointed conversations with unconnected thoughts and speech (Cox et al., 1983). Side effects include an increased heart rate, reddened eyes, and drowsiness. Experiments have demonstrated disturbance of short-term memory (forgetting what was just said, or what one just learned) and impairment of perception, coordination, and motor skills, including skills needed for safe driving (Institute of Medicine, 1982; Jaffe, 1980; Nicholi, 1983). Panic reactions are occasionally reported, with feelings of persecution, confusion, and hallucination, but these are infrequent.

As to marijuana's potential for dependence and other long-term effects, opinion is divided. Some experiments have shown particular withdrawal reactions in animals given very high doses of marijuana smoke or injected THC, but few human users report serious adverse reactions upon cessation of marijuana use (Nicholi, 1983; Khantzian and McKenna, 1979). Although tolerance to marijuana can develop, it does not necessarily lead to increased drug-taking. Toxic effects are infrequently observed, and death is rarely, if ever, attributed to marijuana consumption by itself (Addiction Research Foundation, 1981).

Nonetheless, many scientific and medical authorities feel that marijuana may cause long-term harm, especially if smoked frequently over an extended period. Partly, this view reflects the uncertainty that surrounds the pharmacology of THC and the related cannabinoids (compounds in cannabis); THC was not isolated until 1964 and rather little is known about its absorption, distribution, and mechanisms of action. Partly, also, this reflects the analogy between tobacco smoking and marijuana smoking. For many years tobacco was suspected of harmful long-term effects, yet it was only in the early 1960s that the evidence became so clear that the Surgeon General was able to issue a report to that effect. The evidence on tobacco's effects was obtained only after epidemiological studies were conducted on large populations of chronic cigarette smokers; hence, it is argued, it will be many years before similar data will be available on populations of chronic marijuana users, and in the meantime there is no way to conclusively establish the risks.

In response to the recent growth of marijuana use in Western countries, public and medical concern about these uncertainties has mounted, and several recent prestigious commissions have surveyed the evidence on marijuana's effects. In the U.S., the National Academy of Sciences' Institute of Medicine conducted a detailed review (1982), and similar groups have issued reports on behalf of the British government (Advisory Council on the Misuse of Drugs, 1982) and the World Health Organization (Addiction Research Foundation, 1981). These reviews broadly agreed on the following points:

- Marijuana smoke has a composition very similar to that of cigarette smoke. Since long-term daily tobacco smoking can cause pulmonary disease and lung cancer, daily marijuana smoking probably poses similar risks.
- Marijuana smoking temporarily increases the workload of the heart. These effects pose risks for persons with cardiovascular disease.
- Some studies have found that marijuana impairs the body's immune response system to a small extent. Animal studies consistently show such effects. However, the effect in humans has not been found by all studies and it has not been shown to result in overall higher rates of disease.
- Marijuana reduces the level of sperm production in men. Animal studies have also shown that THC affects male reproductive hormones and female ovulation as well. Such phenomena could have adverse effects on reproductive systems, though the actual effects in humans, if any, have not been demonstrated.
- Marijuana causes short-term impairment of cognitive functions (including learning and memory). If, as contemporary reports suggest, many young people use the drug before or during school hours, it may reduce the amount they learn in school and may impair their long-term cognitive development.

- Marijuana unquestionably reduces motor coordination, tracking ability, perceptual accuracy, and other functions important in driving.

Because of these and other concerns, all of the above commissions recommended avoidance of regular, high-dose marijuana smoking. The U.S. commission, pointing to survey data suggesting that 9 percent of high school seniors smoked marijuana every day, concluded that the evidence on possible adverse effects of marijuana "justifies serious national concern."

A final reason for worry about marijuana's effects grows out of the drug's pattern of distribution in the body. Unlike alcohol, THC is not distributed evenly throughout the tissues, nor is it rapidly eliminated through metabolism. Being fat-soluble, THC is concentrated in certain fatty tissues. It appears to be only slowly removed from those sites, and as a result the metabolites of THC can be detected in the urine up to 10 days after the last administration of marijuana (Blasinsky and Russell, 1981). Moreover, it is suspected that cannabinoids other than THC also act on the central nervous system, and knowledge of their pharmacokinetics is even less complete than knowledge of THC. These considerations suggest that extended, regular marijuana smoking could lead to an accumulation of pharmacologically active compounds, with unknown effects (Addiction Research Foundation, 1981). Experience with other drugs, many of which were once thought harmless but later were found to have serious adverse effects, leads many authorities to be cautious on all these points.

Hallucinogens

The class of drugs known as hallucinogens (literally, "hallucination-creating") includes LSD, PCP, mescaline, and numerous related compounds. These drugs have in common the property of changing one's perceptions (distorting sense of distance, color, hearing, etc.) and of altering thought processes. For that reason they are also known as psychedelics ("mind-revealing") and psychotomimetics ("mimicking psychosis"). Strictly speaking, these drugs do not usually create hallucinations (seeing, hearing, or otherwise sensing things that are not real); most users recognize that their altered perceptions are unreal effects caused by the drug.

History. In traditional Indian cultures of Central America, certain species of mushrooms containing the drugs *psilocybin* and *psilocin* were eaten, usually as part of religious rituals. Other groups used peyote, a cactus variety containing the drug *mescaline*. Both types of natural hallucinogens have chemical properties similar to those of newer synthetic drugs such as lysergic acid diethylamide (LSD), on which a great deal more research has been done (DuQuesne and Reeves, 1982; Cox et al., 1983). LSD was discovered accidentally in the 1930s as a by-product of processing compounds derived from the ergot fungus. One of the most powerful of all drugs (its dosages are measured in micrograms, not milligrams), it was originally thought to produce mental states similar to schizophrenia—hence the term "psychotomimetic." This led to an active period of research predicated on the belief that LSD could be used for experimental manipulation of psychotic-like states that might illuminate the etiology of schizophrenia. However, in the 1960s the drug was discovered by large numbers of young people, and the resulting public concern led to its being reclassified under the Controlled Substances Act, unavailable for public use.

Another hallucinogenic substance that has gained an unsavory reputation is phencyclidine, popularly known as PCP or "angel dust." Introduced as an anesthetic, it was withdrawn after many patients experienced side effects such as dizziness, delusions, and hallucinations. Despite this, PCP was still used as a veterinary anesthetic, and it became a popular street drug in the 1970s, often manufactured in illicit laboratories.

Production. LSD is easily manufactured from readily available precursor chemicals, and at low cost. An active dose of LSD, for example 50 to 100 micrograms, is too small for visual measurement, so the drug is often impregnated into sugar cubes, blotter paper, candy, or on the backs of stamps. It can also be made in tablet or capsule form. Buying it in the illicit market, the user has little knowledge of the exact dose, or even if the drug is what is claimed by the seller.

PCP is also easily and cheaply synthesized, but an effective dose is bulkier than LSD. Originally produced as a white powder, it is frequently sprinkled on tobacco or marijuana, then smoked. It may also be taken orally in capsule or tablet form, sniffed in powder form, or injected. Because of its low cost and availability, it is often misrepresented as LSD, THC, or other drugs that many users prefer. In contrast, the naturally occurring drugs psilocybin and mescaline are rather difficult and expensive to obtain, and they have a very limited market.

Effects of LSD. The most common effect of all hallucinogens is a profound distortion of time, distance, color, sound, and general perception of the outside world. The following psychic effects are often attributed to LSD; effects of other drugs are less well documented (Jaffe, 1980; DuQuesne and Reeves, 1982). Colors may pulsate or seem more intense; two-dimensional objects may seem three-dimensional; sensitivity to music, touch, and taste may be greatly enhanced. Sensory crossover (synesthesia) may occur, with colors being "heard" or sounds "seen." The other main effect is variously known as "depersonalization" or "psychedelic experience." Boundaries between the body and the environment may seem nonexistent. Some users report they see themselves from the outside, or appreciate a new relationship with the cosmos.

Side effects of LSD may include incapacity to judge time or distance accurately, fast heartbeat, and a rise in body temperature. Nausea and other discomforts may be present. In a "bad trip," the user may become frightened of the perceptual changes, resulting in anxiety, panic, or confusion. Instead of appreciating that the altered perceptions are due to the drug, the user may experience true hallucinations. Outright delusions and paranoia have been reported, but controversy exists as to the frequency of psychotic reactions.

Little is known about the long-term effects of LSD. Few users develop dependence in the sense that word is used for opiates or alcohol. No evidence has been reported of a withdrawal syndrome. For many users, the experience is so intense that it is not repeated immediately; moreover, tolerance develops quickly after a few administrations, so the user cannot achieve the desired effect without waiting a few days for tolerance to wear off (Cox et al., 1983). No death has been attributed to the direct physiological effects of LSD, although some have been attributed to psychotic reactions (e.g., jumping out a window under the delusion of being able to fly).

Effects of PCP. PCP also produces changes in perception, but these are often described in less enthusiastic terms. Its effects vary widely, even in the same person at different times. Users report an experience of unreality or depersonalization (e.g., being out of one's body), distortion of space and time, feelings of floating or weightlessness, and changes in vision and sound, sometimes with outright hallucinations. Euphoria, relaxation, and a feeling of intoxication may be felt as well.

Unwanted effects of PCP may include increased heart rate and blood pressure, nausea, loss of coordination, inability to judge distances, anxiety, and acute feelings of isolation, alienation, or depression. The drug is notorious for producing confusion, disorientation, paranoia, and assaultive behavior, especially at high doses; emergencies are common in which the user is severely agitated, unpredictable, and violent. Deaths from drowning, suicide, jumping from heights and other bizarre behavior have been reported. Overdose can cause convulsions, coma, and death (Khantzian and McKenna, 1979). Evidence is lacking on PCP's potential for physical or psychic dependence.

Stimulants

The term "stimulant" is commonly used to refer to a class of prescription drugs that increase the body's capacity to perform, to remain awake, and to resist fatigue. The most prominent drugs of abuse in this class are the amphetamines, which we discuss here. Other drugs with stimulant properties include cocaine, which was discussed above; caffeine, which is found in coffee, tea, and soft drinks; and over-the-counter (OTC) diet aids such as Ayds or Dexa-Trim, which contain the mild stimulant phenylpropanolamine. Although caffeine and OTC diet aids can pose risks—for instance to persons with cardiovascular disease—they are a negligible part of the adolescent drug abuse problem. We shall confine our discussion to the amphetamines, which have a well-documented abuse potential.

History. In the late 1920s the first amphetamine compound was found to have several useful effects: constriction of blood vessels, dilation of bronchial air sacs, and nasal decongestion. In 1932 it was introduced as the Benzedrine inhaler for treatment of bronchial asthma. Consisting of a cotton pad soaked with amphetamine enclosed in a plastic tube, the inhaled vapors helped to constrict the mucous membranes in the nose. It shortly became known that Benzedrine also had stimulatory effects, and soon Benzedrine tablets were on the market. Truck drivers and others with a need to stay awake for long hours began to use the drug in the 1930s, and during World War II it was widely used by the military on both sides to maintain alertness and control fatigue under difficult conditions. In Japan, amphetamines were issued to factory workers in large quantities, and after the war large stockpiles remained. These were disposed of by uncontrolled sale on the open market, which led to a large-scale problem of amphetamine abuse in Japan in the 1950s. Eventually the Japanese government instituted strict controls and penalties, after which the scale of abuse appeared to decline (Smith et al., 1979).

Later in the postwar period, outbreaks of amphetamine abuse surfaced in Sweden, Britain, and other Western European countries; in these cases a prominent cause was unconstrained prescription of amphetamines, ostensibly for appetite control. Today, prolonged and repetitive prescription of stimulants is discouraged. Amphetamines remain available, however, and are still used for treatment of narcolepsy and the childhood hyperkinetic syndrome. Although many authorities warn against use for reduction of appetite even on a short-term basis, some prescriptions continue to be written for that purpose.

Patterns of Use. The amphetamine class of drugs includes amphetamine (trade name Benzedrine); dextroamphetamine (Dexedrine); and methamphetamine (Desoxyn). Related drugs, some widely prescribed, include phenmetrazine (Preludin) and methylphenidate (Ritalin). They normally appear as tablets or capsules to be taken orally. Some abusers prefer to inject them, particularly methamphetamine ("speed"), which is the drug of choice for that purpose.

Effects. Psychic effects of amphetamines, appearing just minutes after ingestion, include a sense of power, well-being, competence, and energy. Amphetamines increase the ability to perform demanding physical tasks without fatigue and to carry out repetitive and moderately demanding mental tasks (e.g., adding columns of numbers). Thus the drugs are useful to long-haul drivers, athletes, infantry soldiers, and others who wish to maintain stamina and performance for long periods of time. Increased attention span is also observed, making the drugs useful, for instance, to a radar operator who must watch a screen continuously for unusual events. Most abusers, however, report taking amphetamines to get feelings of euphoria, energy, and sexual capability. Injected methamphetamine, in addition, is reported to produce an intense "flash" of exhilaration (Nicholi, 1983; Jaffe, 1980).

Side effects can include elevated heart rate and blood pressure, hyperexcitability, inability to sleep, irritability, tension, and anxiety. High doses, particularly if administered intravenously, can lead to violent paranoia, hallucinations, and bizarre stereotyped behavior such as disassembling and reassembling the same object time after time. "Speed freaks," who repeatedly inject methamphetamine over a period of several days, are notorious for developing suspicions and hostility even toward friends; they may believe that they are being watched, that spies or enemies are plotting against them, controlling their behavior with secret transmitters and the like. Cardiovascular collapse and death have been reported.

One of the most certain reactions to an amphetamine use episode is depression as the user "comes down" or "crashes." As the drug wears off, unpleasant feelings replace euphoria, and many users report a strong desire to re-initiate the experience with another dose. Thus psychological dependence can develop rapidly in some people. Tolerance is quickly developed, and speeders may take many times the normal dose to achieve a desired effect (Nicholi, 1983).

Authorities disagree as to whether amphetamines cause a withdrawal syndrome, though depression, disturbed sleep patterns, and great fatigue are often noticed (Jaffe, 1980). Whether these reactions are actual evidence of physical dependence or simply reactions to sleep deprivation is not clear.

Sedatives and Hypnotics

Sedative-hypnotic drugs are those used to induce sleep. Typically, a high dose acts as a hypnotic (sleep-causing agent), whereas a lower dose provides daytime "sedation." These drugs usually depress a broad range of physiological functions, including respiration; hence an overdose can be fatal. They may be broadly grouped into the *barbiturates*, a class of drugs such as secobarbital or phenobarbital, and the *nonbarbiturates*, the most common of which are methaqualone (Quaalude), glutethimide (Doriden), and ethchlorvynol (Placidyl). Here we will describe the barbiturates and methaqualone in some detail, as they are the most frequently abused drugs in this class.

History. In the 19th century the list of hypnotic drugs was very limited, the most common being chloral hydrate, which when added to an alcoholic drink became the "knockout drops" made famous by mystery tales. In the early 20th century, however, the drug phenobarbital was introduced and gained wide acceptance as a treatment for insomnia. Other derivatives of barbituric acid were developed later, many of which were better adapted because of their shorter duration of action. These shorter-acting barbiturates became well known as drugs of abuse in the 1940s; among them are amobarbital (Amytal), secobarbital (Seconal), and pentobarbital (Nembutal). They were soon recognized as very dangerous drugs with a high potential for dependence. Since modern tranquilizers can be used more safely to achieve the same effect, many authorities now regard the barbiturates as obsolescent except for certain specific purposes such as treatment of some forms of epilepsy (Cooper, 1977).

Most of the nonbarbiturate sedatives were formulated as alternatives to barbiturates, and many were heralded as safe and nonaddicting when first introduced. Unfortunately, all have demonstrated potential for abuse. Most notorious is methaqualone, which became widely accepted in Europe and the U.S. in the 1960s and became a frequent cause of drug-related emergencies in the 1970s. Methaqualone has now been restricted by reclassification under the Controlled Substances Act. The clinical utility of the nonbarbiturate sedative-hypnotics is now in doubt, along with barbiturates.

Production. Barbiturates and many nonbarbiturate sedative-hypnotics are marketed as capsules, often identified in street slang by their colors ("red devils," "yellow jackets," etc.). Until recently, methaqualone was marketed as a tablet by several firms under different brand names (Quaalude, Sopor, Parest). The federal government then succeeded in drastically limiting the amount of methaqualone produced legitimately in the U.S., and a brisk illicit market sprang up in which methaqualone was produced in bulk in Europe and shipped to South

America, where it was made into tablets and smuggled into the U.S (NNICC, 1982).

Effects of Barbiturates. Barbiturates, in common with other hypnotic agents, can be taken in moderate doses to produce a feeling described as a state of calm, relaxed, or peaceful intoxication. Side effects superficially resemble those of drunkenness due to alcohol: slurred speech, lack of coordination, unsteady posture, and sluggish movement. Mood may alternate quickly from happy and gregarious to sad and withdrawn. Motor skills, including those needed for driving, are impaired, as are memory and learning. Although barbiturates induce sleep, the sleep is not normal; the REM (rapid eye movement) phase is suppressed, and after the drug is discontinued the subject experiences "REM rebound" sleep that sometimes includes disturbing nightmares. After a night of drug-induced sleep, users report "hangover" effects typified by grogginess and sluggishness (Jaffe, 1980).

Barbiturates have high potential for accidental or deliberate overdose. Tolerance to psychic effects develops with regular use, so the user may increase the amount, but the lethal dose increases more slowly and may be as little as 10 to 20 times the standard therapeutic dose. Thus it is easy for an abuser to miscalculate and overdose. In addition, barbiturates interact with alcohol and several other drugs, multiplying the effects of each. Because many users are unaware of the barbiturate-alcohol interaction, and also may miscalculate their dose when intoxicated, it is easy to ingest a fatal combination.

Barbiturates also have a high potential for physical and psychological dependence. Tolerance is acquired after a few weeks of regular use, as the drug stimulates the liver's capacity to metabolize it. Physical dependence is common among regular users, and the withdrawal syndrome is more dangerous than that of heroin. Withdrawal symptoms include restlessness, tremors, insomnia, weakness, cramps, confusion, delirium, and convulsions, with possible death.

Effects of Methaqualone. Methaqualone shares many of the effects and dangers of the barbiturates. Users seek effects described as feeling loose, relaxed, or euphoric; its reputation as an aphrodisiac gave it a street designation as the "love drug." Drowsiness, lack of coordination, and symptoms similar to alcohol or barbiturate intoxication are common side effects. Toxic effects of high doses include numbness, weakness, tremors, respiratory depression, pulmonary edema, and possible death, particularly when the drug is taken with alcohol, as it often is to increase the psychic effect. With repeated administration over a period of weeks, methaqualone produces tolerance, physical dependence, and a dangerous withdrawal syndrome.

Tranquilizers

Anti-anxiety agents, commonly called tranquilizers, are the most widely prescribed drugs in the U.S., Britain, and many other nations. The best known of these is diazepam (Valium), used to combat nervousness and tension, and useful in treatment of withdrawal syndromes from many other drugs. Diazepam and other drugs with similar chemical properties (the benzodiazepines) are also widely used in higher doses to promote sleep (DuQuesne and Reeves, 1982; Cooper, 1977).

Sometimes these drugs are called the "minor tranquilizers," in distinction to the "major tranquilizers" such as the phenothiazines that are used in treatment of schizophrenia and other serious mental illness. We specifically omit discussion of the major tranquilizers, as they are not often abused.

History. Until about 1950 the only practical drugs for daytime sedation were the barbiturates, with all the disadvantages discussed above. When new drugs with calming effects were discovered, they experienced quick acceptance and popularity for treatment of the large number of patients with emotional problems, tension, and anxiety. Thus, meprobamate (Miltown) was widely used in the 1950s, and Valium has been a best seller since its introduction in the early 1960s. Valium and its chemical relatives have enjoyed general acceptance for several reasons. First, very large doses are required to produce serious toxic effects; thus, they are less apt than barbiturates to cause suicide or accidental death. Second, they do not stimulate increased metabolism, and hence tolerance to them develops much more slowly than to barbiturates. Third, users can perform many normal functions during the daytime while experiencing the calming effects of the drug. Nonetheless, abuse of these drugs has been documented.

Effects. Users report relaxation, mild euphoria, and reduction of tension and minor pain. High doses promote drowsiness and sleep. Side effects, not consistently observed, include dizziness, headache, lethargy, and lack of interest in surroundings. At high doses, the user may experience memory impairment, confusion, lack of coordination, insomnia, and symptoms similar to alcohol-induced drunkenness.

Diazepam and related tranquilizers, like the traditional sedative-hypnotics, create tolerance to many of their effects. Hence abusers may tend to increase the dose. However, the tranquilizers have few toxic effects, and enormous doses are required to cause death unless alcohol or another depressant drug is used at the same time.

Tranquilizers can easily create psychic dependence, and in many cases physical dependence. Because these drugs are so frequently prescribed, they account for large numbers of clinical cases of abuse. However, the risk of physical dependence on tranquilizers appears substantially lower than for the barbiturates (Cooper, 1977). When physical dependence does occur, the withdrawal syndrome is usually less serious than with barbiturates; it is typified by agitation, nausea, tremor, and insomnia, but it can be life-threatening (Cox et al., 1983).

Alcohol and Cigarettes

We will not describe the historical background or usage patterns for alcohol and cigarettes in detail, as these are familiar to most people. However, two points about their effects are important: (1) Both alcohol and tobacco cause serious damage to organ systems when taken in significant quantities. (2) Both substances produce stubborn dependence in some persons.

Excessive alcohol consumption is the prime cause of liver disorders, particularly cirrhosis, and contributes to development of gastritis, peptic ulcer, cardiomyopathy, and several types of cancer. Alcohol is implicated in a high proportion of all types of accidents as well. Among its other adverse effects, regular consumption of high amounts leads to tolerance and craving. In sufficiently high doses, alcohol depresses respiration and causes death. It produces a powerful physical dependence; the withdrawal syndrome is similar to that of barbiturates, and can be equally life-threatening (National Institute on Alcohol Abuse and Alcoholism, 1981). Though a legal and accepted element in Western cultures, alcohol must be ranked as a major drug of abuse.

The smoking of tobacco cigarettes is now generally recognized as a hazardous practice. Among its more well-established risks are those of chronic bronchitis, emphysema, lung cancer, and cardiovascular disease. The psychoactive element in tobacco is nicotine, a mild stimulant that creates a profound psychic dependence. There is also some evidence of physical dependence, which though not conclusively demonstrated, may precipitate a withdrawal reaction including nervousness, anxiety, irritability, difficulties in concentrating, and intense craving for tobacco (Surgeon General, 1979; Cox et al., 1983). Smoking is widely regarded as one of the most tenacious habits and as one of the leading causes of disease.

PATTERNS OF DRUG USE

The way we view drug use depends not only on the pharmacological characteristics of a drug, but also on the number of users. A large user population implies a high number of persons at risk, which may carry important public health implications. For example, a population with 30 million cigarette smokers faces vastly higher rates of future pulmonary disease than a population with 3 million smokers. In addition, the number of current drug users surely affects the probability that other users will be recruited. Indeed, the existence of a "critical mass" of users in a given community may affect local social norms, making drug use more acceptable. This effect is probably more pronounced among adolescents because of their strong peer orientation. For such reasons, the proportion of the population using a drug—known as the "prevalence" rate—is an important factor in deciding on the attention that should be given to each drug.

The prevalence of drug use may be gauged by several indicators. The National Institute on Drug Abuse (NIDA) sponsors surveys of the U.S. household population (Miller et al., 1983) and annual surveys of high school seniors (Johnston et al., 1982), both of which yield self-reported data on drug use. NIDA also publishes data on drug-related episodes in hospital emergency rooms and drug-related deaths reported by medical examiners and coroners (NIDA, 1983a). Below we examine those data to estimate the prevalence of use and the number of users for the drugs that we have identified.

Number of Drug Users

We start by examining data on drug use from the most recent national survey, carried out in 1982. The data cover a representative sample of individuals living in households in the United States (Table 2.3). To maximize response validity, the questions about drug use are asked using a confidential self-administered form that the respondent fills out and seals in an envelope.

The most important feature of Table 2.3 is the wide variation by age group: Young adults are more likely to use each drug than any other age group; adolescents 12 to 17 are second for every illicit drug, but third for the publicly sold drugs (alcohol and cigarettes).[3]

Among adolescents and young adults, by far the most popular drug is alcohol, followed by cigarettes and marijuana. Two classes of drugs with stimulant properties—cocaine and stimulant pills such as amphetamines—are next in popularity, particularly among young adults. Rates for all other drugs are lower.

One difference among the age groups is important: Cocaine is considerably more popular than stimulant pills among young adults (6.8 vs. 4.7 percent) but not among adolescents (1.6 vs. 2.6 percent). We

---

[3]There are few striking variations in reported prevalence rates of current drug use across demographic subgroups of adolescents (Miller et al., 1983). Among the largest differences are those for marijuana use by city size (17 percent for large metropolitan areas, 9 percent for nonmetropolitan areas), and by region (15 percent for Northeast and North Central, 8 percent for South).

Table 2.3

DRUG USE PATTERNS BY AGE GROUP, 1982

	Percent Using Drug Past Month, By Age Group			Estimated Total Number of Users, in Millions (All Ages)[a]	
Drug	12–17	18–25	26 and Over	Past Month	Past Year
Marijuana	11.5	27.4	6.6	20.0	31.5
Cocaine	1.6	6.8	1.2	4.2	11.9
Hallucinogens	1.4	1.7	—	1.0	4.1
Heroin[b]	—	—	—	< 1	< 1
Stimulants	2.6	4.7	0.6	2.9	7.0
Sedatives	1.3	2.6	—	1.6	5.5
Tranquilizers	0.9	1.6	—	1.1	4.1
Alcohol	26.9	67.9	56.7	100.2	124.7
Cigarettes	14.7	39.5	34.6	60.2	69.6
Sample size (number of interviews)	1,581	1,283	2,760		
Population size (number of persons, in millions)	23.3	33.1	126.1		

NOTE: —indicates less than 0.5 percent.

[a]Estimated from 1982 national household survey (Miller et al., 1983; NIDA, 1983b), except as noted.

[b]Figure too small to estimate from survey; based on data in the official Narcotics Intelligence Estimate (NNICC, 1982).

infer that this reflects the high price of cocaine and the limited disposable incomes of adolescents; many young adults, but fewer adolescents, can afford cocaine at perhaps $20-$30 for a one-hour use session.

Table 2.3 suggests that the use of illicit psychoactive drugs is truly a mass phenomenon, particularly for marijuana and cocaine. Indeed, the estimate of 32 million annual marijuana users, as compared with 70 million cigarette smokers, is remarkable considering that twenty years ago (by all accounts) marijuana was still an uncommon drug in most communities.

We have argued that all of these drugs have potential for adverse effects, especially if used regularly in high doses. If we also accept that the risk of harm to the population rises with the number of users, then it is clear that the greatest harm to the population is likely to be caused by three drugs: marijuana, alcohol, and cigarettes. Such views are frequently expressed by public health officials, who argue that cigarette smoking and alcoholism are among the top causes of "preventable" death in Western countries (Surgeon General, 1979), and that daily use of marijuana is a potential danger to the health and development of younger age cohorts (Institute of Medicine, 1982).

Some observers suspect that the rates of drug use estimated from the household survey somewhat understate the true prevalence rates. Some high-risk groups do not live in households (e.g., some students and some military personnel, who make up 5 to 10 percent of the age group 15 to 25 years of age). Among household dwellers, drug users are probably less likely to respond (for example, because of being away from home). Also, respondents may deny or understate their drug use. However, the evidence on the extent of underreporting is mixed. Generally speaking, survey data on sensitive topics such as income, alcohol use, or crime rates do not understate population parameters as compared with estimates from nonsurvey criteria such as official records (Marquis et al., 1981); it has not been shown that survey respondents deny using drugs or engaging in other sensitive behaviors. However, when people are questioned about the *amount* of alcohol or tobacco they have consumed, the results understate total consumption, as estimated by sales records, by at least one-third (Room, 1971; Warner, 1978). That effect may be greater for illicit drugs. Therefore, we regard these survey estimates as reasonably accurate estimates of the number of users, but we suspect that the data may significantly underestimate total consumption of drugs.

Frequency of Drug Use

The national household survey is able to collect very little detail about the frequency or quantity of drug consumption. For such information we must turn to the survey of high school seniors, whose drug use patterns are illustrated in Fig. 2.1. These data suggest that by the time a young person reaches high school graduation, regular use of certain drugs is a common phenomenon. Alcohol, of course, leads the list (70 percent using in a one-month period), but marijuana and cigarettes are also widely used (30 and 29 percent). A rate of 11 percent was reported for stimulant pills (defined in this survey as amphetamines).[4] The survey researchers noted that this rate was adjusted to remove reports of using "look-alike" or diet-aid pills that resemble amphetamines and that have been heavily promoted to teenagers in recent

---

[4]The high school senior data, of course, exclude dropouts, who represent about 14 percent of the 10th grade cohort (Peng, 1983) and a larger proportion of the same-age cohort (*New York Times,* 1984). It seems likely that persons who drop out of school have higher rates of drug use, so the high school senior results may underrepresent the total population use rates for that age group. However, NIDA comparisons between the senior survey and the national household survey suggest that the bias is not large (Mayer, 1982, p. 90).

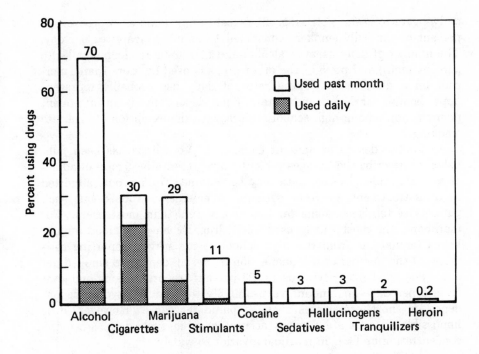

Fig. 2.1—1982 drug use rates among U.S. high school seniors (from
national high school senior surveys, Johnston, Bachman,
and O'Malley, 1982)

years. Such pills actually contain mild stimulants with much less
dependence potential than genuine amphetamines. If all stimulant use
is included, the rate rises to 14 percent (Johnston et al., 1982). However, both the adjusted and unadjusted rates suggest that pills with
stimulant effects enjoy considerable acceptance among adolescents.
Furthermore, as we shall discuss shortly, stimulants have grown in
popularity since 1975.

The most serious concern about public health effects has focused on
frequent use of these substances, particularly on *daily use*. Daily use is
often seen as an indicator that the individual is highly involved with
the drug, possibly to the detriment of other life interests. For many if
not all drugs, daily use also could indicate psychic or physical dependence. The lower portions of the bars in Figure 2.1 show the percentage
of high school seniors who reported daily use of each drug. These rates
follow a very different pattern from the basic use rates. The number of

daily cigarette users is striking: 21 percent of all seniors. Moreover, 75 percent of the daily smokers consumed 10 or more cigarettes per day. The number of daily users of alcohol and marijuana is much smaller (6 percent each), and none of the other drugs is used by more than 1 percent on a daily basis. These rates of daily use probably represent upper bounds for dependence rates. Thus, dependence is an infrequent phenomenon among high school seniors, with the exception of cigarette smoking.

As for the dosage or amount consumed: Very little has been published to describe the dosages taken by a representative group of adults or young people. Dosage data may be obtained from people admitted to drug treatment, or from patients in emergency rooms, but such patients certainly consume far higher amounts than most users. For marijuana, the most widely used illicit drug, we have obtained unpublished tabulations from the high school senior survey, reporting estimates of the number of marijuana "joints" respondents had smoked per day. The great majority of users (83 percent) reported using one joint or less per day—an amount very unlikely to produce psychic dependence or short-term crises such as panic reactions. However, it is impossible to estimate dosages accurately from such data, since the concentration of THC in marijuana varies so widely.

Rates of Medical Crises: Emergencies and Fatalities

To evaluate the seriousness of drug-related problems, many observers examine rates of injuries, emergencies, and deaths due to drug use. Table 2.4 presents information on emergency-room episodes as recorded in the Drug Abuse Warning Network (DAWN), operated by the National Institute on Drug Abuse. The DAWN system includes 819 emergency rooms in a set of 26 metropolitan areas and a randomly selected set of counties outside those areas. Each emergency room files monthly reports detailing the circumstances of visits related to drug abuse.[5] In addition, DAWN receives reports of all drug-related deaths from a sample of 84 county medical examiners and coroners.

Table 2.4 summarizes rates of "mentions" for specific drug groups in emergency room records. A mention for a given drug represents an episode in which the records state that the emergency was related to

---

[5]The number of participating facilities varies by year; the data cited are for 1981, the most recent year for which complete information is published. Based on the populations of the areas served and the participation rate of hospitals in each area, we estimate that perhaps 25 percent of the U.S. population lives in places covered by the DAWN emergency room system. Therefore, if these areas were representative of the nation, the numbers of episodes should be multiplied by 4 to estimate a national total. However, since the facilities and areas are not a random sample, such projections could be in error.

Table 2.4

DRUG-RELATED EMERGENCIES REPORTED TO DAWN SYSTEM, 1981

	Drug-Related Emergencies Reported[a]			
	All Ages		Ages 10-17	
Drug Category[b]	Number of Mentions	Index (Sedatives=100)	Number of Mentions	Index (Sedatives=100)
Sedatives	24,179	100	2,131	100
Tranquilizers	23,769	98	1,759	83
Narcotics	20,067	83	679	32
Amphetamines	6,082	25	942	44
Hallucinogens	5,884	24	1,097	51
Cocaine	4,777	20	158	7
Marijuana	4,671	19	906	43

[a]"Mentions" of the drug in emergency room records of drug-related cases. More than one drug may be mentioned for a given case (e.g., heroin and cocaine).
[b]Selected categories reported to the Drug Abuse Warning Network (DAWN). Adapted from the DAWN 1981 Annual Report (NIDA, 1982b).

abuse of that drug. Because a given visit may be due to multiple drugs (e.g., sedative plus alcohol), a mention of a particular drug does not always mean it was the sole cause of the episode. However, relative rates for different drugs give a rough indication of the importance of the drug in hospital emergencies. To facilitate comparisons among drug classes, we have calculated an index representing the ratio of mentions for each drug relative to the number of mentions for sedatives, which are the most frequently cited class.

These data confirm the life-threatening consequences of overdose from depressant drugs, including sedatives, tranquilizers, and narcotics. All three of those drug classes can depress respiration and central nervous system functioning, either alone or in combination with alcohol. Hence they can cause accidental overdose and can be used in suicide attempts. The hospital records indicate that suicide attempts accounted for about half of the tranquilizer episodes. Among heroin episodes, only 3 percent reflected suicide attempts; 76 percent were attributed to "dependence."

Among all age groups taken together, use of other drugs is associated with substantially fewer emergency room visits, but important differences occur in the patterns for adolescents. First, the rate of adolescent visits related to use of narcotics is much smaller. (Heroin-related visits are even more infrequent, accounting for only about half of all narcotics-related visits.) This confirms our other information suggesting that teenagers use heroin very infrequently. Similarly, cocaine is infrequently seen as a cause of adolescent emergencies.

Second, adolescents are much more likely than adults to go to an emergency room because of taking marijuana, amphetamines, or hallucinogens. Again, this confirms the implications of the survey data and suggests that the immediate drug problems of adolescents grow largely out of abuse of marijuana and pills.

Reports of deaths linked to drug abuse are summarized in Table 2.5. Most striking here is the tiny number of adolescent deaths. For example, among 1360 fatalities recorded for narcotics, only 13 were people 10 to 17 years old.[6] Once again, we see that the narcotics and sedatives have have high rates relative to other drugs, but immediate death is clearly not a major risk of drug use for adolescents.

Table 2.5

DRUG-RELATED DEATHS REPORTED TO DAWN SYSTEM, 1981

Drug Category[b]	Number of Drug-Related Deaths Reported[a]	
	All Ages	Ages 10-17
Narcotics	1360	13
Sedatives	1084	26
Tranquilizers	421	4
Amphetamines	186	3
Hallucinogens	84	1
Cocaine	84	1
Marijuana	9	3

[a]"Mentions" of the drug in medical examiner reports of drug-related deaths. More than one drug may be mentioned in a given death.

[b]Selected categories reported by the Drug Abuse Warning Network (DAWN). Adapted from the DAWN 1981 Annual Report (NIDA, 1982b).

[6]Based on the population of participating metropolitan areas, we estimate that about 20 percent of the U.S. population was covered by the medical examiner reports. Therefore if the sample were representative of all U.S. areas, the numbers in Table 2.5 could be multiplied by 5 to obtain an estimate for the entire nation. However, the data are dominated by results from large metropolitan areas, which are probably more likely than others to record drug-related deaths; hence a factor of 5 may not represent the true value.

Recent Trends

The data in Fig. 2.2, taken from the high school senior surveys, represent the best available information about drug use trends over recent years. Those surveys have collected annual data with stable sample sizes and technical procedures to detect possible trends or sampling biases (Johnston et al., 1982). It is difficult to use recent national household surveys for trend comparisons, even though they would cover a broader age range of young people, because the household surveys have been conducted less frequently (e.g., 1977, 1979, 1982) and their questions have been modified from year to year, leading to possible artifacts in the observed prevalence rates.[7]

The high school senior data reveal a substantial downward trend in cigarette smoking since 1976. At that time about 39 percent of seniors reported monthly cigarette use, a rate that had fallen to 30 percent by 1980. However, the decline seems to have halted thereafter, at least temporarily. Marijuana use appears to have peaked in 1978 and 1979 at about 37 percent; thereafter it rather consistently declined, reaching 28 percent by 1982. It is too soon as yet to tell whether this reduction is a lasting pattern.

In contrast to the recent drop in marijuana and cigarette use, drugs with stimulant effects—cocaine and stimulant pills—appear to have risen in popularity recently. Figure 2.2 shows that current use of stimulant pills rose from 8 percent to 16 percent through 1981 and then dropped slightly. Cocaine use tripled, though from a low level of 2 percent to a high of 6 percent. As we noted above, some of the rise in pill use may be due to respondents' erroneously including diet pills and "look-alike" stimulants, which are not amphetamines, in answers to the stimulant questions. However, the concomitant rise in cocaine prevalence suggests that drugs with stimulant properties have become increasingly attractive and acceptable to young people over the past decade.

Trends for most other drugs have been stable or declining. Current use of alcohol remained virtually constant (between 68 and 72 percent) through the 8-year period when the high school senior surveys were conducted. Figure 2.3 shows the trends for other important drugs. Rates for barbiturates and tranquilizers, the two classes of drugs that produce the most medical crises among young people, have been steadily declining. Until 1980 these declines were countered by a rise in methaqualone, a nonbarbiturate sedative. In 1981 and 1982, however, use of methaqualone declined, a trend that is confirmed by

---

[7]For example, in 1979 the household survey questions on amphetamines, sedatives, and tranquilizers were changed from spoken questions to a self-administered form.

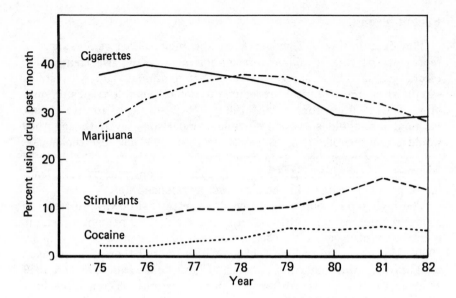

Fig. 2.2—Trends in drug use among U.S. high school seniors (from
national high school senior surveys, Johnston, Bachman,
and O'Malley, 1982)

reductions in emergency room visits (NIDA, 1983a) and data on law
enforcement seizures (NNICC, 1983b) since 1981.

The principal hallucinogens, LSD and PCP, show different patterns.
LSD use rates have been quite stable, hovering at about 2 percent
throughout the period. PCP was specifically measured only since 1979.
Since that time its prevalence rate has declined from about 2.5 percent
to one percent. Although no specific trend data exist to measure attitudes toward the drug, it seems likely that PCP has increasingly
acquired a street reputation as an unpredictable, dangerous drug, and
that fewer young people are inclined to experiment with it.

AVAILABILITY OF DRUGS

Merely outlawing or regulating certain drugs has not made them
unavailable; sources of supply exist to fill the demand. This raises
some questions: How readily available are drugs? Where do they come
from? And how large is the illicit supply system? The answers are
important, not only for background information, but for understanding
our analysis in later chapters.

In this section we lay out what is known and what can reasonably be
deduced about the conditions under which drugs are available to

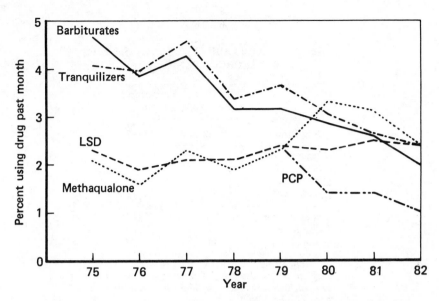

Fig. 2.3—Trends in other drug use among U.S. high school seniors
(from national high school senior surveys, Johnston, Bachman,
and O'Malley, 1982)

consumers. These conditions directly affect usage patterns. Young
people, for example, are more likely to begin using drugs that are
cheap, readily available, and difficult for police to detect. Availability
conditions also constrain feasible methods for control. If a drug is
widely distributed, with a lucrative retail market and a vast network of
local dealers, it will be difficult to reduce the supply for any extended
period of time. These conditions differ sharply among drugs. Therefore, to round out our basic picture of drug use in the U.S. and to
prepare for considering methods of drug control, we examine drug
availability, drug sources, and the scale of the retail drug market.

Table 2.6 shows how high school seniors perceive the availability of
drugs. Both today and eight years ago, 88 percent of high school
seniors reported that they could easily obtain marijuana if they wanted
it. Though no systematic data on purchasing patterns are available, we
suspect that given the large number of adolescent users, they could
readily buy it from friends. The various types of "pills" are also widely
available: More than two-thirds of the seniors report that amphetamines are easily obtained, and although the popularity of barbiturates
and tranquilizers has declined in recent years, more than half of the
respondents report they can locate such drugs.

Table 2.6

PERCEIVED AVAILABILITY OF DRUGS, U.S.
HIGH SCHOOL SENIORS

	Percent Reporting Ready Availability of Drug[a]	
Drug Group	1982	1975
Marijuana	88	88
Cocaine	47	37
LSD	34	46
Heroin	21	24
Amphetamines	71	68
Barbiturates	55	60
Tranquilizers	59	72

[a]Reporting it would be "fairly easy" or "very easy" to obtain the drug. Data from national surveys of high school seniors (Johnston, Bachman, and O'Malley, 1982).

At the other end of the spectrum, heroin appears much more difficult to get. Only one in five seniors reports easy access to heroin, an observation that corresponds with the low rate of use by teenagers and the high degree of police pressure on heroin dealers. Judging by these data, cocaine was formerly rather difficult to obtain, but its recent rise in popularity seems to have opened up more channels of supply to the high school population. Overall, availability closely follows the prevalence of use for each drug. The most striking points are the nearly universal availability of marijuana and the low availability of heroin.

Where does this material originate, and how does it reach the users? Answers to those questions are essential for informed control policies, but difficult to come by. Obviously, suppliers have every incentive to conceal their sources and distribution patterns. Law enforcement agencies obtain some intelligence from seizures, arrests of dealers, and undercover purchases. Table 2.7 summarizes official estimates made by the government interagency National Narcotics Intelligence Consumers Committee (NNICC), indicating the original sources of production for most drug classes as of 1980. The specific foreign countries that provide a particular drug may vary from year to year.

Some marijuana is grown in the United States, and the amount may be increasing, but official intelligence estimates still hold that 75 percent is cultivated in Colombia and exported directly to the U.S., largely by boat. Jamaica is estimated to supply less than 10 percent of the U.S. market, but in both Jamaica and Colombia marijuana is perceived to be a major source of foreign exchange earnings and the economic

Table 2.7

SOURCES OF DRUG SUPPLIES, 1980

	Percent of Total Supply, by Source[a]			
Drug	Foreign Countries	Illicit Domestic Production	Diversion from Licit U.S. Production	Principal Foreign Sources
Marijuana	91	9	0	Colombia, Jamaica, Mexico
Cocaine	100	0	0	Peru, Bolivia, Colombia
Heroin	100	0	0	Pakistan, SW Asia, Mexico, SE Asia
Hallucinogens	0	100	0	—
Stimulants				
Amphetamines	20	80	0	Uncertain
Methamphetamine	5	95	0	Uncertain
Depressants				
Methaqualone	85	5	10	Colombia
Barbiturates	0	0	100	—
Tranquilizers	0	0	100	—

[a]Adapted from data reported in NNICC, *Narcotics Intelligence Estimate, 1980,* Washington, D.C., 1982.

and political support for growers appears strong. Mexico used to be a larger supplier, but in recent years its production has waned. The Mexican central government, unlike the governments of many producer countries, mounts substantial efforts at production control and crop eradication (NNICC, 1983b).

Cocaine and heroin are thought to derive entirely from foreign sources; there is no evidence of coca or opium poppy cultivation in the U.S. At present coca is refined into cocaine hydrochloride in South America and smuggled into this country. Authorities believe that the vast majority of the coca is grown in Peru and Bolivia, but that most of it is shipped through Colombia to the United States (NNICC, 1983b). Opium production and refining is more dispersed. Over the past few years the principal heroin sources have shifted from Mexico and Southeast Asia to Southwest Asia (Pakistan, Iran, and Afghanistan), but these patterns have been extremely volatile. Like cocaine, heroin is an extremely potent drug (doses are measured in milligrams) and can be readily concealed within other cargo, personal luggage, or even body cavities.

Virtually all of the rest of the psychoactive drug supply comes from inside the U.S. Though illegal, LSD and other hallucinogens are manufactured in clandestine laboratories and distributed on the black market. Most if not all PCP is produced in the same way; PCP is still used in veterinary medicine, but legal channels are not thought to supply any significant amount to the illicit market.

The illegal circumstances of domestic production of hallucinogens have resulted in a very unreliable supply for these drugs. PCP is often misrepresented as another more desirable drug (NNICC, 1983b). Such distribution patterns suggest the difficulty in warning young people against specific drugs; though a person may rightly fear PCP's unpredictable effects and avoid the drug, he may get it anyway as a counterfeit.

A modest proportion of illegal stimulants is derived from foreign nations, but the Drug Enforcement Administration (DEA) believes that the vast majority comes from domestic clandestine laboratories. Because it is more difficult to interdict or trace shipments inside this country, it appears that the government has very little information about domestically produced supplies. DEA regularly reports seizures of large quantities of such "dangerous drugs," but official estimates suggest that these represent less than 10 percent of total consumption (GAO, 1983). Recently, DEA has pursued a policy aimed at control of "precursor chemicals"—compounds essential for manufacturing the drug. To that end, increasing attempts have been made to reduce domestic and foreign supplies of P2P, an essential precursor of amphetamines. The response of drug suppliers is to smuggle in P2P, and high school students still find amphetamines readily available (Table 2.6).

In contrast to stimulants, the depressants and tranquilizers have found widespread use in medical practice. For that reason, supplies of the barbiturates (e.g., Seconal) and tranquilizers (e.g., Valium) are thought to originate almost entirely from the legal domestic distribution system. Users may maintain a habit by obtaining legal prescriptions from physicians, or from clinics ("scrip mills") that specialize in easy provision of psychoactive drugs. Alternatively, a user may forge a prescription or steal from a pharmacy. Wholesalers may fraudulently obtain large quantities from manufacturers and sell them on the illicit market. Little reliable information is available on the extent of such practices.

The situation is different for one of the most prominent depressants, methaqualone (Quaalude). Methaqualone was formerly popular as a sedative and sleeping aid until its abuse potential became widely known to the medical profession. Today, government sources estimate that only about one-tenth of the methaqualone supply is derived from the regulated market. In 1980 the majority of the supply came from European manufacturers who (perhaps unwittingly) sold bulk powder to Colombians, who then pressed counterfeit tablets to be smuggled into the U.S. Since then the European sources have been subjected to closer controls, so the supply may be reduced or may be derived from other channels.

Extent of the Drug Market

Perhaps the best appreciation for the extent of drug use can be gained from examining the size of the "retail" drug market, that is, the point at which a supplier sells drugs to the consumer. Our later analysis of drug control procedures will rely heavily on an understanding of this retail market, especially the price and the total value of retail drugs sold.

There are basically two ways of estimating the size of the drug market. One is to estimate the amount of drugs produced. Government agencies have used that method in the past but have found it rather unsatisfactory. To estimate cocaine production, for example, one must know the acreage cultivated, the yield of coca leaf per acre, the efficiency of refining operations in extracting cocaine from the leaf, the extent of losses along the distribution chain, and—most important—the amount consumed outside the U.S. Few if any of these parameters can be measured with confidence. For many other drugs, such as domestically produced amphetamine, the data are entirely lacking.

A second method is to estimate U.S. consumption of the drug. This is done by combining estimates of the number of users (e.g., from a national survey) with data on frequency of use and quantity consumed per session. Such procedures appear more reliable than production estimates, though the resulting figures are still subject to considerable variation depending on assumptions about drug purity and the habits of heavy vs. average users (NNICC, 1983b). Given this uncertainty, we will first present current official estimates prepared by NNICC and then discuss what we view as a reasonable range of variation that should surround those estimates.

Table 2.8 presents recent estimates published by NNICC. The government attempts consumption estimates only for marijuana, cocaine, and heroin; for other drugs the data are insufficient. For each drug, the estimation procedure begins with data on the number of regular users (for cocaine and marijuana, derived from surveys; for heroin, based on NIDA's estimates of the number of "active addicts"). Then, estimates of drug consumption rates per user are applied, yielding a figure for the total quantity consumed in the nation. Total quantity

40

consumed is then multiplied by average retail price to produce total retail value.

In these estimates the figures for retail price are probably the most reliable, as they reflect assembled information from actual police undercover purchases. However, prices may vary substantially by market levels, between areas, and even across dealers in the same area (Carlson et al., 1983).[8] The figures for quantities consumed and total retail value are the product of rather involved calcuations requiring numerous assumptions, some of which are hard to test. Thus, these are truly estimates, intended to convey the magnitude but not the precise level of drug consumption and sales.

What shows through clearly is the vast size of the drug market. Law enforcement authorities acknowledge that in the face of this extensive distribution system they intercept and confiscate only a modest fraction of drugs in the illicit market (GAO, 1983). The volume of imports alone suggests the difficulties in attempting to "seal off" the borders. The retail value estimates indicate that very large sums are at stake, and dealers have strong financial incentives to overcome any obstacles the police may place in their way.

Table 2.8

OFFICIAL ESTIMATES OF DRUG SUPPLY SYSTEM CHARACTERISTICS

Item	Marijuana 1980[a]	Cocaine 1981[b]	Heroin 1980[a]
Number of monthly users (millions)	25.0	6.7	0.5
Quantity consumed (000 kg)	12,600	34.4	4.0
Retail price per kg	$1700	$625,000	$1.9 million
Total retail value ($ billion)	22.5	21.5	8.7

[a]Midpoints of ranges reported in the federal Narcotics Intelligence Estimate for 1980 (NNICC, 1982).

[b]Number of users (6.7 million) inferred from the Narcotics Intelligence Estimate of 15 million annual users for 1981, of whom 55 percent did not use in the past month (NNICC, 1983b). Retail price taken from DEA data cited by the General Accounting Office (1983) and Carlson et al. (1983). Total retail value inferred from price ($21.5 billion = 34,400 kg × $625,000/kg).

---

[8]Retail prices also vary by the purity and potency of the active ingredient; for instance, DEA reports prices up to $7000 per kg for high-potency *sinsemilla* marijuana (NNICC, 1982). We have cited prices for the commonest type (Colombian).

Table 2.8 also shows that these three drugs vary widely in many important respects. For example, heroin commands a price of almost $2 million for one kilogram (about 2.2 lb.), whereas the same weight of marijuana goes for less than $2000, only one-thousandth as much.[9] Yet the size of the marijuana user population is so large that the total retail value of all marijuana consumed is more than twice that of heroin. The quantities also vary enormously: To service the demand for marijuana, smugglers are estimated to import about 12 million kilograms, while cocaine and heroin smugglers move much less volume. These differences show why we must analyze each drug separately.

Other observers of the drug market have arrived at rather different values for some of these parameters. The official NNICC report for 1980 noted that the Internal Revenue Service had commissioned a separate evaluation, which produced considerably lower estimates of consumption and retail value for cocaine and marijuana. In 1981 NNICC revised its estimation procedure and incorporated some of the IRS methodology (NNICC, 1982, 1983b).

We too hold reservations about the magnitude of the NNICC estimates. For marijuana and cocaine, the NNICC estimates have assumed there are substantially more users than are shown by recent survey data. As an example, the NNICC 1981 cocaine calculation started with 1979 survey data and projected a rapid growth in cocaine use, concluding that there would be 6.7 million cocaine users by 1981. Actually, the 1982 survey revealed only 4.2 million users. In the case of marijuana, a recent study by Abt Associates used the 1982 survey to calculate that U.S. marijuana consumption was about 4,330,000 kilograms rather than the NNICC figure of 12,600,000 kilograms (Carlson et al., 1983; NNICC, 1983b).[10]

A brief examination of heroin addict behavior also raises concern about the official figures on the addict population. Several independent studies have suggested that active heroin addicts commit crimes such as robbery at very high rates (Ball et al., 1982; Inciardi, 1979; Chaiken and Chaiken, 1982). If the nation really possessed 500,000 addicts who committed robberies at the rates reported in these

---

[9]Prices, of course, must be interpreted with respect to dosage. NNICC (1983b) suggests a typical cocaine use session requires 45 mg (3 administrations of 50 mg at 30 percent purity); at $625 per gram such a session would cost $28. From unpublished data in the 1982 high school senior survey (Johnston et al., 1982), we calculate a typical marijuana cigarette contains about .44 grams; at $1.70 per gram, such a dose would cost only $0.75. Heroin doses vary widely, but a 20-mg dose at $2000 per gram would cost $40.

[10]Among the important refinements made during this process was segregating the consumption and price calculations into groups of heavy users, infrequent users, etc. In the most recent work (Carlson et al., 1983), it is assumed that very heavy users pay lower-than-retail prices, corresponding to the tendency of such users (who themselves may be retail dealers) to have access to higher-level suppliers.

42

samples, the national robbery rate arising from adult addicts alone would be higher than the actual rate of robberies by all adults (Reuter, in press).[11] Therefore, we regard the official NNICC estimates of consumption and retail value as upper bounds for the true values.

The uncertainty about the true scale of the drug market is not merely an academic question. The larger the market, the less effect will any given attempt at supply control have. As we shall see in Chap. 3, the effect of, say, doubling the arrest rate of cocaine dealers depends intimately on the current retail value of the cocaine market. For our argument in the remainder of this report, it is crucial to have an estimate of the reasonable range of variation for these figures. Table 2.9 shows the lower-bound estimates we will use. By employing lower-bound values, we overstate the true effect of supply control, but as we shall see, the effects are small even with overstatement.

Because the data for heroin are less complete and not essential to our analysis, we do not attempt an independent estimate for the heroin market.[12] For marijuana and cocaine, we shall take the Abt estimate as the lower bound. Note that the Abt estimates do not contain any upward adjustment for survey underreporting of consumption, so they might be too low. When necessary, in the analysis below we will show results assuming the lower-bound estimates (which are probably too low) and the upper-bound estimates (which are probably too high). Thus we will be reasonably confident that the size of the true effects falls within the range we will identify.

Table 2.9

ALTERNATIVE ESTIMATES OF DRUG SUPPLY
SYSTEM CHARACTERISTICS

Item	Marijuana	Cocaine
Number of monthly users (millions)[a]	20.0	4.2
Quantity consumed (000 kg)[b]	4,330	23.1
Total retail value ($ billion)[b]	7.4	11.3

[a]Estimated from responses to the 1982 national household survey (NIDA, 1983b).

[b]Adapted from Abt Associates estimates for 1982 (Carlson et al., 1983).

[11]These calculations allow for the fact that much of an addict's time is spent in prison, treatment, or otherwise in situations where high-rate criminal activity is unlikely.

[12]There is great uncertainty about the number of active heroin users. However, the Abt estimate of heroin's 1982 retail value ($7.9 billion, from Carlson et al., 1983) was very close to the official estimates for 1980 and 1981.

SUMMARY

The principal psychoactive drugs of abuse fall into three broad categories: (1) strictly controlled or illegal drugs, including marijuana, cocaine, heroin, and the hallucinogens (such as LSD and PCP); (2) drugs regulated by prescription, including stimulants (such as amphetamines), sedative/sleeping pills (such as barbiturates and methaqualone), and tranquilizers; and (3) over-the-counter preparations, the most prominent of which are alcoholic beverages and tobacco cigarettes. These drugs vary widely in their short-term effects, long-term effects, and potential for dependence. Heroin, sedatives, alcohol, and cigarettes frequently produce physical dependence, whereas the others may produce only psychic dependence (i.e., a desire or tendency to continue taking the drug). Many of these drugs, especially alcohol, cigarettes, and sedatives, cause known adverse effects on body tissues and organs; the others are widely suspected of causing harmful effects on the body if used over long periods of time. Because most drugs cause short-term impairment of memory, learning capacity, and ability to concentrate, they appear to pose special risks for adolescents in school.

Despite legal prohibitions against many psychoactive drugs, they are widely used. National surveys lead to an estimate of 32 million annual marijuana users and 12 million cocaine users; for other illicit or regulated drugs, the numbers are between 1 and 10 million. Use rates are highest among young adults (age 18 to 25) and adolescents (age 12 to 17). Among adolescents, alcohol is the leading drug (used by 70 percent of high school seniors), followed by marijuana and cigarettes (29 or 30 percent each). Stimulants (11 percent) and cocaine (5 percent) are next in popularity. The rate of daily use, which may indicate serious potential for dependence, is substantial only for cigarettes (21 percent), alcohol (6 percent), and marijuana (6 percent).

Recent trends suggest that adolescent use of marijuana and cigarettes peaked in the 1970s and has since declined somewhat. Use of cocaine and stimulants has risen since 1975. Both of these trends may have stabilized in the past one to two years; sufficient data to project the future are lacking. Most other drugs, including PCP and methaqualone, which were popular among teenagers in the 1970s, have been on the decline in the past five years. Heroin, the drug most closely associated with addiction and crime in the public mind, is used by very small numbers of adolescents (fewer than 0.5 percent) and causes few deaths or injuries among that group. From all of the data we have reviewed, we conclude that the greatest short-term risks for adolescents are those created by alcohol and marijuana (impaired learning and driving ability); the greatest long-term risks come from cigarette smoking (respiratory and cardiovascular disease). Stimulants, including cocaine, also pose significant short-term risks because of their tendency to lead to increased dosage. The other drugs also create risks, but those risks appear less substantial.

Most of the above drugs are readily available to adolescents. Among the more popular drugs, 88 percent of high school seniors report that marijuana is easy to obtain; even for cocaine, 47 percent report easy access. This widespread availability arises from sources of supply that are difficult to control and that differ sharply across drugs. Marijuana and cocaine, for example, originate largely from foreign countries and are smuggled into the U.S. Hallucinogens, stimulants, and sedatives are produced for the most part within the U.S., either by illegal secret laboratories or by diversion from legal pharmaceutical supplies. The market for these substances is vast; official government estimates of the retail value of drugs actually consumed are $22 billion for marijuana, $22 billion for cocaine, and $9 billion for heroin. In each case our analysis suggests the above estimates may be too high, but the scale of the market is still very large. Its very scale presents a formidable problem for attempts to control drug use.

Chapter 3

DRUG LAW ENFORCEMENT

As Chap. 2 makes clear, drug use has created a large and very profitable drug market in this country, a market linked with a larger, international, illegal drug "industry." U.S. drug policy has historically focused on controlling that market through aggressive enforcement of laws against manufacture, sale, and possession of prohibited drugs. Indeed we have seen (Fig. 1.3) that the federal government has put new emphasis on law enforcement in the past five years, on the assumption that this can (1) reduce the quantity of drugs coming into the country; (2) make it more risky and more difficult for traffickers to distribute drugs; (3) create shortages of drugs in the illicit market; and (4) raise the price of drugs to consumers, hence ultimately reducing consumption.

Are these assumptions justified? The evidence on the effectiveness of drug law enforcement to date is very mixed. On the one hand, it is true that in the case of heroin, the consumer price is many hundreds of times its production cost and obtaining the drug is both risky and difficult. Those conditions can be attributed in large part to law enforcement efforts against dealers and users. Presumably the high prices, frequent shortages, and serious risks confronting users have kept heroin consumption much lower than it would otherwise be. In the case of other prohibited drugs, law enforcement pressure has been less intense, but we assume it has restricted their consumption somewhat.

On the other hand, there is serious doubt that tighter law enforcement can reduce the availability of drugs much further. The greatly increased federal enforcement effort since 1978, aimed particularly at cocaine and marijuana, has not dried up drug supplies. We have already seen, in Chap. 2, that 88 percent of the high school seniors reported in 1982 that they could easily obtain marijuana if they wanted it. That percentage was the same as in 1975. The number of cocaine users has not declined. Moreover, prices have not increased, when inflation is taken into account. For example, the inflation-adjusted retail price for cocaine actually declined between 1979 and 1982 (from $865 to $625 per pure gram in 1982 prices).[1]

---

[1]Real prices for marijuana were stable ($1.71 per gram in 1979, $1.70 in 1982); the heroin price declined ($2,980 per gram in 1979, $2,130 in 1982, expressed in 1982 prices) (General Accounting Office, 1983, p. 16).

We argue below that, for several reasons, intensified law enforcement is not likely to make large inroads against drug use. Existing strategies cannot eliminate or even tightly constrain the production of drugs. Marijuana, cocaine, and heroin can be cheaply and easily produced, and there is no feasible method of creating an "absolute scarcity" of supply, either through crop reduction or the seizing of drugs in transit. The most law enforcement can do is to increase dealers' risks, thus driving up retail prices—but probably not by much, because the scale of drug dealing has become so great. Moreover, drug dealers may be able to adapt their procedures to reduce the effectiveness of intensified or innovative law enforcement.

THE NATURE OF DRUG LAW ENFORCEMENT

Principal Drugs Targeted

Law enforcement has concentrated on three principal drugs: heroin, cocaine, and marijuana.[2] We deal here primarily with marijuana and cocaine. As we saw in Chap. 2, marijuana is the most widely used illicit drug among young people. Fewer use cocaine, but the rate of use has risen in recent years, and its popularity among the 18-to-25 age group suggests that it may become more of a problem among the younger group—if it follows the pattern of marijuana use. In addition, we have seen that the trade in these drugs supports a mass market with millions of regular users. This mass market makes it particularly likely that the drugs will continue to be readily available.

Although the police have historically devoted a great deal of attention to heroin, we will discuss heroin only to a limited extent. The principal reason for this is our focus on adolescents: Few teenagers use heroin, and few experience medical crises related to heroin use. Moreover, the heroin market differs in kind from the other two in its relation to property crimes, its vulnerability to police informants, public attitudes toward it, and the character of its dealers and users. However, the heroin market does have some characteristics that provide instructive analogs for the marijuana and cocaine markets, and we note these in our discussion.

---

[2]Although enforcement agencies also attempt to disrupt the trade in "dangerous drugs" (which includes all controlled substances other than heroin, cocaine, and marijuana), it appears that only a small portion of effort goes into these drugs and little information is available to document law enforcement activities directed at them. Dangerous drugs accounted for 15 percent of local drug arrests in 1980 (FBI, 1980).

Enforcement Against Levels of the Drug Market

Law enforcement agencies tend to specialize at different levels of the drug market. Table 3.1 shows characteristics of the various market levels and law enforcement agencies concerned with them. The federal government strives to reduce foreign drug crop production, to interdict imports before drug shipments reach the U.S., and to attack drug distributors and wholesalers ("high-level dealers"). State and local authorities carry out street enforcement against drug retailers and other low-level dealers. As Table 3.1 shows, federal agencies spent almost $600 million on drug law enforcement in Fiscal Year 1982, mostly on interdiction and operations against high-level dealers. No data are available for drug-related expenditures of local law enforcement agencies, but the amount is surely large; drug arrests accounted for 6 percent of all arrests in 1981 (FBI, 1981), and total local police expenditures amounted to $11.8 billion. Not all arrests have the same cost, but even if each drug arrest cost only one-fourth as much as other arrests, the total cost allocable to local drug enforcement would represent over $175 million.

The scale of the federal government's antidrug effort is significant by various other measures as well. For instance, the DEA Fiscal Year 1982 budget of $208 million may be compared with the total FBI budget of $740 million. Drug defendants accounted for 18 percent of the 36,000 defendants in federal court in 1982, and persons convicted of drug violations made up 25 percent of the federal prison population (Flanagan and McLeod, 1983). Federal spending on drug enforcement has been increasing very sharply in recent years, and this trend may continue.[3]

Enforcement Against Adolescent Markets

Clearly, most law enforcement activity is aimed at the general drug market and not specifically at adolescents. It seems reasonable that a given price increase for drugs (say, due to law enforcement) might inhibit youthful consumption more than adult consumption, since the incomes of youth are smaller. However, we lack evidence about the responsiveness of consumption to price changes among either youth or adults.

Besides the police, schools could possibly play an important enforcement role in adolescent drug markets. It seems likely that a great deal of drug use, and certainly some of the most troubling use, takes place

---

[3]President Reagan announced a new regional Task Force program in October 1982. Congress appropriated an additional $127.5 million for this in FY 1983 and the figure may rise to $200 million in FY 1984.

Table 3.1

LAW ENFORCEMENT AGAINST LEVELS OF THE DRUG MARKET

Market Level	Main Law Enforcement Activity	Principal Government Agencies	Federal Government Expenditures, FY 1982 ($Million)[a]
Production	Crop eradication, substitution	Department of State, foreign governments	61
Import	Interdiction: seizure of goods, couriers, vessels	Coast Guard, Customs Service	278
Domestic Distribution	Arrest of "high-level" dealers; seizure of dealer assets	Drug Enforcement Administration, Internal Revenue Service	244[b]
Retail Sales	Arrest of retail ("low-level") dealers	Local police	—

[a]Estimated by the General Accounting Office (1983), p. 11. Includes investigative functions, but not prosecution, court, or prison costs.

[b]Includes GAO estimate of $208 million spent by DEA, plus White House estimate of $36 million spent by IRS (Drug Abuse Policy Office, 1982). Excludes small amount spent in FY 1982 by FBI, which did not devote major resources to drug investigations until FY 1983.

in schools. Schools may also be a convenient site for drug sales to young people. However, we have found no evidence on how effective school policies are in reducing drug use. Apart from occasional press reports on incidents at specific schools (e.g., *Los Angeles Times*, 1983), we lack even a description of existing school policies. Some schools are apparently aggressive in their enforcement of bans on use or possession of drugs, occasionally conducting random searches of student lockers and expelling or suspending students found in possession of drugs. Other schools appear to make little effort either to detect or to punish violators. Because we have no systematic information on the effects of school policies, we will confine our analysis to efforts by federal, state, and local law enforcement authorities.

The Possibility of Legalization

One alternative to continued drug law enforcement is legalization or regulation of currently illicit drugs. Legalization has been considered by several observers who note that current drug control policies have numerous undesirable consequences, such as creating criminal records for otherwise law-abiding persons, producing large criminal incomes with associated police corruption, and generating property crimes committed by heroin addicts (National Academy of Sciences, 1982; Drug Abuse Council, 1980). Clearly, legalization would reduce some of these economic and social costs, but with unknown effects on consumption. We have not attempted to estimate these possible effects because there are simply no convincing data to suggest what would happen under a legalization plan.[4] We presume that increased availability would lead to increased consumption, even if sales were regulated. The adverse effects arising from higher exposure to risks would have to be weighed against the benefits of reduced costs. In our judgment, the best evidence on these costs and benefits—perhaps the only credible evidence—would be obtained from an experiment in a restricted geographic area. However, we see no feasible method of controlling the flow of drugs out of such a restricted area, given the high demand for drugs and the permeability of state borders. Hence even an experiment would yield very imperfect data. Because of the absence of any credible data on this subject, we have not attempted to evaluate the consequences of legalization programs.

Risks and Drug Prices

To trace the possible outcomes of continued drug law enforcement, it is important to understand how police activity affects the drug market. The immediate objectives of law enforcement are to seize drug supplies, to apprehend and punish dealers, and to make successful cases against those arrested. Ultimately, accomplishing those objectives is expected to reduce drug use by restricting the availability of drugs. There are two ways in which enforcement could affect availability: It could limit or eliminate the physical supply, or it could increase the risks of trading in drugs.

---

[4]Studies of the effect of decriminalizing possession of small amounts of marijuana have found that this has little effect on prevalence of marijuana use. However, decriminalization, with sale still subject to criminal sanction, provides little evidence on the effects of complete legalization, since most of the current risk of punishment is borne by dealers. The British experience with medically dispensed heroin (Trebach, 1982), undertaken initially when the nation had a very modest addict population, provides only slight evidence as to its potential impact in the U.S.

We shall see that there is little prospect that any strategy can create an absolute scarcity of drugs. The other effect of law enforcement, namely increasing the riskiness of being a drug dealer, is the more important. (We use the term "dealer" to include all participants in the drug trades, apart from final users.) By threatening dealers with penalties, ranging from arrest, through seizure of drugs and financial assets, to imprisonment, law enforcement can raise the price of drugs. The higher the risk, the higher the price that dealers will demand; and the higher the price, the less will be consumed.

It is important to note that drug dealers face two types of risk. One is the set of risks imposed by others in the business. Suppliers may sell dealers a lower quality or quantity of drugs than had been agreed upon, competitors may use violence against other dealers to increase their own share of the market, and customers may steal drugs or money from dealers. Dealers lack many of the protections of the law that permit legal commerce to operate smoothly. Some of their income is compensation for this kind of risk. We have no systematic data on the significance of these events, but it is quite plausible that dealers face very considerable risk as a result of the actions of other participants.

The other type of risk comes from law enforcement agencies. The more resources are devoted to drug law enforcement, the higher the probability that a dealer will be arrested, imprisoned, or deprived of drugs or financial assets. We shall be focusing on these risks, since they are directly affected by law enforcement efforts.[5]

Law enforcement agencies have long recognized the appropriateness of price as an indicator of availability, and frequently rate their success in terms of the change in price of drugs.[6] We shall follow that practice, and in some of our analysis we will attempt to estimate the effect on prices of various efforts to increase the extent or effectiveness of drug law enforcement.[7]

----

[5]The two kinds of risk are clearly related. It is only because drugs are expensive and somewhat difficult to obtain that dealers face such high risks from other participants. Nonetheless, we shall deal only with the second type because it seems plausible that the risks from other participants are not very responsive to marginal changes in the risks imposed by law enforcement.

[6]Purity is also cited for heroin and (less frequently) for cocaine. It is usually assumed that price and purity are negatively related, so that purity thus adds no new information.

[7]There are two caveats about using price as an indicator of law enforcement efficacy: (1) The demand for heroin, in the short run, may be insensitive to price since many addicts may be unable to moderate their usage levels when the price rises. In the long run, the increased price would dampen sales since it would reduce the flow of new users into the addict pool. This argument, of course, does not apply to marijuana and cocaine use, because few such users are as dependent as heroin addicts. (2) More intense enforcement might make it more difficult for users to find dealers. If so, users would have to invest more time to find the drug, and this may lower the cash amount they are

We now turn to an evaluation of the prospects for each of the major types of enforcement.

REDUCING FOREIGN CROP PRODUCTION

The most appealing method of controlling drug use would be simply to cut off the source of supply—if only that were possible. U.S. policy statements have historically claimed that the nation can never hope to solve its drug problem unless the countries where drug crops are grown reduce production and control exports (Musto, 1973). Leading law enforcement officials continue to emphasize that enforcement within the U.S. alone cannot solve the problem (Mullen, in U.S. Senate, 1981, p. 242). Unfortunately, although production control efforts have worked in a few countries, there is little prospect that they could be extended widely enough to put much of a dent in the U.S. market.

Approaches to Controlling Foreign Drug Production

The U.S. government has used two main approaches to reduce export of drugs to this country: law enforcement assistance and crop reduction. Law enforcement assistance is the easier to carry out. The Drug Enforcement Administration has offices in many of the major producer countries and assists their police agencies in conducting investigations (U.S. Senate, 1981). It also provides these agencies with funds for equipment and training. But there is little optimism even among U.S. officials that law enforcement alone can have much impact on production.

To encourage crop reduction, the United States provides some foreign governments with resources for eradicating crops, for example, by spraying with herbicides or manually uprooting plants. The United States has also funded a number of projects (directly or through multilateral agencies such as the United Nations Fund for Drug Abuse Control) aimed at providing farmers with alternative commercial crops; these are called crop substitution programs. This approach is the most costly, but it is often justified as the only long-range solution to the problem. To date, most of these projects have involved opium production, and our evaluation of this approach will rely largely on its effects on heroin export.

---

willing to pay for a given quantity of the drug. However, the networks for marijuana and cocaine are less susceptible to police disruption, so law enforcement may not be able to raise the time needed to find a source by much. Thus, this effect is probably also significant only for heroin traffic.

Impediments to Control of Production

The federal government now has over a decade of experience with attempts to control drug production and export in other countries (Pekkanen, 1980), but the result has often been disillusionment where the programs confronted difficulties rooted in the economic and political conditions of the producer countries. Using the case of opium as an example (since experience is richest for that crop), let us examine several reasons why most foreign control programs have failed to make a lasting impact on the U.S. drug market:

- Economic importance of the drug crop for growers;
- Lack of skills or resources for growing substitute crops;
- Lack of infrastructure that permits delivery of alternative crops to market;
- Existence of legal uses for the illegal crop;
- Weak control by goverments in producing areas;
- Complexity of U.S. relations with producing countries; and
- Abundance of potential supply countries.

To take basic economic considerations first: Unless farmers are given other productive opportunities, law enforcement will do little more than make production more covert. Many farmers have no other way to earn money. In remote areas of Burma and Thailand, for instance, poppies may be the only crop that be can be relied on to provide a steady cash income. Under these circumstances, it is difficult to motivate local police to attack their neighbors' livelihood.

Furthermore, poor farmers in remote areas may have neither the agricultural skills nor the resources to grow an unfamiliar crop. Even if they could and would grow it, many of these areas lack the infrastructure (roads particularly) that permits the efficient delivery of bulkier and more perishable crops to distant markets. It would take years to overcome these problems, and even then drug production may continue to flourish. Nowhere, as yet, has development of alternative cash crops reduced opium production in a substantial area.

Besides, poppies provide animal feed, cooking oil, and fuel— legitimate uses that make it more difficult for governments to ban poppy growing.

Another major problem in reducing crops is the generally weak control of governments in producing areas. For example, the Thai and Burmese governments have long been fighting insurgent movements in the hills inhabited by the poppy growers. And the Pakistani and Laotian governments have little effective control in the remote regions that produce opium. Even where governments are strongly motivated and have feasible plans, they are likely to have great difficulty implementing them.

Opium crop reduction has been further impeded by the complex relations between the United States and many of the producer countries, and by the fact that many of them do not take the drug problem very seriously. The United States would like Pakistan to adopt certain policies toward Afghanistan. It seeks to retain bases in Thailand. It would like Mexico to support its policies in Central America. Consequently, it is awkward to exert heavy pressure on such governments to deal with what they view as primarily a U.S. social problem. At Congressional prompting, restrictions have been placed on U.S. aid to those nations involved in drug production, but these have been as difficult to maintain as restrictions related to human rights policies in other nations (U.S. Senate, 1981, p. 230). Producer governments can be expected to accept whatever aid is offered for the purpose of suppressing the drug trade, and to pass much legislation at U.S. insistence, but translating that into a sustained program of crop substitution incentives and law enforcement is another matter.

Nonetheless, some optimism prevails in the U.S. government about the prospects for more effective diplomatic efforts. For instance, State Department representatives have told us that in the past few years senior U.S. government officials have shown increased interest in discussing drug-related issues with their foreign counterparts and that the latter are more willing to follow up on promises of action (personal communication, Department of State). Pakistan's recent success in reducing the area under illicit poppy cultivation is cited as an instance of effective diplomatic pressure. However, it is also possible that this cooperation reflects Pakistan's awareness of its own growing population of heavy heroin users, rather than increased compliance with U.S. wishes (Trebach, 1982).

It is also important to note that U.S. heroin consumption accounts for a small portion of the total world opium production. At its peak, U.S. heroin consumption is estimated to have been five tons, requiring about 50 tons of opium (NNICC, 1982). Yet world opium production fluctuates between 1000 and 2000 tons per year, much of it consumed in the producer countries. Even large production cuts might have little effect on heroin availability in the U.S., since American addicts are likely to be the wealthiest and therefore able to outbid other user groups.

Advocates of crop reduction efforts might argue that these impediments could be overcome—if the United States, and other countries, could devote enough resources and provide enough pressure and incentives to make producer countries cooperate. However, unless every producer country cooperates, cutting off supplies from one country simply spurs production and export in another. Both Turkey and Mexico succeeded in reducing opium production, but ironically, both "success stories" illustrate the problems that prevent more dramatic reduction in supplies.

Because Turkey was reputed to produce 80 percent of the opium used for American heroin supply, in 1971 the U.S. government signed a treaty to compensate Turkish poppy growers in return for a Turkish government prohibition on poppy farming. The ban appears to have succeeded: Very little opium was grown in Turkey while the treaty was in force (Epstein, 1977). Although Turkey abrogated the treaty after three years, it subsequently imposed stringent controls on poppy production, designed to assure that there was little leakage from the legal opium market. The penalties for violating these laws were sufficiently harsh to discourage widespread illegal production. It is generally believed that Turkey now provides only negligible amounts of opium for the illicit market (personal communication, Department of State).

Unfortunately, the development of Mexican heroin production rapidly compensated for whatever shortfall the Turkish ban caused in the U.S. heroin market. By 1973, Mexican heroin accounted for 80 percent of total U.S. heroin consumption (NNICC, 1982), which regained the level prevailing before the Turkish ban.

In response, the United States made an agreement to supply Mexico with equipment and training to help in eradicating poppy fields. The Mexican government also attacked marijuana cultivation by spraying with the herbicide paraquat. Evidently, its interest in eradicating marijuana was based largely on concern about rising use of the drug in Mexico. Nevertheless, the spraying had a very important effect on the U.S. marijuana market. The demand for Mexican marijuana fell drastically among U.S. consumers because of widespread belief that smoking marijuana that has been sprayed with paraquat is hazardous (Institute of Medicine, 1982; U.S. House of Representatives, 1978).

Although the United States did not prompt the spraying of marijuana in Mexico, the program was successful in reducing the consumption of supplies from a source country. Consequently, it is germane to our point about the impediments to control: Colombia, which had previously been a minor supplier, quickly replaced Mexico as a major source (NNICC, 1982). Thus, as in the case of Turkish opium, effective action by a single producing nation was quickly negated by increased supply from another source country.

Cocaine and Marijuana Production

Most of the problems discussed above have been illustrated by U.S. attempts to control the supply of heroin. Do we have any reason to be more sanguine about reducing production of marijuana and cocaine? To answer that we need to characterize the production and control of each in the source countries.

Cocaine is produced from the coca leaf, which is grown only in Peru, Bolivia, and Colombia. Although no one knows for certain whether it can be grown readily in other locations and other environments, there is plenty of room to increase production in the present growing areas. The coca leaf is cultivated by numerous peasant farmers, generally in very small plots. By one estimate, Bolivia has 23,000 coca farmers (U.S. Department of State, 1983). There is no comparable estimate for Peru, but the area under cultivation in 1980 is estimated to have been about 50,000 hectares. In both countries, the growing area has expanded rapidly since the late 1970s, spilling over into Colombia, which was not listed as a coca producer until about 1980 (NNICC, 1982). This expansion of coca production has been at the expense of other crops.

The coca leaf itself has been used by Peruvians for at least 500 years as a mild stimulant, and chewing the leaves is still legal in Peru above a certain altitude. The leaf is also used to produce substances for non-stimulant purposes. For example, with certain constituents removed, the processed leaf is used as a flavoring in Coca-Cola; and refined cocaine is used as a therapeutic drug in a number of countries. However, the vast bulk of coca leaf is processed into coca paste where it is grown, and then shipped to Colombia, where it is refined into cocaine hydrochloride.[8] It enters the United States in this form.

Unlike coca, marijuana can be, and is, grown throughout the world in a variety of environments. Most U.S. supplies come from Colombia, Jamaica, and Mexico, in descending order of volume. Domestic U.S. production is still believed quite low but is increasing, mostly on the West Coast. The Middle East and North Africa have long been major producers for local and European markets. Also unlike coca, marijuana has few legal uses,[9] requires no processing once the plant is harvested, and has a relatively short life unless stored in proper conditions. There are no adequate estimates of total production in the major

---

[8]Some 200 to 500 kg of coca leaf produces 2.5 kg of coca paste, which, in combination with acetone and ether produces 1 kg of cocaine hydrochloride (NNICC, 1982).

[9]The hemp plant was formerly grown for production of fiber for rope and twine, use of the seeds in bird and other feed, production of oil for paints, etc. Today these uses are rare in the U.S. Although it may still be put to such purposes in some Third World countries, they do not generally grow it as a commercial crop.

export nations.[10] Even with good acreage estimates, the lack of adequate data on the yield per acre prevents valid production estimates.

In both Colombia and Jamaica, marijuana exporting is associated with significant official corruption. At the urging of the U.S. government, the Colombian national police mount high-visibility campaigns against the trade, and in some years seize thousands of tons. However, the fact that price in producer countries has increased very little over the last few years suggests that production is still considered a low-risk activity.

Prospects for Control of Marijuana and Cocaine Production

To date, U.S. crop-reduction efforts have concentrated on opium. Until recently, neither the State Department nor Congress gave much attention to control of either marijuana or coca production (U.S. Senate, 1977). However, there is little reason to believe that dedicating more resources to control their production would much reduce availability of the two drugs in the U.S.

Marijuana, like opium, can be grown virtually anywhere. Even if U.S. efforts could stop production in the current source countries, others may well take up the slack, just as Colombia quickly replaced Mexican supplies after the paraquat spraying. At the very least, we would expect U.S. domestic production to increase. Under the circumstances, dedicating resources to overcome other impediments to control in any given country would seem wasteful.

Because coca is presently produced only in the Andean regions of three countries, crop reduction efforts there might appear more promising. The fact that coca is grown nowhere else raises the hope that it is more difficult to produce elsewhere and, therefore, that alternative sources of supply would be more costly if the current producer countries could mount effective crop reduction programs. However, as our description of the crop implies, other impediments are quite strong: The production and use of the crop are deeply ingrained in the native culture; it has a large legitimate market; the governments have weak control in the remote growing areas; and it has unique attraction as a cash crop.

That last obstacle has considerable significance for any alternative crop programs. Coca is, indeed, a traditional crop, and many small farmers in remote regions of the Andes probably do not have the skills or resources to grow other crops. However, for other farmers coca is a

---

[10]The most recent *Narcotics Intelligence Estimate* (NNICC, 1983b) notes that prior acreage and production estimates are implausibly high and that U.S. officials making on-site inspections found much lower than reported acreage under cultivation.

new crop that has replaced more "traditional" crops because it is so much more profitable—even at the low prices farmers are paid. It may well be that efforts to raise the skill of peasant farmers have the negative consequence of raising their receptivity to shifting to the most profitable crop, coca. Consequently, any alternative crop progams might have to be accompanied by strong government control and law enforcement,[11] which has proven difficult to deliver in a sustained fashion. Much the same could be said about marijuana, especially since the development of new Colombian strains suggests the presence of sophisticated business interests rather than traditional small farming.

For the marijuana and coca producing countries, the greatest impediments to crop reduction are probably weak government control and ineffective law enforcement. As our descriptions above suggest, the governments involved lack strong incentives for mounting crop reduction programs; and they have strong economic and political incentives for not doing so.[12] In economies that are otherwise rather weak, these crops provide a noticeable share of national income. Actions to reduce them would be unpopular not only with farmers, but also with those involved in exporting the drug. Unless the foreign governments perceive some other pressing reason for crop reduction programs—as Mexico did in 1973—U.S. efforts will have little effect. They may produce no more than the highly visible, but ineffectual, Colombian seizures of marijuana mentioned above.

This is not to say that the United States should give up all programs aimed at crop reduction. However, it should be recognized that they serve largely symbolic purposes. The rationale for these programs cannot be found in their effect on domestic U.S. drug consumption. Nevertheless, these programs may help producer countries deal with their own drug abuse problems, and they indicate to the rest of the world that the United States takes its own and the international drug problem seriously.

---

[11]Turkey offered rather extreme disincentives in its attempt to prevent leakage from the legal opium market: According to a USAID official, one was the threat to tear up the authorized poppy crops of all members of a village if one member was caught growing unauthorized poppies.

[12]In one case, Bolivia in 1980 and 1981, high-level government complicity in cocaine trafficking was a contributing factor leading DEA to close its offices and withdraw its personnel (U.S. Department of State, 1983, p. 2).

ENFORCEMENT AGAINST RETAIL DEALERS

The failure of crop reduction efforts in the producer countries indicates that it would be impossible to cut off the entire supply of drugs at the source; some supplies will always be available. The best that law enforcement can do is to increase dealers' risks and thus drive retail prices higher.

Risks of Arrest and Incarceration for Retail Drug Dealers

As Table 3.2 shows, local police make a great many arrests, but the numbers become less impressive when we consider that there are 20 million regular marijuana users and over 4 million regular cocaine users. Certainly, arrests can make hardly a dent in these user populations; accordingly, most police activity is aimed at dealers.

But dealers are not likely to find the threat of arrest very worrisome. Over 80 percent of arrests are for drug possession, not for sale; and most (72 percent) are for marijuana possession, which rarely results in jail or prison time.[13] Therefore, it cannot be taken as a serious sanction

Table 3.2

ARRESTS FOR DRUG LAW VIOLATIONS: U.S. TOTAL, 1981

Drug Arrest	Number of Arrests by Local Police[a]		Number of Regular Users[b]
	Possession	Sale	
Marijuana	344,000	56,000	20,000,000
Cocaine and heroin	49,000	23,000	4,200,000 to 4,700,000

[a]FBI Uniform Crime Reports (1981).

[b]Marijuana and cocaine monthly users estimated from 1982 national household survey (NIDA, 1983b). Number of regular heroin users reported in federal Narcotics Intelligence Estimate for 1980 (NNICC, 1981). Range reflects the possible overlap between numbers of cocaine and heroin users, which are combined in drug arrest statistics.

---

[13]We have been unable to locate any source of data on disposition of misdemeandor arrests for marijuana possession, but several state criminal justice officials agreed on this assessment. State data for California show that none of the 1054 *felony* marijuana possession arrests in 1982 resulted in prison terms.

for dealers. Arrest for possession of other drugs or for sale of any drug can result in significant penalties.

Table 3.3 presents our estimates of the risk of arrest that dealers currently face. No systematic data are available on how many dealers are arrested, but we can make reasonable estimates for marijuana, at least, based on the arrest statistics and results from the 1982 national household survey.[14] We start with the household survey figure of 20,000,000 "regular" marijuana users (those who use the drug at least once a month). A recent study by Abt Associates, estimating parameters of the illicit market, suggested that each retailer may sell to 7 or 8 frequent users—those who use more than once per month (Carlson et al., 1983). The 1982 household survey data indicate twice as many regular users as frequent users (Miller et al., 1983). These two figures together imply that each retailer serves about 15 regular users. Another basis for comparison is the heroin market, which certainly is subject to greater police pressure. In studying heroin distribution, Moore (1977) estimated that each retail dealer sold to about 10 regular customers. Since marijuana dealing is much less risky, we assume that each marijuana retailer sells to at least 15, but no more than 40 users. Using those figures for upper and lower bounds, we calculate there may be as many as 1,300,000 or as few as 500,000 marijuana dealers. Given the number of arrests for marijuana sale, these results imply that only 4.3 to 11.2 percent of dealers are arrested annually.

Not only is the risk of arrest rather low, but so also is the likelihood of a jail or prison sentence. Again, only limited information is available on sentences imposed for nonfederal drug convictions. Nationwide, in 1978, an estimated 15,000 people were serving state prison sentences (i.e., sentences of one year or more) for drug violations (Flanagan and McLeod, 1983). However, there is no estimate for the number of persons in jail on drug violations (i.e., with sentences of less than one year), nor any breakdown of prison inmates by type of drug involved in the offense.

Fortunately, we do have detailed data on the outcome of felony drug arrest cases for California, which permit us to estimate the risk of incarceration, given arrest, for that state. As Table 3.4 shows, in 1981 a person arrested for felony marijuana sale in California had a 29.7 percent chance of going to jail and only a 1.2 percent chance of going to prison. If we multiply these probabilities with the probability of being arrested (from Table 3.3), it becomes clear that a typical marijuana dealer faces a low risk of being imprisoned—or even jailed—for his drug sales. If the California data represented nationwide patterns, the risk of imprisonment for a marijuana dealer would be at most 0.1 percent.[15]

---

[14]Cocaine is unfortunately lumped with heroin in the arrest statistics.

[15]The probability of a jail term—typically 30 to 90 days—is about 3 percent.

Table 3.3

ESTIMATED ARREST RATES FOR RETAIL MARIJUANA DEALERS

Item	Lower Bound Estimate	Upper Bound Estimate
Number of users[a]	20,000,000	20,000,000
Number of users per retail dealer (estimated)[b]	15	40
Number of dealers	1,300,000	500,000
Number of arrests[c]	56,000	56,000
Percent of dealers arrested	4.3	11.2

[a]Based on report of monthly drug use in 1982 national household survey (NIDA, 1983b).

[b]Lower bound based on estimates by Carlson et al. (1983). Upper bound estimated by authors.

[c]FBI (1981).

Table 3.4

INCARCERATION RATES FOR DRUG OFFENSES: CALIFORNIA, 1981

Item	Marijuana Sale Felonies	Other Drug Felonies
Arrest Dispositions		
Not indicted	2,168	10,122
Indicted, not convicted	1,682	6,838
Convicted, not jailed	1,633	5,095
Jail sentence	2,364	7,504
Prison sentence	93	982
Total dispositions	7,940	30,541
Rate of incarcerations per arrest (percent)		
Jail	29.7	24.5
Prison	1.2	3.2
Total incarcerations	30.9	27.7

SOURCE: California Department of Justice, Offender Based Transaction System, unpublished tabulations, 1983.

Specific data on arrest rates for cocaine offenses are not available. Presumably there is greater police pressure against the cocaine market simply because the drug is regarded as more dangerous. That might result in somewhat higher rates of arrest, but it is still unlikely that any given dealer faces a great risk of arrest.[16] For incarceration rates, our California data show that among all persons arrested on non-marijuana felony drug charges (mostly cocaine and heroin), 24.5 percent were jailed and 3.2 percent were imprisoned.[17] Given any reasonable assumption about arrest rates, these figures suggest that for cocaine dealers, as for marijuana dealers, the risks of imprisonment are exceedingly small.

Feasibility of Increasing Risks at the Retail Level

These results naturally raise the question: Could local police increase those risks by stepping up drug enforcement activities? Our analysis suggests not, because the tools available to the police are not very appropriate to the nature of the marijuana and cocaine retail markets.

The tactics that police most often use are patrol, searches incidental to other arrests, and inducing users to inform on dealers. These practices are effective against heroin because the characteristics of users make heroin dealing a risky street activity (Goldstein, 1981). Because heroin users generally are poor, and have erratic incomes but a compelling need for the drug, they typically have to make frequent, small purchases on short notice. Street trading is also dictated by the fact that many users have no fixed residence; dealers do not encourage meetings at their own residences because the police often know users and can follow them. Finally, many heroin users commit numerous property crimes to get money for drugs (Moore, 1977). When they are caught, they may be willing to cooperate in police investigation of a dealer.

These characteristics—poverty, transiency, and criminality—make local police efforts quite effective against the heroin trade; the drug is both exceedingly expensive and rather difficult to obtain. The picture is much different for marijuana and cocaine. Cocaine buyers tend to be

---

[16]A rough estimate of cocaine dealer risk can be made, but it requires several uncertain assumptions. Some cocaine dealers are arrested for possession instead of sale, and cocaine possession arrests can lead to stiff penalties. If we assume that 50 percent of all heroin/cocaine arrests in Table 3.2 are for cocaine and that 50 percent of the possession arrests are of dealers, we get 23,750 arrests of cocaine dealers per year. If the 4,200,000 cocaine users are served by 280,000 dealers (1 dealer per 15 users), the arrest rate for dealers would be 8.5 percent. Such calculations are very speculative, however.

[17]Since heroin dealers are likely to be treated more severely than cocaine dealers, these rates probably overstate the risk of incarceration on a cocaine charge.

reasonably affluent. Marijuana is bought by a broad cross-section of the adolescent and young adult population. Marijuana dealers commonly sell the drug from their own residences, and cocaine dealers are reputedly willing to make trips to their customers' offices or residences (*Wall Street Journal*, 1983). This willingness reflects the lower risk posed by the police, the greater stability of their clientele, and the larger size of individual transactions.

Even if local tactics were effective against marijuana and cocaine dealers, local agencies face another constraint—resources. Under present budget constraints, it seems unlikely that police and courts can increase pressure on drug dealers unless they reduce pressure on other offenders. Moreover, state prisons are already overcrowded, so much so that many states are now faced with court suits based on inadequate prison space (Blumstein, 1983). Without expensive building programs, imprisoning more drug dealers would mean sending other felons to jail rather than prison, reducing their original sentences, and/or putting them back on the street sooner. Given the current low rates of imprisonment for serious crimes such as burglary and robbery, that tradeoff may be inappropriate.

Would Increased Risk Affect Price?

Finally, we must consider the ultimate effect that law enforcement is expected to achieve—a steep rise in drug prices. Suppose that, despite the problems cited above, the criminal justice system could find effective methods for arresting, convicting, and imprisoning more low-level drug dealers. Would the increased risk of prison time boost the retail price enough to affect consumption of marijuana? Our calculations in Table 3.5 indicate that the effects would be modest, at best. Even if police could double the risk of arrest and could imprison 5000 dealers per year, instead of a mere handful, the effect on price would be minimal. We assume, generously, that dealers value an arrest at $5000 and a year in prison at $50,000, and that they compensate for this risk by raising the price to buyers.[18] Under these assumptions, dealers would have to charge consumers, in the aggregate, $480 million more for marijuana. However, this increase is small compared with the

---

[18] This figure takes into account the fact that most marijuana retailers probably do not receive large incomes from their dealing activities. If there are indeed 500,000 marijuana retailers and their share of the final price is one-third (representing a 50 percent mark-up), then their average annual income from sales is between about $5,000 and $15,000. The lower figure, based on the Abt estimate of total marijuana sales, is more plausible. Dealers tend to be young and probably have modest incomes from legal activities.

current aggregate sales value. The resulting rise in retail price would be between 2 and 7 percent.[19]

We are not suggesting that local enforcement activities are futile or should be abandoned. By making dealing as risky as it is, the police do make it harder for users to find dealers, and do discourage open trading of cocaine and marijuana. Our point is that local enforcement should not be expected to achieve a great deal more; if enforcement is to make inroads into marijuana and cocaine consumption, it will be through some agency other than the local police.

ATTACKING THE IMPORT AND DISTRIBUTION LEVELS

The most promising targets of law enforcement are at the import and distribution levels. Federal agencies direct the bulk of their activities against these levels, and have stepped up their efforts in recent years.

Table 3.5

HYPOTHETICAL EFFECT OF INCREASED ARRESTS AND
INCARCERATIONS ON MARIJUANA PRICE

Item	Value
Arrests	
Number of arrests, current conditions	56,000
Number of arrests under hypothetical conditions (increased enforcement)	112,000
Dealers' valuation imputed to the increase in arrests @ $5000	$280,000,000
Incarcerations	
Number of incarcerations, current conditions	1,000
Number of incarcerations under hypothetical conditions (increased enforcement)	5,000
Dealers' valuation imputed to the increase in incarcerations @ $50,000	$200,000,000
Increase in retail marijuana value[a]	$480,000,000
Percent increase in retail marijuana price[b]	2% to 7%

[a]Sum of valuations for arrests and incarcerations.

[b]Increase in retail value, as percent of current retail value ($7.4 billion to $22.5 billion).

---

[19]The calculation of the price effect ignores the decline in usage caused by the increased price. This leads us to overestimate the price change arising from increased enforcement.

Federal law enforcement uses three main strategies: interdiction, investigation of high-level distributors, and seizure of dealer assets. The agencies have confiscated large shipments of marijuana and cocaine, made some spectacular cases against high-level dealers, and seized considerable assets (U.S. Senate, 1981). Nonetheless, the price structure and adaptability of the drug trade limit the effectiveness of such interventions. We will illustrate the main problems facing intensified interdiction and then discuss additional limitations that apply to other actions against high-level distributors.

Analyzing the Effect of Interdiction

Interdiction aims to intercept drug shipments just as or just before they enter the United States. It is expected to raise retail prices by (1) imposing costs to replace confiscated shipments; (2) raising the risk of imprisonment for people who transport drugs; and (3) increasing the uncertainty of dealer supplies and income. As we saw in Table 3.1, interdiction expenditures account for about 50 percent of total federal drug enforcement costs, and are increasing rapidly (GAO, 1983).

The Coast Guard and the Customs Service carry out most interdiction operations. The Coast Guard concentrates on sea patrols around Florida and the Caribbean, through which most Colombian and Jamaican marijuana passes. In the last few years, especially, it has seized enormous quantities of marijuana, but little else. The Customs Service also patrols, and it conducts inspections at ports of entry. Its patrols account for the majority of all federal cocaine seizures, and its inspections at port of entry intercept significant quantities of marijuana.

As Table 3.6 shows, the combined efforts of the Customs Service, the Coast Guard, and DEA have resulted in substantial seizures of marijuana and cocaine, with a sharp upward trend for cocaine.[20] These amounts represent a significant proportion of total shipments of drugs destined for the U.S.: between 10 and 27 percent by our estimates in Table 3.7. To make these estimates, we first reduced reported seizures to correct for the overlap between the various agencies' reports, using data from the General Accounting Office audit (1983). We then calculated the seizure rate as a proportion of all imports (those shipments that were successfully imported plus those that were seized). Although the range of results indicates some uncertainty in these parameters, it is clear that federal interdiction efforts are having an immediate effect on drug smuggling. Despite this, recent studies express continued

---

[20]Most DEA seizures took place during investigations, not interdiction. We discuss the effectiveness of investigations later.

Table 3.6

DRUG SEIZURES, 1979–1982

Drug	Quantity of Drug Seized (kg)[a]			
	1979	1980	1981	1982
Marijuana	2,082,000	1,350,000	2,837,000	2,203,000
Cocaine	1,234	3,778	2,932	7,340
Heroin	293	312	271	448

[a]Total quantity seized by the Coast Guard, Customs Service, and Drug Enforcement Administration (Source: General Accounting Office, 1983).

Table 3.7

ESTIMATED INTERDICTION RATES, 1982
(In thousand kilograms)

Item Estimated	Cocaine		Marijuana	
	Lower Bound	Upper Bound	Lower Bound	Upper Bound
Seizures				
Reported seizures[a]	7.3	7.3	2,203	2,203
Less overlap in reporting[b]	1.5	1.5	753	753
Estimated actual seizures	5.8	5.8	1,450	1,450
Shipments				
Total estimated consumption[c]	34.4	23.1	15,000	4,330
Less domestic production[d]	0.0	0.0	1,350	390
Estimated amount successfully imported	34.4	23.1	13,650	3,940
Total shipments to U.S. (actual seizures plus imported amount)	40.2	28.9	15,100	5,390
Seizures as percent of shipments	14%	20%	10%	27%

[a]Total seizures reported by federal agencies (GAO, 1983).

[b]For cocaine, the amount double-counted (i.e., reported by two agencies) in one large seizure in 1982. For marijuana, based on the proportion of seizures double-counted (one third), as shown by an audit of 1981 seizure records (GAO, 1983, pp. 35-37).

[c]From Tables 2.8 and 2.9.

[d]For marijuana, 9 percent of total consumption.

skepticism about the ultimate effects of interdiction (GAO, 1983; Mitchell and Bell, 1980).

The reason for skepticism is rooted in the drug market's price structure, which is steeply graduated for all illicit drugs. Table 3.8 illustrates the structure for cocaine. Note that most of the retail price goes to domestic intermediaries, not to the grower, exporter, or importer, despite the fact that these latter parties bear the costs of production, processing, and international transportation. The sharp increase within the U.S. arises from the risks that dealers face. Paradoxically, this means that changes in the cost of drug distribution at the highest levels—interdiction and high-level dealing—may have little effect on the consumer price.

Effects of Drug Seizures. Confiscation of drugs is one of the principal risks for importers. A simple analysis illustrates the consequence of such a seizure for retail prices. Table 3.9 shows what happens when importers compensate for interdiction seizures. We assume that under current circumstances the interdiction rate is 20 percent. Thus an importer must arrange for 125 kg of cocaine to be shipped from Colombia in order to receive 100 kg "on the beach" in the U.S. On the average, the other 25 kg will be lost to seizure. The cost of the lost cocaine is, at most, $50,000 per kg (the price the importer charges

Table 3.8

PRICE STRUCTURE OF THE COCAINE MARKET

Level of Seller	Selling Price per Pure Kg
Peruvian refiner	$ 5,000
Colombian exporter	$ 20,000
U.S. importer	$ 50,000
Domestic distributor	$100,000
.	
.	
.	
[possibly 2 or 3 other levels]	
.	
.	
.	
Retailer	$625,000

SOURCE: Adapted from the 1980 *Narcotics Intelligence Estimate* (NNICC, 1982); retail price estimate from GAO (1983).

Table 3.9

EFFECTS OF INCREASED INTERDICTION SEIZURES
ON COCAINE PRICE

Item	Current Situation	Hypothetical Situation (Increased Interdiction)
Interdiction rate	20%	40%
Amount exported to land 100 kg in U.S.	125 kg	167 kg
Amount seized	25 kg	67 kg
Amount landed in U.S.	100 kg	100 kg
Replacement cost of seizures (@ $50,000 per kg)	$ 1.25 million	$ 3.35 million
Total retail price (100 kg)	$62.5 million	$64.6 million
Increase in retail price	—	3.4%

his customer). Actually, the cost is presumably less, but since we do not know the details of importers' costs of operation we assume $50,000 as an upper bound; this will cause our analysis to slightly overstate the effect on retail price. Under these conditions, we observe that the retail price for 100 kg of cocaine is $62.5 million ($625,000 per kg).[21]

Now suppose that a government crackdown increases the interdiction rate to 40 percent. The importer must then order and pay for 167 kg from Colombia to receive 100 kg in the U.S. His costs increase because he must pay for the additional 42 kg of lost cocaine. At $50,000 per kg, this causes a total increase of $2.1 million for a 100 kg shipment. However, this addition raises the retail price by only 3.4 percent.[22]

How do we explain this small effect on retail price? There is little evidence of any monopoly power in the cocaine market. Consequently,

[21]It is important to note here that enforcement agencies have almost universally adopted the policy of valuing seized drugs at retail or "street" price. This has the effect of greatly exaggerating the impact of drug seizures on drug dealers; one kg of cocaine seized in a 10-kg shipment at the border is valued at $625,000 instead of $50,000. As Pekkanen (1980) says, "It is equivalent to valuing rustled cattle at the price of prime ribs in a restaurant." This procedure may lead the federal government to overemphasize interdiction in its strategic choice.

[22]In a slightly more complex model, we can assume that the importer has to pay for the replaced cocaine at the exporter's price ($20,000 per kg), plus other transportation costs and cost of capital. However, the basic result changes very little: a retail price rise of 1 to 3 percent.

we assume that the importer passes only his increased cost on to the domestic distributors, and that they, in turn, raise their prices to dealers only enough to compensate for the higher cost of purchase. If importers and dealers try to charge more than enough to compensate for the increased cost of importing 100 kg, they may be undersold by their competitors. Thus, the interdiction "tariff" simply gets passed down the line; intermediate dealers cannot much increase it; and consumers see little "inflation" in the retail price beyond the impact at the import level. Actually, the retail price increase may be somewhat more than the absolute increase in the import price because capital costs and financial risks of dealers will rise.[23] However, the increase at retail will be much less than proportionate to the change at the import level.

For marijuana, interdiction may produce a slightly stronger effect. Nevertheless, it is still unlikely to affect consumption significantly. Looking at Table 3.10, we can see that the marijuana market has a price structure somewhat different from that of the cocaine market.

Table 3.10

PRICE STRUCTURE OF THE MARIJUANA MARKET

Level of Seller	Selling Price Per Kg
Colombian broker	$ 55
Colombian exporter	$ 125
U.S. importer	$ 500
Domestic distributor	$ 750
.	
.	
.	
[possibly 2 or 3 other levels]	
.	
.	
.	
Retailer	$1,700

SOURCE: Adapted from the 1980 *Narcotics Intelligence Estimate* (NNICC, 1982).

---

[23]The higher purchase price raises the capital costs of domestic dealers; they must hold more expensive inventory. This effect is likely to be slight since cocaine appears to move relatively quickly through the distribution chain. If it takes three months for cocaine to move from importation to sale and cocaine dealers can earn 25 percent on their money, adjusting for the added cost would make our estimated change in the retail price 6.25 percent larger. Both three months and 25 percent are probably too high, leading to an overestimate of the total effect.

While the price of cocaine increases 31-fold between export and retail sale, the price of marijuana increases only 13-fold. Presumably, this reflects the greater risks of arrest and imprisonment for trafficking in cocaine. Because marijuana's price does not rise so astronomically at the intermediate levels, interdiction has a more direct and proportionately greater effect on the retail price. As Table 3.11 illustrates, if the interdiction rate rose from 20 to 40 percent, the cost of importing 100 kg of marijuana would increase by $21,000. Assuming that marijuana dealers also operate in a competitive market, this increase would raise the retail price by about 12 percent. However, given that a marijuana cigarette currently costs perhaps 75 cents (e.g., 0.44 grams at $1.70/gram), the price increase represents about 9 cents—probably not enough to discourage much consumption.[24]

Effects of Arresting Couriers. So far, we have considered how interdiction of drugs affects the market. However, interdiction is also supposed to work by increasing the risk for couriers—that is, pilots of small aircraft carrying cocaine and crewmen on vessels carrying marijuana. Couriers are often captured along with the drugs during interdiction, and their treatment, once caught, will affect their perceptions of risk. Raising their risk might be expected, a priori, to affect the price of the drug.

Table 3.11

EFFECTS OF INCREASED INTERDICTION SEIZURES
ON MARIJUANA PRICE

Item	Current Situation	Hypothetical Situation (Increased Interdiction)
Interdiction rate	20%	40%
Amount exported to land 100 kg in U.S.	125 kg	167 kg
Amount seized	25 kg	67 kg
Amount landed in U.S.	100 kg	100 kg
Replacement cost of seizures (@ $500 per kg)	$ 12,500	$ 33,500
Total retail price (100 kg)	$170,000	$191,000
Increase in retail price	—	12.4%

[24]We can speculate, however, that it might significantly affect some heavy users, possibly including some adolescents who may already be spending a large share of their disposable income on marijuana.

It is very difficult to obtain data on the risks faced by couriers. Records of the disposition of interdiction arrests are incomplete, and the various agencies disagree on estimates of the most basic parameters, such as rates of indictment, conviction, and imprisonment (GAO, 1983). From the fragmentary available evidence, it seems that an arrested marijuana courier faces less than a 40-percent chance of going to prison.[25] If his probability of arrest is the same as the seizure rate (20 percent), that would imply a less than 8-percent risk of imprisonment per trip. Whatever the assumptions, a marijuana courier coming by sea faces only a modest risk of imprisonment on any trip.

What if the government could raise that risk radically—say, from 8 percent to 20 percent? The result would probably differ between marijuana and cocaine, because different types of couriers may be involved. Most marijuana arrives by sea, generally in small vessels operated by unskilled Colombian or other foreign nationals. A large proportion of cocaine is smuggled in dedicated airplanes by skilled pilots.

In the case of marijuana boats, it is unlikely that many crewmen have other opportunities that pay nearly as well as smuggling. For this reason, the supply of Colombian seamen competent to man smugglers' boats is probably very elastic at the current price—that is, raising the risk of a prison sentence for seamen who get caught will not greatly increase the cost of smuggling marijuana.

To suggest the magnitude of the effect, we can use a model similar to that we used to evaluate raising the risk for retail dealers. A study for the Coast Guard concerning seized marijuana boats shows that the average crew numbered about 6 (Mitchell and Bell, 1980). On the average, such boats may carry about 10 metric tons (10,000 kg) of marijuana, a figure that Mitchell and Bell estimated from seizure data. If interdiction and prosecution rates could be raised to make crewmen face a 20 percent chance of imprisonment instead of 8 percent, and if the average crewman values his freedom at $50,000 a year, each crewman would have to get $6,000 more (0.12 × $50,000) per trip to compensate him for the additional risk of prison time. For a crew of 6, that would raise the cost of shipping 10,000 kg by $36,000. That would increase the cost of shipment per kg by only $3.60—which is 0.7 per-

---

[25]Coast Guard information for 1981 shows that in the one district for which data are available (the district including South Florida, where most large Coast Guard seizures are made), 68 percent of arrestees were indicted and 86 percent of indictments resulted in convictions (GAO, 1983, App. X). The GAO examined records of 128 individuals who were arrested and convicted as a result of seizure operations; of these, 67 percent received a prison sentence. These rates are likely to be upper bounds (since, for example, the GAO sample was missing information for many other arrestees), but taken together they suggest a maximum rate of imprisonments per arrest equal to 0.39 (i.e., 0.68 × 0.86 × 0.67).

cent of the importer's selling price and only 0.2 percent of the retail price.

Interdiction of cocaine couriers may be another story. At least some pilots bringing in drugs receive severe sentences (U.S. Senate, 1981). Pilots skilled enough to fly small planes into remote airstrips at night probably have substantial alternative earning opportunities. With a high enough interdiction rate and severe enough penalties, it might be possible to deter most or all of them. Few skilled pilots are likely to be willing to incur a high probability of a long prison sentence. However, the dent in the market would last only as long as it took the cocaine trade to adapt, by replacing planes with boats; the two are completely interchangeable for cocaine smuggling.

The Possibilities for Adaptation. That consideration brings us to the last point concerning the effectiveness of interdiction: the ease with which cocaine and marijuana smugglers could adapt to interdiction pressure. Even if we assume that present interdiction efforts could be greatly intensified, we cannot assume that drug smugglers would go on using the same methods that would now hurt their business and expose them to inordinate risks. If the seizure rate rises sharply they can always change their importing procedures.

Adaptation would be easier for the cocaine than for the marijuana trade. Like heroin, cocaine is a highly concentrated drug. Consequently, cocaine smuggling could adopt the procedures of the heroin trade, bringing in the drug in small units in unspecialized vessels or cargo planes, using unskilled couriers, and often concealing the drug inside other cargo. We estimate that this would raise the price of cocaine at most by $80,000 per kg or about 12 percent.[26]

The marijuana trade would have more trouble adapting to enforcement pressure. The bulkiness of the drug, per unit value, means that the value of much smaller units (one or two kg that can be hidden on the body or in luggage) simply would not compensate for the risks of smuggling them. Moreover, marijuana has a distinctive odor that is hard to mask. But importers could shift to forms of cannabis that have less bulk for a particular quantity of THC—hashish or hashish oil, for example. Under current conditions, the higher labor costs of hashish production make it unattractive to import, but that could change if the risks of transporting marijuana rose.

---

[26]This estimate is based on the cost of bringing heroin from Europe to New York, about $150,000 per kg (NNICC, 1982, p. 30). Heroin is smuggled in smaller units than cocaine; two kg is a typical heroin shipment, compared to 20 kg for cocaine. If cocaine dealers adopted the heroin importation mode, then the highest domestic distribution level would be eliminated. Thus the price of cocaine at the two kg level would rise by $80,000.

The optimal adaptation may simply be to scale down the size of shipment brought in by specialized vessel. Instead of the present (average) 10-ton shipment that requires a very sizeable vessel, importers may drop down to a one-ton unit that can be shipped in a much smaller boat or more effectively concealed on a boat of the current size. Although this would raise transportation costs, it is less feasible to stop many small boats than a few large ones. Since a major portion of the cost in interdiction is a Coast Guard ship's "waiting time" between boarding a smuggling vessel and returning to patrol (personal communication, Coast Guard), a switch to smaller smuggling craft might require much greater interdiction resources to attain a given interception rate. Furthermore, with this mode of transportation, the drug passes through one less distribution level, since it arrives in smaller bundles, thus avoiding the mark-ups at that level. Since we have already estimated that, without adaptation, doubling the interdiction rate would raise the retail price by less than 13 percent (Table 3.11), it is clear that adaptation of smuggling technique to intensified interdiction would lead to a smaller increase.

Finally, higher interdiction could result in higher domestic production. This is not strictly an adaptation by the import business, but it could frustrate the ultimate objective of interdiction. We have little systematic data on either current or potential domestic production, but the recent increase in apparent availability of *sinsemilla*, Hawaiian, and other high-THC specialty varieties of marijuana suggests that expansion in domestic capacity is a very real possibility (NNICC, 1983b).

Actions Against High-Level Domestic Distributors

The federal government has for many years conducted investigations aimed at arresting and incarcerating high-level distributors. It recently intensified that effort, as indicated by increases in the number of arrestees classified as high-level dealers (U.S. House of Representatives, 1978–1982). DEA now devotes most of its resources to making cases against such dealers. The Customs Service and the Internal Revenue Service also conduct their own investigations against major dealers. These actions take the form of undercover investigations, "sting" operations, use of Currency Transaction Reports (CTRs), asset seizure, and taxing drug-related income (NNICC, 1983b).

Types of Actions. In many recent successful investigations, federal agencies have mounted sting operations that capitalize on the drug trade's requirements for certain services. Cocaine smugglers need to obtain planes and pilots. Marijuana importers need to offload tons of the drug very rapidly once it comes ashore and to find safe warehouses where it can be stored until sold. And high-level dealers in both trades need financial services to protect their enormous incomes from detection and to invest them profitably. In buying these services from independent entrepreneurs, dealers make themselves vulnerable to investigators. In a number of cases, DEA agents have set up transportation and financial "firms," building strong cases against dealers who sought their services. In addition, federal agencies continue to use their more traditional undercover techniques.[27]

Apart from undercover operations, federal agencies have also begun regularly using Currency Transaction Reports. Federal regulations require financial institutions to file CTRs for transactions of $10,000 or more. Agents have analyzed CTRs to identify members of major dealer organizations and locate their assets for later seizure and taxation. In addition, failure to file CTRs has served as the basis for prosecution, and bribery attempts to keep bank officials from filing them have provided investigative leads.

Law enforcement agencies also have authority to seize the assets of drug dealers, including vessels, aircraft, vehicles, real estate, front businesses, cash, and bank accounts. For example, DEA can seize assets if they are used in the drug traffic or if they were purchased with drug-produced income. The Customs Service can confiscate vehicles, aircraft, and boats used in attempts to smuggle contraband and also seize cash entering or leaving the country in violation of currency reporting laws (reports must be filed for all cash or bearer-negotiable instruments exceeding $5,000). The IRS uses other procedures, such as jeopardy-assessments, which enable the government to freeze assets during protracted litigation to show that they were obtained from unreported and untaxed drug distribution.

Effects of Asset Seizures. Let us consider the effects of asset seizures first, because they are the most straightforward. The various asset-seizure programs have an obvious attraction as devices for attacking the drug trade. They are faster than the trials of well-defended traffickers. They immobilize assets during court proceedings, thus disrupting the cash flow of criminal organizations. They serve as condign punishment: Given that dealers get into the drug trade because they

---

[27]It has been argued that the newer investigative approaches such as sting operations have an additional virtue, namely, that they produce large effects because they are targeted on organizations rather than individuals (*Miami Herald*, 1981). It takes time and money for traffickers to recreate large organizations because of the need to rebuild contacts, relationships of trust, etc. Thus, removing 50 individuals from one organization may have a greater effect than removing 50 randomly selected individuals from many organizations. However, despite the success of such techniques in building cases, we are skeptical that eliminating organizations has much additional effect, simply because there are currently many successful dealers who operate on a much smaller scale. If the large-scale organizations were eliminated, smaller-scale ones would replace them.

want large incomes, it seems appropriate that they lose the assets generated by that trade.

Nonetheless, it appears that seizure programs could do little to force up the retail price of drugs. The amounts seized may not represent the actual financial penalty imposed on a trafficker. These procedures typically involve two phases: In the first phase (seizure), the agency freezes the assets to prevent the dealer from removing them beyond the government's reach; in the second phase (forfeiture), ownership finally passes to the government, usually after conviction or lengthy civil proceedings. After litigation, the amount the trafficker loses may be substantially lower than the amount originally seized.[28] In fact, counting actions for all types of drugs, in 1981 DEA obtained only $43 million in forfeitures from its asset removal program; closed tax cases yielded only $41 million to the IRS (NNICC, 1983b).

These amounts are trifling in relation to the retail value of all drugs (at least $27 billion for marijuana, cocaine, and heroin together, according to the lower-bound estimates in Table 2.9). Even if these amounts rose considerably in the future, the effect on final retail price would be modest. For example, let us suppose that the agencies could triple the value of the dealers' assets that are forfeited or taxed, and that 50 percent of that value came from marijuana dealers. Although those would be improbably high figures, they would raise the retail price of marijuana by only about 1 percent.

The Possibilities for Increased Investigative Effort. The prospects for investigations may be better. Unlike local authorities, the federal agencies have been very successful in prosecuting drug offenders. In the 12 months ending in June 1982, U.S. district courts disposed of 7981 indictments against drug violators.[29] Convictions were obtained for 79 percent of those indictments, and of those convicted, 72 percent were imprisoned. The average prison sentence was 61 months (Flanagan and McLeod, 1983).[30] Moreover, in contrast to state prisons, federal prisons are not overcrowded, and the federal government presumably has the resources to construct additional prison space for many more drug violators should that be deemed desirable. This suggests that federal law enforcement agencies might find it feasible to

---

[28]For instance, if a seized house is mortgaged, the bank may successfully petition for return of the property. Valuation of real property may be overstated at the time of seizure. In tax proceedings, IRS may seize large amounts of assets before closure, but the amount seized may bear no relation to the actual tax assessment. In addition, the agency may lose its claim in court.

[29]At the federal level, the number of indictments is almost equal to the number of arrests. At the local level, less than half of arrests may lead to indictment.

[30]However, drug violators, like other federal prisoners, are released after serving, on the average, only half their sentence.

imprison a substantially larger number of high-level dealers, if they could carry out more investigations.

It would be very expensive, however, to increase investigations of high-level dealers. Operating undercover, conducting electronic and physical surveillance, obtaining and analyzing financial documents, acquiring and assembling the props for a successful sting operation, are all activities that absorb large numbers of skilled agents—not to mention the agent time needed for trial preparation and presentation. No cost data are available, but it seems likely that scores of person-years, largely professional, are required to conclude one case. In addition to the personnel, these investigations have an array of other resource and administrative costs. And, of course, after investigation there are costs of prosecution and imprisonment.

To see how large such costs might be, one can examine current expenditures. In Fiscal Year 1982, approximately $403 million was spent for drug law enforcement by the DEA, IRS, FBI, the Criminal Division of the Justice Department, U.S. Attorneys, and Bureau of Prisons (Drug Abuse Policy Office, 1982). Below we will show that to make even a modest difference in retail drug prices, these agencies would have to triple the amount of prison time they impose on dealers. It is likely that each additional case would be more difficult and hence more costly than the typical case currently made. Thus, to triple the number of persons incarcerated on federal drug charges could mean spending an additional $800 million on drug law enforcement, perhaps much more. The magnitude of this incremental investment is striking; it would exceed, for instance, the FBI's total 1982 budget.

In addition, we must consider the possibility that high-level distributors might adapt their operations to increased investigative pressure. Many of the newer and more successful techniques, such as sting operations and analysis of CTRs, are susceptible to adaptations. Large smuggling or distributing organizations are vulnerable to undercover operations (e.g., selling financial or transportation services) precisely because of their scale. If these investigations present too much risk, organizations can simply handle smaller quantities of both goods and money. It is useful to note here that these investigations appear to have had little success against the heroin trade, which is handled by much smaller organizations.

As for the analysis of CTRs, a dealer can avoid the CTR requirement by converting currency into other negotiable instruments without ever making a $10,000 transaction; it simply takes slightly smaller transactions with different financial institutions. Consequently, the effectiveness of CTR analysis may be self-limiting. Ease of entry into the marijuana and cocaine markets has meant that some people who have little education or familiarity with U.S. institutions and finances have amassed considerable wealth. Thus, the real effect of the CTR requirement may be to weed these traders out of the market, leaving a more sophisticated dealer population. It is likely that there are enough potential dealers to keep the removal of the less competent from making a difference in the market.

Price Effects of Intensified Investigations. Despite the difficulties just enumerated, it is conceivable that federal agencies could, through greatly increased efforts and expenditures, make many more cases against high-level dealers. Let us suppose that they achieved a very large increase, say tripling the number of drug violators now sent to prison. What effect would that have on drug prices?

As before, our approach to answering that question is to estimate the additional compensation that dealers would require to cover the increased risks of spending time in federal prison. From the sentencing data cited earlier, we estimate that federal judges sentenced drug dealers to about 22,000 years of prison time in 1982 (Flanagan and McLeod, 1983). Given that dealers serve, on the average, only about half their sentence, this implies about 11,000 actual years of imprisonment. Now assume that number were tripled, i.e., 22,000 more years were imposed on dealers. In response, dealers would require extra compensation for the added risk of imprisonment. Since these are high-level dealers, many of whom are earning very large incomes, it is reasonable to impute higher values than those we used for retail dealers. For the highest-level dealers (Class I violators as defined by DEA), we use a figure of $250,000; for second level (Class II) dealers, $125,000; and for the remainder, $75,000. Assuming the distribution of classes of dealers remained the same under the new situation as it was in 1982, the added years of imprisonment would result in a total of $3.6 billion added to retail prices.[31] Compared with the total retail value of drugs, this added cost would represent a price increase of 13 percent.[32]

Even this modest increase would probably not appear for a few years. There would presumably be a substantial time lag between increasing expenditures and completing cases. It takes time to build a network of informants, to accumulate a pool of experienced agents, and to mount investigations. These considerations must be taken together with the possibilities of dealer adaptations and the probability of very

---

[31]In 1982 DEA estimated that of 7300 total domestic drug arrests it initiated, 3380 were of Class I dealers, 1040 of Class II, and 2880 of Classes III and IV (U.S. House of Representatives, 1982).

[32]This is a maximum value for the price increase, based on our lower-bound estimate of $27 billion for the retail value of marijuana, cocaine, and heroin. It also ignores enforcement against other drugs, which accounts for a non-trivial (but unreported) share of federal prison sentences.

high costs. Of course, there are numerous uncertainties here; it may be that dealers will not readily adapt, that the agencies could accommodate large budget increases quickly, or that further innovations in investigative techniques, such as targeting organizations, will pay off more than we expect. However, with currently available information there is little to suggest that even a large expansion of investigative effort against high-level drug distributors would have a very substantial effect on availability or price of drugs.

WHAT IS NEEDED TO GUIDE FUTURE POLICY

Ever since heroin became illegal in the United States, federal and state governments have relied primarily on law enforcement to control the supply and consumption of illicit drugs. We have seen that law enforcement has succeeded in making drugs expensive—and therefore has presumably held consumption substantially below levels it otherwise might have reached. But there is little reason to believe that further intensification of any particular law enforcement activity would have a great impact on the availability of drugs.

It may be that a suitable combination of increased activities could raise consumer prices for drugs somewhat, but at this point we lack the essential information to specify the best combination. For instance, we have concluded that substantial increases in local drug enforcement might raise retail marijuana prices by 2 to 7 percent; that doubling interdiction seizures might raise prices by 12 percent; and that tripling federal investigative effort might raise them by 13 percent. Conceivably, then, a coordinated increase of all these activities might lead to a retail price increase of perhaps 30 percent. Moreover, we are least certain about the possibilities for increasing investigations against high- and mid-level dealers; it could be that the federal agencies will continue to develop new tactics for such investigations, or dealers will not adapt quickly. Thus, though we cannot be optimistic, it may be possible, given much greater amounts of resources, to make some difference in retail drug prices. The important questions are how much money would be needed to make a given difference, and which policies are likely to pay off most—questions whose answers require more information than we now have.

To guide future policy, higher priority should be given to improving the information base. At present, many of the basic parameters of the drug market, such as prices in various areas and at various levels, are estimated from fragmentary data. This is acknowledged even by the government organizations that must make the estimates (NNICC, 1983a). As a result, it is impossible to say, for example, whether interdiction efforts should be reduced to permit more investigations of high-level dealers (or vice versa). Although policymakers must make such trade-off decisions frequently, up to now there has not been a substantial analysis of these issues.

Below we outline a few of the most important items that are needed for a full analysis of drug enforcement policies. We start with the requirements for basic but essential data, and then outline what additional information is needed for analysis of strategic issues such as the structure of dealer networks and the adaptability of dealer behavior to law enforcement tactics.

Data Requirements. Law enforcement agencies face uncertainties about many specific parameters of the drug market. To design an effective enforcement program, a data-based estimate of those parameters is essential. Here we will mention only three data items needed, each related to an important strategic issue.

1. *Prices and competition by market level.* More complete and reliable information is needed on price levels and the extent of competition at various levels of the drug distribution system. Our analysis of the effects of interdiction depends on price data reported by law enforcement authorities. It also depends on the assumption of competitiveness among dealers. We have asserted that competition in drug distribution at different levels would ensure that, except for possible inventory and associated risk costs, an increase in the import price of drugs would lead to a similar absolute rather than proportionate increase in the retail price. Only by systematic collection of price data from different levels of the market can this critical assumption be verified.

2. *Number of retail dealers.* Our analysis of effects of local law enforcement is very sensitive to the number of retail dealers. We have assumed reasonable ranges of consumer/dealer ratios in our analysis— for example, from 15 to 40 customers per retail marijuana dealer. However, if it turned out that marijuana or cocaine dealers had an average of 100 customers, we would estimate there were many fewer dealers in the country, and we might find the effectiveness of increased local law enforcement would be much greater. In addition, incarcerating a significant percentage of a small dealer population might be feasible.

3. *Consumption and interdiction rates.* More care needs to be taken in collecting and reporting data on drug consumption and interdiction. Official estimates of total drug consumption are made informally and irregularly; the methods used are not fully documented; and the methodology varies from year to year and from study to study (NNICC, 1983a; Carlson et al., 1983). In the case of interdiction statistics, the

General Accounting Office reports that the various federal agencies involved in joint operations double-count a significant portion of the drugs seized (GAO, 1983). Our analysis of interdiction has shown how important these figures are. We do not believe that our substantive conclusions are affected substantially by errors in the data, because we have made various adjustments for them in the analysis. However, if consumption and interdiction data are to be tracked over time for evaluation of federal policies—as they should be—the data should be more carefully and consistently collected and reported.

Strategic Information About Dealer Networks. Law enforcement has a fundamental need to better understand the structure and behavior of dealer networks. This is essential to evaluate allocations of law enforcement resources across different activities. As an example of why this is important, consider the current strategic focus of federal enforcement against high-level dealers. At present a large fraction of federal antidrug resources is devoted to making cases against national or regional dealers. Such cases involve the penetration of large-scale dealer networks and often the seizure of huge amounts of drugs. These are visible outcomes that have an obvious attraction for investigative agencies. But it may turn out that it is quite easy for the illegal drug market to replace national or regional dealers. An organization handling just 20 kilograms of cocaine per month accounts for 1 percent of the national market. It seems plausible that the organization's customers, themselves experienced mid-level dealers, have a number of other sources of cocaine—given the inherent unreliability and instability of deliveries in an illegal business. If several mid-level dealers have the requisite knowledge and skills to move up and replace a top-level dealer who is convicted, then making such cases may prove futile.

Knowledge about the dealer network could point to more efficient allocations of law enforcement dollars. For example, it is possible that the investigative resources now used for a single high-level case might be better used to make a number of lower-level cases focused in a single metropolitan market. Low-level dealers are likely to be less resourceful and knowledgeable than their high-level peers. If so, using those resources to remove a dozen mid-level suppliers in Cleveland might do more to disrupt supplies and discourage new users than does the single glamorous case.

Understanding Dealer Adaptability. The issue of adaptability provides another illustration of the importance of understanding dealer behavior. Earlier, we cautioned that high-level drug dealers are likely to learn and adapt to particular tools of enforcement, such as interdiction of cocaine-carrying airplanes or investigations using currency transaction reports. Unfortunately, while we can be certain this will happen in some cases, we have no data on how many dealers may prove adaptable, or in what ways they will adapt.

Dealer responses could be crucial to the success or failure of law enforcement actions that increase their risk. If high-level dealers were to respond to increased risk by exiting from the business earlier than they otherwise would—say, as soon as they earned a comfortable nest egg—then adaptation may not pose a serious problem for enforcement. This would be true, of course, only if the exiting dealers failed to pass on their accumulated information to their successors. It may also be that dealers' impatience would inhibit their responsiveness; for example, cocaine dealers may be unwilling to incur the delays involved in using the heroin mode of smuggling and may continue to use the increasingly risky bulk import mode on dedicated vessels. Because of uncertainties like these, it is very desirable to develop a better understanding of dealer careers, organizations, and tactics in response to changes in law enforcement strategies before spending large sums on those strategies.

SUMMARY

In this chapter we have considered the possible effects of intensified law enforcement against each of the main levels of the illicit drug market. In every case, we conclude that even large increases in law enforcement expenditures would be unlikely to greatly reduce drug use.

The Production Level

The federal government has attempted to control production in source countries through drug law enforcement assistance, diplomatic pressure, and crop reduction programs. However, these programs have not controlled and probably cannot control supply because:

- Drug crops are more lucrative than other crops.
- Governments are typically weak in the growing areas.
- Some producer nations do not give high priority to solving what they consider to be a U.S. problem.
- If there is a legal market for a drug, it is almost impossible to prevent spillover into the illegal market.
- If one nation reduces crop production, others quickly increase production to make up the shortfall in supply.

Enforcement Against the Retail Market

At the retail level, local police seek to limit the availability and raise the price of drugs primarily by increasing risks for dealers. Our analysis indicates that intensifying enforcement against retail dealers has dim prospects:

- Marijuana and cocaine dealers now face low risk of arrest and very low risk of going to prison.
- Stepping up patrol and incidental search activities would have very little effect on marijuana and cocaine trading because, unlike heroin dealing, they are not street activities.
- Given resource constraints, increasing enforcement against retail dealers would mean decreasing the risk of arrest and imprisonment for other kinds of felons—a tradeoff that might not be in the best interests of society.
- Even if local enforcement could raise those risks considerably, retail prices would not increase enough to much reduce consumption. The total value of drugs consumed is too high, and competition would restrict dealers from compensating themselves by raising the price very much.

Enforcement Against Importers and High-Level Distributors

Federal agencies also try to reduce availability and raise the retail price by increasing the risks of importing and distributing drugs. Their primary tactics are interdiction, investigation of high-level distributors, and seizure of dealers' assets. The agencies have had some highly visible successes using these tactics, and we are more optimistic about the prospects for intensified investigations at this level than about the other law enforcement strategies. However, we have concluded that even here, the ultimate effect of intensified enforcement on retail price would be modest, because:

- The price structure of the drug market keeps enforcement against importers and high-level dealers from having much effect on retail price.
- Doubling the interdiction rate, even if feasible, would raise prices by only about 3 percent for cocaine and 12 percent for marijuana.
- Increasing the chances of incarceration for couriers who import drugs will not deter them all, and the amount required to compensate them for that risk has an extremely small effect on retail prices.

- Even if federal agencies could seize a much larger amount of dealer assets than they now do, retail prices would probably rise very little.
- Importers and dealers may find it easy to adapt their practices if increased interdiction and investigative activities begin taking too high a toll.
- Increasing investigative effort against high-level distributors would be very costly—perhaps requiring triple the current expenditures or more—yet it would increase the retail price of drugs by at most 13 percent. Like other tools available to law enforcement, these procedures simply impose very small penalties on a very large market.

Chapter 4

TREATMENT OF ADOLESCENT DRUG ABUSERS

This chapter examines the treatment given to adolescent drug abusers. We will show that although drug abuse treatment constitutes a rather large industry in the United States, spending at least $500 million annually, there is little scientific evidence to suggest how effective treatment is for adolescents, or which treatments work best for them. Most treatment research has concerned adults, usually heroin users, and only a small fraction of patients admitted to drug treatment are under age 18. Some approaches to adolescent drug treatment seem more promising than others, but much more treatment research, preferably including randomized controlled experiments, is required to identify the most effective forms of treatment for adolescent drug abusers.

We first discuss the difficulties in defining adolescent drug abuse and its treatment, and then describe the extent of treatment in the United States. We also show how treatment of adolescents differs from that of adults, and discuss the applicability of the major current modalities of treatment to the problems of adolescent drug abusers.

We then examine treatment effectiveness by reviewing problems of measurement and method, summarizing the major nationwide studies, and presenting what is known about the effectiveness of general drug treatment programs and drug treatment programs targeted at adolescents.

WHAT IS ADOLESCENT DRUG ABUSE?

An initial difficulty in assessing drug abuse treatment is the conceptual confusion about what constitutes "use" vs. "abuse" of a drug, especially for adolescents. Is the junior high school girl who smokes marijuana with friends about once a month a drug abuser? Certainly, she is violating the law, and it is possible but not proven that she is endangering her physical health (Secretary of HHS, 1982). She may be putting herself at risk for other problems as well. But can we say that she has a drug problem requiring treatment?

Most definitions agree that drug abuse is ingesting substances of a nature and in a quantity that produce harmful or dysfunctional effects.

Beyond that, there is no consensus on what the problem to be treated is. Lettieri, Sayers, and Pearson (1980) surveyed 43 modern theories on drug abuse, which they classified into four categories:

1. *Biological Explanations.* These include genetic explanations for predispositions to abuse drugs, biochemical models of physical addiction, and explanations of drug use in terms of sensory excitation and deprivation.

2. *Personality Explanations.* These models of drug abuse attempt to explain the propensity for abuse in terms of dysfunctional individual personality characteristics.

3. *Interpersonal Explanations.* These theories view drug abuse within the framework of an individual's relationships with significant others. Parental and peer influences play a prominent role in these theories. Many of these models view drug abuse as a way of maintaining one's identity in the family or community.

4. *Social/Cultural Explanations.* This last group of theories views the role of drugs in the larger social context of economic, racial, and cultural differences in American society.

Prevailing opinion among drug treatment professionals holds that drug treatment, especially for adolescents, requires adjustment of an entire lifestyle, not just treatment of a physiological dependence on a substance. In this sense, the problem of adolescent drug abuse is one of the latter three of the above categories, with particular emphasis on individual and family/peer relationships. Smith, Levy, and Striar (1979) note that some adolescent programs do not label themselves as drug treatment programs at all, but rather as more general programs to treat adolescent "life problems." Miller (1973, p. 309) states this view most succinctly:

> Drug abuse is a regressive symptom and the basic issue is the treatment of the underlying conflicts. It has meaning in relationship to the intrapsychic state of the patient as well as his intrafamilial conflicts and environmental stresses.

Much of the literature discusses the problem of adolescent drug abuse as a general developmental problem, and makes general recommendations based on classical psychiatric techniques (e.g., Amini, Salasnek, and Burke, 1976; Bennett, 1983; Gibbs, 1982; Hartmann, 1969; Unger, 1978; Wieder and Kaplan, 1969). Pediatricians addressing the question of youthful drug abuse emphasize that the drug abuse itself cannot be treated apart from family problems, school problems, and the influence of peers and the larger community (e.g., Macdonald and Newton, 1981; Mackenzie, 1982; Monopolis and Savage, 1982). Amini and Salasnek (1975) identify the targets of treatment as the youth's lack of motivation, early deprivation of family interaction, the inability to manage internal conflict, and the normal problems of adolescence. Gottesfeld, Caroff, and Lieberman (1973) assert that parental involvement is mandatory in the drug treatment of adolescents and that drugs are almost always hiding some other problem, which itself will require treatment even if the drug abuse problem is completely solved. Coupey and Schonberg (1982) recommend that the problem issues in the adolescent drug abuser's life should be addressed before the topic of the substance abuse itself is tackled. All of these viewpoints suggest that treatment of adolescents should go well beyond substance use to address underlying problems if treatment is to have long-term impact.

WHAT IS TREATMENT?

Many intervention programs could be classified as either treatment or prevention. Whether an intervention is called drug abuse treatment or drug abuse prevention depends less on the actual mode of intervention than on the perceived degree of involvement in the drug by the person being treated. Less drug-involved people receive preventive measures while more drug-involved people receive treatment. Often the distinction between treatment and prevention is drawn from the frequency of use and/or the problems (dysfunctions) caused by excessive use. Some authors also consider the situation in which the drug is used (e.g., as a concomitant of a social event); the motivation for use (e.g., whether the drug is sought out as an end in itself); or the function that the drug serves for the user (Brill, 1981; Bukoski, 1981; Cross and Kleinbessilink, 1980; Ungerleider and Beigel, 1980). Generally, treatment is given to individuals who use drugs frequently, who take large amounts, and who experience significant dysfunctions or adverse effects as a result. We shall follow this terminology and examine those interventions directed at individuals whose drug use is frequent, regular, dominant in their lives, and, at least to some degree, dysfunctional.

Not surprisingly, preferred treatments heavily depend on the theoretical orientation of the treatment provider. Theories with biological bases will be cited by proponents of chemotherapy or detoxification treatments. Personality-based theories will be cited by treatment professionals who speak in terms of relearning behavior patterns and who define goals in terms of individual changes that obviate the need for drugs. Interpersonally based theories lead to treatments designed to alter the drug user's relationship with family and friends, and society-based theories are cited when treatments have large community support components. Of course, few drug treatment programs are founded on a single theoretical base; in practice they may draw on several.

Most programs provide a mix of services. Table 4.1 presents the services listed in the 1982 National Drug and Alcoholism Treatment Utilization Survey (NDATUS) data base (NIDA, 1983c), reorganized here by type of service. Virtually all treatment facilities offer some form of psychological therapy or counseling, and most combine multiple forms of treatment. Medical care is less prevalent, a fact which led to the recommendation by a recent Congressionally mandated evaluation of drug treatment (General Accounting Office, 1980a) that medical care be available for all drug abusers. Social assistance is equally sporadic, with only 35 percent of facilities offering some form of job placement and half offering education; other services are offered even less frequently.[1] Almost all facilities will refer patients or clients to outside services, and most provide information on the availability of services. Although almost three quarters of all facilities have training programs for their employees, only one quarter are involved in research and evaluation.

The very term "treatment" is not well specified in the typical treatment program (Einstein, 1981; GAO, 1980a; Sells, 1979). How the many services listed in Table 4.1 are combined in a plan for any individual client is not clear. Important distinctions among categories of services (Sells, 1979) are generally not available to investigators of treatment effectiveness, especially when multiple treatment sites are included in the evaluation.

Although there are acknowledged differences between abusers of opiates and abusers of other drugs, this difference does not necessarily result in differential treatment. A NIDA Services Research Report (1979) compared treatment of nonopiate drug abusers in nondrug, drug, and mixed mental health treatment facilities. In all three types, staff lacked familiarity with treatments specifically aimed at nonopiate abuse. Only rarely did staff receive special training for treating nonopiate drug abusers.

Generally, medical care and crisis-oriented psychotherapy characterize the early phases of treatment, with general social services and supportive psychotherapy used when the client becomes stabilized as a nonabuser. The percentages shown in Table 4.1 support the

---

[1]The Supported Work Demonstration Project (Manpower Demonstration Research Corporation, 1980), which claimed to significantly improve the employment status of drug abusers, only enrolled abusers who had been in earlier treatment. Moreover, no effect of the program on drug use was found.

87

Table 4.1

TREATMENT SERVICES PROVIDED

Type of Care	Percent Providing
Medical	
Intake and screening	85
Physical examinations	44
Emergency care	32
Other medical services	30
Psychotherapy and Counseling	
Individual	99
Group	93
Family	90
Psychological testing	53
Social Assistance	
Education	50
Legal aid	15
Job counseling, placement	35
Vocational rehabilitation	21
Child care	3
Transportation	24
Referral	88
Aftercare follow-up	69
Community-Based Services	
Outreach	61
Alternatives	24
Information	78
Early intervention	43
Employee assistance	24
Self-help groups	38
Occupational alcoholism program	9
DWI program	20
Other	
Research/evaluation	26
Training	70
Total Number of Facilities	3018

SOURCE: National Drug and Alcoholism Treatment Utilization Survey for 1982 (NIDA, 1983c).

observation of the GAO's Report (1980a) that present treatment efforts focus on the short-term aspects of treatment, but there is little other information about the precise nature of services provided or the effectiveness of different treatment combinations.

Not only the means, but also the goals of treatment are in part theory-driven and are often ill-defined (Einstein, 1981). Lavenhar (1979) notes that there is a lack of agreement on the aims, objectives, and criteria for the effectiveness of treatment. While most treatment professionals would advocate freedom from drug dependence as a short-term goal and a functioning, mature lifestyle as a long-term goal, they would differ about the particulars, especially as reflected in the measures taken as indicators of program success.

TREATMENT IN THE UNITED STATES

For all the ambiguity about what constitutes drug treatment, it is a major activity in the United States, involving government at all levels, private charitable organizations, private for-profit organizations, individual health care professionals, and concerned lay people. This multiplicity of service providers prevents knowledge of the extent of drug treatment. For example, if the child of a well-paid and well-insured lawyer obtains individual psychotherapy because cocaine use has caused a drop in high school grades, neither the treatment nor the money expended on it is likely to be incorporated into any statistical description of the extent of drug treatment. However, a lower bound on the extent of drug treatment can be found in the various data bases collected until 1982 by the National Institute on Drug Abuse (NIDA).

What is the Extent of Treatment?

The largest data base collected by NIDA was the Client Oriented Data Acquisition Process (CODAP). Until funding was shifted to block grants in 1982, CODAP forms were required to be filled out for each admission and discharge to any federally supported program. These forms contained information about client statistics and treatment such as history of drug use, type of drug treatment program at admission and discharge, degree of involvement with the criminal justice system, and demographic characteristics such as as sex, race, age, employment status, and marital status.

The second data base maintained by NIDA is the National Drug and Alcoholism Treatment Utilization Survey (NDATUS), which considers the treatment facility as the unit of measurement. NDATUS collects, on a voluntary basis, information from all types of facilities associated with drug abuse and alcoholism. This information includes the location and ownership of the facility, the population it serves and type of services it offers, and for a single point in time, client census data by treatment modality.

The NDATUS survey of 1982 (NIDA, 1983c) recorded 3018 drug abuse treatment units in the United States, serving 173,479 registered clients (out of a capacity of 196,289).[2] These facilities were funded at a level of $533 million; Table 4.2 breaks this amount down by funding source. Government expenditures predominate, although private facilities may be underrepresented in these data, and noninstitutional treatment is not reported. Since 1980, federal expenditures dropped by 37 percent, but increased state and local spending made up the difference (NIDA, 1981b).

Table 4.2

DISTRIBUTION OF TREATMENT FUNDING: SEPTEMBER 1982

Funding Source	Funding per Year (in $ thousand)		Treatment Units Supported[a]
	Amount	%	
ADAMHA[b] support	79,376	15	1,228
Other federal funds	46,070	9	369
State government	165,412	31	1,732
Local government	41,423	8	973
Other direct party funds	22,400	4	482
Health insurance	105,742	20	1,135
Client fees	52,200	10	2,007
Private donations	17,358	3	694
Other	3,651	1	190
Total	533,631	100	2,875

SOURCE: NIDA (1983c).

[a]Units that receive funds from more than one source are counted for each source. Excludes 143 units that did not report funding data.

[b]Alcohol, Drug Abuse, and Mental Health Administration. The majority of these funds is in the form of block grants.

---

[2]The number of facilities has dropped from the nearly 3500 facilities participating in the 1980 NDATUS survey. The difference may be partly due to the shift toward block grant funding and reduced federal reporting requirements.

Who Receives Treatment?

As described in Chap. 2, a third data base operated by NIDA is the Drug Abuse Warning Network (DAWN), which surveys selected hospital emergency rooms and medical examiners in order to identify new drug abuse patterns and trends. These agencies report all drug-related admissions or deaths, the particular drug abused, the route of drug administration, whether the abuse was connected to a suicide attempt, what type of treatment program, if any, had been treating the person, and demographic data.

Table 4.3, which merges information from the NDATUS and DAWN data bases, shows the distribution of clients in treatment by sex, age and ethnicity. Although many clients are adolescents, they are underrepresented with respect to their frequency in the general population because of the heavy preponderance of young adults in treatment facilities. Note also that while the great majority of clients in drug treatment centers are men, more women are admitted to emergency rooms, where treatment is more for overdoses of legal drugs than for dependence on illegal drugs.

Table 4.3

DEMOGRAPHIC DISTRIBUTION OF CLIENTS IN TREATMENT

Sex, Age, and Race	NDATUS, 1982 Treatment Units (percent)	DAWN, 1981 Emergency Rooms (percent)
Sex		
Male	70	46
Female	30	54
Age		
18 years and under	12	16
19 to 44 years	80	74
45 to 59 years	7	8
60 and over	1	2
Race/Ethnicity		
White, not of Hispanic origin	53	58
Black, not of Hispanic origin	29	24
American Indian or Alaskan native	1	—
Asian or Pacific islander	1	1
Hispanic	17	6
Other, unknown	—	11

SOURCE: NIDA (1983c, 1982b).

Drug treatment in the United States was traditionally oriented towards opiates, and the popular image of drug treatment still envisions heroin addiction. Moreover, the vast majority of research and evaluation of treatments has dealt with heroin addiction and heroin treatment centers. This emphasis is changing, as attention turns toward abusers of multiple substances ("polydrug users"), as other drugs such as cocaine and PCP come to public awareness (Davis, 1982; Drug Abuse Council, 1980; Heilig, Diller, and Nelson, 1982), and as the relationship between alcohol and drug use is studied (Greene, 1979; Kaufman, 1982). Treatment for marijuana use is also discussed in the literature (e.g., Hendin et al., 1981; Wolf, 1981), but efforts have concentrated on epidemiology and prevention (e.g., Janeczek, 1980; Manatt, 1979; Penning and Barnes, 1982). In 1983, NIDA invited research proposals for treatment of marijuana use, calling for research on the utility of various psychotherapeutic strategies, on the use of alternative treatment settings to traditional drug abuse centers, and on the effectiveness of various behavior modification strategies in the treatment of (almost universally youthful) marijuana abusers.

Table 4.4 looks at the 1981 reports of primary substance abused by patients admitted to federally funded treatment facilities. There are great differences in primary drug of abuse between young persons and overall client admissions: First, although opiate problems account for 44 percent of admissions overall, only 1.5 percent of adolescent admissions are for those substances. Second, over three-fifths of all adolescent admissions are for primary marijuana abuse, over three times the corresponding overall rate. For young people, then, marijuana is the drug of greatest abuse, with everything else coming well behind. It follows that treatments addressed to nonopiate drugs, marijuana in particular, will be most relevant to the majority of juvenile drug abusers.

Comparisons of Adult and Youthful Drug Abusers

Few studies have attempted to identify the differences between adolescent drug abusers and their adult counterparts. There has been one recent major effort to examine adolescent drug treatment on a national scale, the National Youth Polydrug Study (NYPS) conducted in the late 1970s (Santo, 1979).[3]

---

[3]The NYPS built upon the CODAP data base, supplementing that information with interviews from a nationwide sample of 2750 youthful (12 to 18 years old) newly admitted clients from 97 volunteering treatment facilities. The client population and characteristics of volunteering facilities did not differ from facilities that declined to participate except that smaller drug treatment centers were less likely to volunteer.

Table 4.4

CLIENT ADMISSIONS BY SUBSTANCE ABUSED

Primary Drug of Abuse	Percent of Total Admissions to Treatment Facilities	
	All Ages	Age Under 18 Years
Heroin	35.9	1.0
Other opiates	8.2	0.5
Marijuana	19.1	61.8
Barbiturates	2.9	2.3
Amphetamines	7.7	10.0
Alcohol	8.5	5.6
Cocaine	5.8	2.9
PCP	2.2	1.6
Other hallucinogens	1.8	4.1
Tranquilizers	2.5	1.3
Other sedatives	3.1	4.0
Other, unknown	2.3	4.9
Total sample size	249,762	29,813

SOURCE: Facilities reporting to the CODAP system (NIDA, 1982a).

The NYPS study confirmed the drug usage patterns found earlier in CODAP data; fully 86 percent of clients used marijuana, 80 percent used alcohol, and one-quarter to one-third of clients reported using amphetamines, barbiturates, and various hallucinogens; heroin use was low, with only 8 percent of the respondents reporting any use (Farley, Santo, and Speck, 1979). Smith, Levy and Striar (1979) summarized the nature of treatment services for youthful drug abusers. First, a youthful abuser was more likely than an adult abuser to be forced to attend the program by criminal justice authorities, parents, or schools. Possibly for this reason, motivation to participate was often quite low. Second, while some youths felt comfortable in "traditional" treatment, many preferred alternative agencies embodying a counterculture atmosphere. This was provided by such innovations as peer counseling, where young people who were themselves former users act as paraprofessionals, by Transcendental Meditation (TM) programs, substituting yoga and relaxation for drugs, by runaway houses for adolescent users who have left home, and by free clinics oriented to countercultural, "naturalistic," antitechnological lifestyles. However, even given all of these programs, a substantial proportion of youth are treated in unsuitable programs designed for heroin addicts, which may be unresponsive to the particular needs of adolescents, and where older drug abusers might provide an undesirable influence. Smith, Levy, and Striar (1979, pp. 566–567) conclude,

> There has been a great diversity of services and modalities established to treat adolescent drug abuse, but thus far there has been a failure to design and test distinct treatment models that can be replicated in the field. Most youth programs in existence have not evaluated their services because of a lack of resources and research capability . . . The youngster is often forced to conform to the program rather than having the services structured or adapted to address his or her unique problems and needs.

Studies of youthful drug abusers other than the NYPS have been strictly local in scope, and few in number. Holland and Griffin (1983) conducted a methodologically sophisticated study that directly compared youthful and adult drug abusers undergoing treatment in the Gateway House therapeutic communities in Illinois. They found that the two groups were similar with respect to the number of drugs used, how often drugs were used, extent of psychosocial problems due to drug use, and number of prior treatments for drug abuse before entering Gateway House. This last is somewhat surprising, given that the adults, older than the adolescents by definition, might have been expected to have been involved in drugs for a longer period of time. Differences were found between the two groups on age at first use (adolescents began younger), duration of use (adults had been abusing longer), drug preference (adolescents used opiates less), and medical problems associated with drug use (adults had more, including more physical addiction to drugs). Adolescents were more likely to abuse alcohol as well as illicit drugs, and reported greater distress in their families of origin than adults. Holland and Griffin comment that the prognosis for adolescent drug abusers is poor; many of their characteristics, notably early onset, are associated with poor outcomes. They note, however, that their sample was biased toward severe problems, because only serious abusers perceived to be in difficulty are led to all-encompassing residential treatment programs such as Gateway House.

MODES OF TREATMENT

There are four generally recognized *modalities* of treatment programs (Brill, 1981; Drug Abuse Council, 1980; Einstein, 1981; Guess and Tuchfeld, 1977; Henry, 1974; Secretary of HHS, 1980; Sells, 1979).

These are detoxification (DT), methadone maintenance (MM), thera-peutic communities (TC), and drug-free (almost always outpatient) treatment (DF). Each of these modalities has several major variations. Einstein (1981) has characterized the differing theoretical assumptions, intake criteria, goals, techniques, and treatment foci of the four approaches.

Detoxification (DT)

DT is a medical treatment intended to terminate current drug use via a safe withdrawal procedure. It largely involves heavily supervised abstinence from the substance, with such medical and psychological support as necessary while the person goes through the trials of physi-cal withdrawal. As such, DT is strictly physiological in orientation, and does not address the patient's psychosocial or economic well-being; these latter are deferred to post-DT treatment, if any. The early treat-ment programs at federal hospitals in Lexington, Kentucky, and Fort Worth, Texas, were stereotypical examples of detoxification institu-tions, spawning the popular image. However, these were institutional-ized treatment programs enmeshed with the criminal justice system; presently, over two-thirds of DT is done on an outpatient basis (Secre-tary of HHS, 1980). Although many different drug programs have detoxification as the initial step in an overall treatment plan, a modal-ity is classified as DT only if detoxification is the principal or only treatment provided.

Although detoxification followed by outpatient aftercare was once the dominant treatment modality for drug abuse (Brill, 1981), its effi-cacy has been questioned over time. Lipton and Maranda (1982, p. 53), in a careful review of the literature on DT programs, conclude:

> ... detoxification fails as a *treatment* procedure for heroin-dependent persons in the sense that it has not produced satisfactory retention rates nor lasting abstinence from opiate use for the majority of addicts. Detoxification seems most appropriate, rather, as a prelim-inary step in the treatment process.

Others (e.g., Brill, 1981; Sells, 1979) concur in this judgment. In light of this consensual finding of the inefficacy of DT as a treatment program *per se*, the GAO's Report (1980a) recommended that federal funding for DT treatment centers be ceased.

Methadone Maintenance (MM)

MM is a treatment in which a synthetic opiate is administered to the client as a substitute for the opiate of abuse, typically heroin. Although the client remains dependent on the substitute, there are several clear advantages to the change of opiate:

- The synthetic does not produce the "highs" or other sensations of the original drug of abuse.
- It blocks the effects of any other opiates taken during treatment, thus eliminating some motivations to continue those drugs.
- It is administered orally instead of by injection.
- It is longer-acting, therefore requiring fewer administrations than the typical opiate of abuse.

The underlying idea is that MM frees the client from the pressures of obtaining illegal heroin, from the dangers of injection, and from the emotional rollercoaster that most opiates produce. Even though addicted to a substance, the client can muster the effort required to gain social stability. Since its development in New York City by Dole and Nyswander, it has become one of the most widely accepted of the treatment modalities for opiate addiction (Brill, 1981). It should be noted that MM is appropriate only for opiate addiction, and not for the treatment of abuse of other drugs such as cocaine, hallucinogens, or marijuana.

The synthetic originally used in MM treatment was methadone, hence the name now generically applied to substance substitution treatment. Recently, methadone has been supplemented by new substances that serve the same function but offer additional advantages. For example, LAAM (L-acetylmethadol) is quite similar to methadone in form and effects, but is longer-acting, thus necessitating fewer administrations. Presently, any drug-substitution treatment of this form is known as MM. In a typical MM treatment, the addict comes to a clinic regularly (e.g., daily for methadone, or three times a week for LAAM) for administration of methadone and an inspection (typically urinalysis) to check that other drugs are not being used. Virtually all MM programs serve clients on an outpatient basis.

Many clinics provide long-term MM programs in keeping with a philosophical view of addiction as a long-term chronic condition (Brill, 1981; Einstein, 1981). The original MM model offered chronic maintenance, with little or no psychosocial intervention. A second model, now more popular than the first, offers both psychosocial interventions and plans to taper off and withdraw all drug maintenance.

Therapeutic Communities (TC)

A TC is a residential treatment center in which the drug user lives, sheltered from the pressures of the outside world and from drugs, and in which he can learn to lead a new, drug-free life. The goal of TCs is to resocialize the drug abuser by creating a structured isolated mutual help environment in which the individual can develop and learn to function as a mature participant (Einstein, 1981).

TCs developed during the 1960s in part as a reaction against the authoritarian treatment structure of the DT approach. The original TC was Synanon; other communities, notably Daytop Village, Phoenix House, and Odyssey House, have achieved some reputation for success. Most TCs are largely staffed by ex-addicts. Some even view professional providers of drug abuse treatment with disdain, although professionals have had critical roles in the establishment of successful TCs such as Phoenix House. The original TC approach sharply restricted the personal freedom of people undergoing treatment and emphasized public self- and other-criticism, with severe sanctions for violations of the community rules and norms. This practice has waned over time, with many present TCs replacing confrontational criticism with more supportive strategies.

Although originally used almost exclusively by heroin abusers, TCs have come to be a modality for pill takers, alcoholics, marijuana users, and even people who wish to change their food-taking habits. Many present-day TCs report large populations of polydrug users. Moreover, TCs have been founded to serve specialized communities such as blacks, women, youth, and born-again Christians who suffer from drug abuse.

In the analyses below, TCs will refer to drug-free residential programs in the CODAP and NDATUS surveys, as opposed to outpatient, hospital, prison, or other programs. Although it is likely that some of these residential programs may not be technically therapeutic communities, the term is sufficiently broad and the use of such communities so widespread that the data are likely to be representative.

Drug-Free (Outpatient) Programs (DF)

DF is a generic term for all of the remaining modalities of treatment, which are noninstitutional, nonresidential, and do not provide alternative drugs. Over 50 percent of all treatment is in this category, as is virtually all of the treatment of nonopiate drug abuse (Kleber and Slobetz, 1979). Among the more commonly used techniques, especially with youthful drug abusers, are:

- *Crisis intervention centers.* These are locations where users in distress can turn for help. They include walk-in centers, 24-hour telephone hot lines, "crash pads" for emergency living arrangements, and referral centers. They deal with overdoses, help during "bad trips," and other short-term services. As with TCs, crisis intervention centers are largely staffed by nonprofessionals with whom the clients can identify.
- *Psychotherapy and counseling.* Talking with abusers is the most common form of treatment, and occurs in every modality. As a primary mode of treatment, psychotherapy tries to help the individual behave in normatively healthy ways.

Additionally, many different types of therapeutic intervention have been attempted under DF. Among these are behavior therapies (both reinforcement and aversive), biofeedback, and hypnotherapy. In reinforcement behavior therapy, the client is placed in a controlled environment where drug-related stimuli are presented to him, and is rewarded or punished depending on his response to the stimuli, so that the client learns appropriate (drug-rejecting) responses. In aversive behavior therapy, the client is presented with drug-related stimuli concomitantly with a noxious condition (such as being induced to be nauseous or receiving mild electric shocks), such that the drug-related stimuli become associated with the noxiousness and produce avoidance reactions (via conditioning). In biofeedback, clients are presented with information based on electronic monitoring of biological processes (such as blood pressure, heartrate, or various brainwaves), and learn to maintain levels of these processes that are consistent with drug avoiding behaviors. Hypnotherapy uses posthypnotic suggestion in conjunction with behavior therapy techniques to reduce the psychological craving for drugs.

Sells (1981) notes that the DF modality of treatment is currently breaking down into two separate modalities as opiate-abusing clients come to be treated not only differently from nonopiate-abusing clients, but also in separate facilities. This development is too new to have been evaluated, and available data on treatment facilities do not make this distinction.

As used below, DF will refer specifically to outpatient drug-free programs, not residential or institutional programs. Residential programs are subsumed under the TC modality, discussed above, and institutional (largely hospital and prison) programs are both idiosyncratic and such a small proportion of active treatment as to not fit within the present discussion.

Comparisons Among Modalities

The four modalities of DT, MM, TC, and DF treatment are out-growths of different theoretical orientations towards drug abuse. DT and MM are largely based on theories of biological malfunctions, and treat the abuser as having chemical dependencies in need of correction. TCs, on the other hand, are founded on theories of interpersonal problems and treat the abuser as needing resocialization. DF treatment is based on theories of personality or interpersonal difficulties; the more the problem is viewed as one of self, the more treatment is individual or group psychotherapy as opposed to family or other systems-based therapies (Einstein, 1983).

Just as few treatment facilities work entirely within one theoretical orientation, few treatment programs have components distinct from those in alternative modalities. Thus, group psychotherapy is a common part of treatment in TCs, with the therapist being a professional or lay counselor, depending on the philosophical orientation of the particular TC. Similarly, crisis intervention centers will often detoxify clients. Purely medical detoxification in a hospital unaccompanied by medication and psychotherapy is rare. However, the modalities differ enough to make comparisons meaningful.

Table 4.5 presents the distribution of clients over the four modalities on the basis of age, prior treatments, and primary drug of abuse. Nearly half of all admissions were to one or another type of outpatient DF program; the remaining admissions were divided about equally among the other modalities. DF was the dominant treatment modality for young abusers, and was the most common for individuals entering treatment for the first time. For drugs that youths are likely to abuse, such as cocaine, PCP, or marijuana, again DF was the likely treatment. For older and repeat clients and for heroin addicts, alternative modalities, particularly MM and DT, were employed.

Table 4.6 shows percentages of different types of clients within each modality. In this table, each column should be read independently. Thus, only about 20 percent of clients in DF treatments were under 18. White clients were overrepresented in DF compared with other modalities. Fewer DF clients were opiate users, although even here the majority did abuse opiates. DF clients were more likely to be engaged in productive as opposed to criminal activities than clients in other modalities.

The four treatment modalities differ not only in clients' admission characteristics, but also in length of treatment, as shown by Table 4.7. DT is typically of short duration, given its medical orientation, while MM, as implied by the term "maintenance," lasts longer. This holds

Table 4.5

DISTRIBUTION OF CLIENTS BY TREATMENT MODALITY

Variable	Percent of Clients, by Modality[a] at Admission			
	DF	TC	MM	DT
All clients	48	14	12	17
Clients under age 18	79	12	—	—
Clients age 30 or over	35	11	19	26
0 prior treatment	63	13	5	10
1 prior treatment	44	17	13	17
2-3 prior treatments	29	15	24	26
4+ prior treatments	19	11	28	37
Primary heroin use	18	12	27	39
Primary cocaine use	65	26	—	—
Primary PCP use	65	27	—	—
Primary marijuana use	82	10	—	—

SOURCE: Facilities reporting to the CODAP system (NIDA, 1982a).

NOTE: — indicates less than 0.5 percent.

[a]Modalities: DF = Outpatient drug-free; TC = therapeutic community/residential; MM = methadone maintenance; DT = detoxification. Other modalities, not listed, account for 8 percent of all clients (primarily prison, hospital, and day care settings).

Table 4.6

CLIENT CHARACTERISTICS WITHIN TREATMENT MODALITIES

Characteristic	Percent of Clients with the Characteristic			
	DF	TC	MM	DT
Male[a]	71	76	69	72
Under 18[a]	20	10	—	2
Age 30 or over[a]	25	27	54	51
White[a]	71	59	55	43
Black[a]	18	27	30	36
Hispanic[a]	9	12	14	20
Other races[a]	2	2	1	1
Daily opioid use[b]	35	63	94	88
Nonopioid only[b]	48	17	1	7
Working, at school, or homemaking[b]	62	35	38	30
Supported by illegal activities[b]	23	54	47	64

NOTE: —indicates less than 0.5 percent.

[a]NIDA (1982a).

[b]Simpson et al. (1976).

true both for all admitted clients and for those who have completed the prescribed term of treatment. The last part of Table 4.7 shows emphatically a disturbing characteristic of all treatment programs: Regardless of modality, more than half of all admissions terminate treatment prematurely, either by dropping out or by being dismissed by the treatment facility for rule violations.

DOES TREATMENT WORK?

There is no general consensus on the current state of drug abuse treatment. Some authors find that no general evaluation can be made (Einstein, 1981; Ungerleider and Beigel, 1980), some find that there is no evidence that treatment does any good at all (Ogborne, 1978), some do not discuss empirical evaluation (Brill, 1981), and some claim that treatment programs have been shown to be effective (NIDA 1981a).

Table 4.7

TREATMENT DISCHARGE STATISTICS, BY MODALITY

Item	Percent Distribution of Clients, by Modality			
	DF	TC	MM	DT
Weeks in treatment—all clients				
2 or less	14	31	8	50
3 to 18	24	27	17	38
9 to 16	22	15	16	5
17 to 26	6	10	13	2
Over 26	24	17	46	5
Weeks in treatment—completing treatment				
2 or less	3	4	3	33
3 to 8	14	24	10	55
9 to 16	22	12	11	4
17 to 26	21	16	11	2
Over 26	39	44	65	6
Reason for discharge				
Completed treatment	29	14	13	20
Transferred to other program	11	17	23	17
Left or dismissed	56	68	55	61
Other	4	2	9	2

SOURCE: Facilities reporting to the CODAP system (NIDA, 1982a).

The field of drug treatment is in the stage that its cousin, psycho-therapy, was in 20 years ago. Each of a variety of treatment approaches claims for itself at least some degree of success (Brill, 1981), but our review suggests that few if any treatments are backed up by persuasive scientific evidence of effectiveness.

In this section, we shall examine the research that leads to the con-clusion expressed above. First, we shall assess the state of treatment evaluation, upon which any assessment of treatment effectiveness rests. Then, we will look at the Drug Abuse Reporting Network (DARP) study, the largest nationwide study to date to attempt to evaluate drug treatment programs. Finally, we will examine in summary form those smaller scale evaluations and experimental studies that address treat-ments that could be applicable to youthful drug abusers.

Evaluating Drug Treatment

Federal officials recognize that evaluation is an important com-ponent of the drug treatment process. NIDA has developed standard-ized treatment evaluation protocols (Guess and Tuchfeld, 1977), and, before the transfer of support for drug treatment programs from direct NIDA funding to block grants, had begun to require evaluations from treatment programs desiring continued support. In the ideal case envisaged by NIDA, treatment facilities would regularly report the number of clients entering their programs, the number successfully ter-minating, the number dropping out, and the number of all other termi-nations. Outcome measures would be taken, including followup infor-mation on the percentages of patients drug free, opiate free, free of criminal arrests and charges, and free from alcohol abuse. In addition the average percentage of time gainfully employed or in school would be reported. All of this would be tabulated by basic client categories such as drug usage pattern, race, age group, and gender.

But these goals have not been achieved. Lavenhar (1979) noted the generally lamentable state of treatment evaluation, observing a general lack of agreement on the aims, objectives, and criteria for the effective-ness of treatment. The GAO Report (1980a) noted that required data keeping was often not maintained. Tims (1982) reported that only 44 percent of 341 programs receiving federal funds in 1979 reported at least one program evaluation in the previous year. Larger treatment facilities were more likely to have evaluations; with increasing size comes increasing differentiation of staff roles, and a class of workers who can concern themselves more with administrative concerns such as recordkeeping instead of having a primary focus on the day-to-day problems of clients.

Thus, evaluation is not routinely done. To discover whether treatment programs have any benefit, we must rely mostly on few specially designed large-scale evaluations of drug treatment programs that have been done within the past decade, supplemented by a number of smaller studies of individual programs.

National Evaluations of Drug Treatment Programs

The largest evaluation project to date has been the NIDA's National Followup Study of Admissions to Drug Abuse Treatments in the Drug Abuse Reporting Program (DARP). Although the clients followed up by DARP were in treatment over ten years ago, this project provides much of what is known about treatment program effectiveness. In this study, data were collected from almost 44,000 clients admitted to 52 different programs. The program obtained longitudinal data for clients admitted between 1969 and 1973, including followup interviews with 4,627 clients from 34 different treatment agencies. Reports of analyses of the DARP project have been extensively published and frequently summarized (e.g., NIDA, 1978, 1981a; Sells, 1979; Sells, Demaree, and Hornick, 1980; Simpson and Sells, 1982). In a main analysis comparing treatment modalities, the outcome factors of employment, opioid use, nonopioid use, alcohol consumption, criminality, and return to drug treatment were combined into a single summary favorableness-of-outcome measure, which was then divided into four categories:

- Most favorable outcomes, characterized by drug abstinence and little or no criminal activity;
- Favorable outcomes, in which there might be some drug use, and moderate levels of unemployment, and in which there might be return to treatment;
- Unfavorable outcomes, in which there was continued opioid use, but not nonopioid drug use, criminality, and unemployment; and
- Most unfavorable outcomes, characterized by moderate to heavy drug use, criminality, unemployment, and a return to treatment

Table 4.8 shows the percentages of the DARP sample that fell into each of the four outcome categories, by treatment modality and, for TC and DF, for the total group and the subgroup who were not opioid addicts. Note also that a No Treatment control group was included in the sample, consisting of people who had completed an intake into an agency, but then did not receive treatment. The data base has acknowledged methodological limitations, including oversampling more successful clients on followup measures and nonrandom assignment of

Table 4.8

PATIENT OUTCOMES AS A FUNCTION OF TREATMENT MODALITY

Group	N	Most Favorable			Favorable			Unfavorable			Most Unfavorable		
		Obs.	Exp.	O/E[a]	Obs.	Exp.	O/E	Obs.	Exp.	O/E	Obs.	Exp.	O/E
Total sample	1923	31.1			20.3			32.2			16.4		
No treatment	143	20.1	32.9	0.61	16.1	23.8	0.68	38.4	22.4	1.71	24.5	21.0	1.17
DT	153	19.6	34.7	0.56	15.6	21.6	0.72	39.3	31.4	1.25	25.5	12.4	2.06
MM	773	29.5	26.6	1.11	25.6	17.0	1.51	30.8	37.6	0.82	14.0	19.0	0.74
TC—all	613	36.9	34.4	1.07	15.9	19.8	0.80	31.1	29.1	1.07	16.1	16.5	0.98
TC—nonaddicts	69	39.2	47.9	0.82	26.1	46.4	0.56	24.7	4.4	5.61	10.2	1.5	6.80
DF—all	241	34.4	33.7	1.02	19.1	29.8	0.64	31.1	27.8	1.12	14.6	8.7	1.68
DF—nonaddicts	55	49.2	31.0	1.59	32.7	63.6	0.51	16.4	5.5	2.98	1.8	(b)	(b)

SOURCE: DARP study, reported in Sells, Demaree, and Hornick (1980).

[a]The ratio of the observed to the statistically expected percentage; see text for an explanation.

[b]Too few expected to calculate a ratio.

clients to treatments, but the authors provide statistical and logical arguments that lend credence to their conclusions.

Table 4.8 presents the observed percentages in each outcome category, accompanied by an expected percentage. This expected percentage was based on a discriminant function analysis of demographic and other characteristics of the sample that predicted outcome favorability assuming no differences in treatment modality effectiveness, and goes a considerable distance towards resolving the problems posed by the inability to randomly assign people to treatment modality. In other words, statistical corrections were incorporated into the data analyses to accommodate the fact that clients who are expected to do well in treatment were not uniformly distributed in treatment conditions. For example, there is evidence that clients who are young, employed, or nonopiate abusers will do better in treatment than older, unemployed, or opiate abusers. But these people for whom the prognosis is more favorable are more likely to be in a DF than an MM treatment program. This would, if uncorrected, seem to suggest that DF works better than MM. The statistical calculations in the DARP study were designed to correct for this bias.

The statistical correction is shown in the O/E ratio in the table, which is the ratio of the *observed* percentage in each outcome category divided by what would be *expected* in each category, given all of the factors such as age, employment, drug of abuse, etc., that influence treatment outcome. The observed percentage measure in the table provides an absolute measure of client success, while the O/E measure assesses success relative to what we would predict if all treatments had the same types of clients. Ratios greater than 1.0 indicate that more people than expected were present in that category; this indicates efficacy of a treatment modality for favorable outcomes and inefficacy for unfavorable outcomes.

Table 4.8 supports the contention of Sells (1979; Sells, Demaree, and Hornick, 1980) that No Treatment and DT are poor treatment alternatives compared with MM, TC, and DF. In the latter three categories, the most favorable outcome rate is slightly higher than its expectation, with the O/E ratio above 1.0. By contrast, the No Treatment and DT modalities have O/E ratios considerably below 1.0 for the most favorable outcome.

The table also shows that overall about half of the clients in treatment were rated in one of the two favorable outcome categories. Nonaddicts had an even greater success rate; over two-thirds of them were in the favorable outcome categories. However, based on the demographic and other predictors, one would have expected over 90 percent of the nonaddicts to fall in one of the favorable categories. So, although most nonaddicts had favorable outcomes, even more of them should have been so classed, if treatments were generally effective for these clients.

A comparison of the nonaddicts with the total sample of DF patients shows that the opiate addicts do poorly in DF compared with TC or MM. From this finding, one might recommend that DF programs be reserved for nonaddicted drug abusers, with the treatment of opiate addicts best left to TC and MM programs. The converse of that recommendation is also true, as the table shows. The prognosis for nonaddicts in TCs is much worse than in DF. Considering that the resident patients and staff of most TCs are addicts or former addicts, and that the ties of community are the strongest feature of TCs, this finding is not surprising.

A considerable part of the DARP evaluation effort was devoted to an understanding of what types of clients were most benefited by which treatment modalities. These analyses provide valuable information, but are beyond the scope of this report. In general, though, the less problems a client had upon admission, the more likely he was to benefit from the program. One major finding of the DARP study is that for MM, TC, or DF treatment programs, favorableness of outcomes with respect to continued abstinence from drugs, stable employment, and avoidance of criminality was found to increase linearly with the amount of time spent in the treatment program (Simpson, 1981). Clients who were in programs for less than three months had poor outcomes and did not differ from intake-only control clients or DT clients. Although this observation could be due to a client self-selection bias (Raymond and Hurwitz, 1981) this finding suggests that program research in this area should be directed towards being able to attract and keep clients in the program long enough for the desired changes to take effect.

The DARP study, which analyzes data from cohorts entering treatment ten years ago, is dated. NIDA recently initiated a new data collection effort called TOPS (Treatment Outcome Prospective Study).[4] TOPS will trace three years of treatment cohorts, from 1979 to 1981; currently, intake and in-treatment results are available for the 1979 cohort (Bray et al., 1981) and the 1980 cohort (Craddock et al., 1982), but post-treatment outcomes are not yet available. Although the TOPS effort aims at comprehensiveness, all treatment programs and clients within those programs are volunteers, so once again the

---

[4]Other evaluations of treatment have been on smaller scale than the DARP or TOPS evaluation efforts. For example, the California Civil Addict Program (McGlothlin, Anglin, and Wilson, 1977) examined adult male opiate addicts convicted of crimes in California; the results of this study are complex and not germane to the treatment of youth.

problem of respondent self-selection will qualify any findings that arise.

The 1979 TOPS cohort includes 3389 clients from 27 drug treatment centers in six cities; the 1980 cohort increased sampling to 3908 clients, 32 treatment centers, and eight cities. Extensive data on the background characteristics of the clients are being collected so that the concomitants of successful treatment may be examined; the study has been designed to explore complex multivariate relationships among background variables, nature of treatment, and outcomes. One preliminary finding corresponds with earlier information: Only a small percentage of clients entering treatment remain with the program for six months. Given the finding reported earlier that the probability of remaining drug free increases with length of treatment, it is unlikely that TOPS will conclude that fully effective treatment methods have been developed.

Smaller-Scale Studies

In this section, we summarize a number of smaller-scale studies assessing effectiveness of treatments that either were addressed specifically to adolescents or might be relevant for them. As explained earlier, we will not examine detoxification any further; nor will we examine MM programs, because methadone maintenance is a treatment for opiate addicts and few adolescents have an opiate as the primary drug of abuse.[5] Most remaining studies are unreplicated reports on the efficacy of one particular treatment at one particular facility, or on improvement based on an outcome measure unique to the study at hand. Since these studies must be regarded as presenting unsubstantiated data, we pass over them and focus instead on findings that have been replicated in a number of independently conducted studies.

Length of Stay in Treatment. Several studies have found that better outcomes are associated with longer time in treatment. DeLeon, Wexler, and Jainchill (1982) performed a five-year followup study of two waves of Phoenix House completers and dropouts. Fully 75 percent of the TC program graduates were successful, in that they were opiate-free, were employed fairly regularly, and were not involved with the criminal justice system; and an additional 18 percent were improved over their condition upon admission to the program. By con-

---

[5]The elimination of MM programs from consideration drastically reduces the number of studies to be considered. A substantial proportion of the drug treatment research is devoted to MM, including effects of alternative synthetic substitutes, effects of different dosages of medication, the effects of monitoring client behavior, and the effects of supportive psychotherapeutic treatment given in addition to the chemotherapy.

trast, only 31 percent of program dropouts were successful, although another 25 percent were labelled improved. Van Ryswyk et al. (1981), examining 641 former residents of eight halfway house TCs, report similar results. Coombs (1981) interviewed 208 dropouts and graduates from two California TCs for opiate abusers, one a long-term program and one a short-term program. Fully 80 percent of the graduates of the long-term TC were opiate-free at the time of the interview, but only 50 percent of the short-term graduates. Dropouts from both programs fared worse than their graduating counterparts. Although program graduates were opiate-free, only nine of the 208 interviewees remained totally drug free, and all nine still continued treatment.

Further evidence for a length-of-treatment effect comes from a NIDA Services Research Report (1977) evaluating the Teen Challenge treatment program.[6] Seven years after program entry, graduates were more likely than dropouts to be drug free. Moreover, the closer to graduation a client had come, the greater the likelihood of a favorable outcome.

Perhaps the most methodologically sophisticated examination of the effects of length of stay is a study by Holland (1981), who evaluated four entering cohorts from the Illinois-based Gateway Houses, with followups taken from one to ten years after treatment. Clients were mostly heroin abusers. Pre-treatment measures from clinic records were compared with post-treatment measures, including measures of alcohol and drug use, criminality, employment, and social stability. The longer a client stayed at Gateway, the better was the outcome. Even after controlling for such factors as client self-selection, client maturation, socioeconomic status, family background, and previous drug, alcohol, and criminality history, time in program remained a statistically significant predictor of followup success.

Raymond and Hurwitz (1981) investigated the antecedents of length of stay in a DF treatment program. At the time of admission, they measured the treatment protocol preferences of 136 clients. Clients who received their preferred treatment remained in treatment longer than those who did not; this could be due to the client's really knowing what is best for himself, or, as the authors posited, to a self-fulfilling prophecy.

The studies above all indicate that the longer clients remain in treatment, the better are their outcomes. Although this consensus must be qualified because there are methodological problems in

---

[6]Teen Challenge is a religiously oriented program with a fundamentalist philosophy, and demands adoption of its religious philosophy as the path to abandonment of drug abuse. In spite of its name, the median age of clients in the facility evaluated was in the mid-20s.

obtaining followup measures from program dropouts, it is implausible that program dropouts who could not be reached were doing better than those who could be. A more serious qualification is that we do not know whether the length-of-treatment effect is due to the increased benefit of more treatment or to self-selection on the part of clients, whereby clients who are predisposed to success are the ones who remain in treatment and would improve anyway. None of the studies above compared treated clients with a control group of treatment candidates assigned to a waiting list, and, of course, dropping out from treatment was not a variable under the control of the investigator. To the extent that self-selection is a factor, treatment programs should concentrate more on motivating clients to become interested and involved in their own treatment, so that they become more predisposed to gain the benefits offered by treatment.

Client Control and Program Style. Several studies have assessed the efficacy of treatments that provide differing levels of control and surveillance over the client's life. More authoritative programs are impersonal, confrontive, and controlling, not trusting the client; other programs are noncritically supportive, and basically trusting. Vaglum and Fossheim (1980) examined two TCs set up in two different years within a Norwegian psychiatric hospital. Using a "quasi-experimental" design[7] that contrasted a traditional confrontive style TC with one that was more supportive, they found that opiate abusers appeared to respond better to the former while psychedelic drug abusers seemed more receptive to the latter. The quasi-experimental design enhances the methodological validity of the study, although random assignments of clients to treatment would have strengthened the conclusions.

Milby et al. (1980), in one of the few studies to employ control groups, randomly assigned 29 polydrug users completing detoxification to one of three treatment groups: DF with surveillance in the form of urine monitoring, DF without surveillance, and waiting-list control. The DF treatment used individual outpatient psychotherapy for three months. The surveillance group showed less barbiturate use and fewer drug-using friends than the other two groups, but the two DF treatment groups together showed no drug-related differences from the control group. The authors conclude that surveillance as an adjunct to treatment has promise.

Anker and Crowley (1982) examined the use of contingency contracts for cocaine abusers. Program clients were offered the

---

[7]The two TCs were in successive years at the hospital; the different styles reflected differing philosophies as the staff turned over.

opportunity to sign contracts containing punishments if they showed evidence of cocaine use in urine monitoring. For clients who agreed, the punishments were individually tailored, and were severe. For example, some clients deposited letters addressed to legal authorities admitting to drug dealing, to be mailed if they violated the contract; thus they invited arrest if the letters were mailed. Clients signing contracts maintained abstinence from cocaine more than refusers; however, a treatment effect cannot be separated from the effect of selectivity of volunteers. As a possible claim for the effect of the treatment, the authors note that more clients signed contracts over the life of the program, with no reduction in the efficacy of the treatment and with a consequent overall improvement in outcome for the treatment.

As yet, we are not in a position to advocate one type of program over another. It appears that style of treatment is strongly client-dependent, some clients faring better with strong supervision and strict control, while others require a more relaxed treatment environment.

Behavior Modification. Although behavior modification is considered a promising treatment for drug abuse, there are few treatment evaluations.[8] Kleber and Slobetz (1979) reviewed several studies in which behavior modification was shown to be inferior to methadone maintenance in reducing drug usage among opiate addicts. Hedberg and Campbell (1974) compared systematic desensitization, covert sensitization, aversive shock treatment, and family behavior reinforcement treatments for alcoholism, with random assignment of male alcoholics to 6 months treatment in each type. They found that about 70 percent of the patients in the systematic desensitization and family reinforcement treatments were able to fulfill their own goals of abstinence or limited drinking. Covert sensitization did not produce such an improvement, while patients in the shock treatment largely dropped out of the program. The extension of behavioral modification techniques to substances other than alcohol is still experimental, with reports consisting of small-sample case studies (e.g., Polakow and Doctor, 1973) or nonevaluative descriptions of pilot programs (e.g., Gotestam and Melin, 1980).

---

[8]Behavior modification refers to various psychological techniques that attempt to change the client's behavior by patterns of rewarding desirable behavior and punishing undesirable behavior. The theoretical rationale is that the client becomes conditioned to this pattern, and thereafter will avoid the undesirable behavior. Desensitization treatments are those that associate stressful situations and stimuli with peaceful relaxed (rewarding) images, so that the anxious reactions will no longer accompany the situations. Aversive treatments associate a painful stimulus (e.g., shock) with undesirable behavior (e.g, taking or thinking about the experience of taking drugs). Reinforcement treatments provide physical or verbal rewards in return for desired behavior.

Treatment Programs Designed for Adolescents

Just as with drug treatment in general, few empirical studies have investigated the effectiveness of treatment for adolescent drug abusers. Miller (1973) reviewed the medical and psychological treatment available for adolescents and concluded that therapy techniques were generally unsatisfactory. Stein and Davis (1982) reviewed over a dozen recently reported treatment approaches to adolescent substance abusers. None of these approaches were supported by analytic evidence of success; either a very small number of case history successes or diffuse impressions were reported. Stein and Davis agree that the extent of the problem far exceeds treatment efforts, and call for development of better methods of treatment as an urgent priority. Here, we will examine two treatments that particularly address adolescent drug abuse: early intervention treatment and family therapy.

Early Intervention Treatment. Considerable effort is devoted to early intervention treatment with adolescents, before the effects of abuse become severe. Blum and Richards (1979) note that few objective data exist on the effectiveness of these programs. There are a few studies, however. Gottheil et al. (1977) report on a DF program specifically aimed at adolescent students. High school students using drugs but not yet manifesting severe problems were recruited into a program that met for a half day once a week for group psychotherapy and counselling. No formal evaluation of the program was presented, but the authors report improved school attendance. Because one of the bases for recruitment into the program was deficient school attendance, this finding could be a regression artifact. In general, other measures of behavioral improvement showed no differences between beginning and end of program.

Iverson et al. (1978) report on an early intervention program that used family and peer pressures on adolescents who were beginning drug use, in an effort to halt criminal drug involvement, reduce school problems, raise the youth's self-esteem, and improve communication patterns between parents and children. The program comprised six counselling sessions in which the adolescents and what parents could be recruited were educated on family structure, communication patterns, and drug knowledge. The recruiting efforts for parents were apparently not very satisfactory, as only 71 parents were seen along with 70 adolescents. Results were not promising; parents reported greater drug knowledge and felt that familial communication patterns were improved, but the adolescents showed no difference after the program on any variable.

Chasanoff and Schrader (1979) reported on another early intervention program for adolescents that used contingency contracting, assertiveness training, relaxation training, and cognitive restructuring. Behavioral measures showed lower frequencies of problems, including drug use, during treatment, but no post-treatment data were reported.

Therefore, in spite of the considerable investment in early intervention, the findings of the few studies examining that treatment are not promising; none of the studies presents reliable evidence that early intervention reduces drug abuse or prevents the effects of continued drug use.

Family Therapy as a Treatment for Drug Abuse. There seems to be considerable interest in family therapy as a treatment for adolescent abusers.[9] NIDA has a number of recent publications (e.g., Ellis, 1980; Ferguson, Lennox, and Lettieri, 1974; Glynn, 1981) that are specifically addressed to family issues in drug abuse. Coleman (1977) reports that most drug treatment programs employ family therapy as a technique; however, this typically means that most programs sometimes see the families of patients as well as the patients. The increased use of family therapy has been accompanied by an increased tendency for professionals treating adolescent drug abuse to prefer interpersonal rather than psychological theories (e.g., Baither, 1978; Clayton, 1979; Kaufman and Kaufmann, 1979a; Kenward and Rissover, 1980; Klagsbrun and Davis, 1977; Stanton, 1979b; Steinglass, 1976, 1977; Usher, Jay, and Glass, 1982). It is widely believed that families play a central role in the genesis of drug abuse problems (Reilly, 1975; Kaufmann, 1979; Kaufman and Kaufmann, 1979a; DeAngelis and Goldstein, 1978).

Huberty (1975), citing family therapy as the single most important treatment for adolescent drug abuse, outlined the problem areas that are to be addressed in treatment

- The family's ignorance of the child's dependence;
- A denial of that dependence, when ignorance was impossible;
- Failure of the parents to accept responsibility for the child's drug dependence problems;
- A general family inability to sort out emotions of anger and hostility from those of love and affection;

---

[9]Family therapy is a philosophy of psychotherapeutic intervention in which the nuclear family of an identified patient (parents and siblings) is regarded as the unit of treatment. The individual whose problems resulted in the initiation of therapy is not singled out as "diseased," but is viewed as a symptom carrier for what is a family problem (e.g., Hoffman, 1981). Treatment can take many forms, of which the most common is *conjoint family therapy,* where the entire family, including identified client, parents, and siblings, are seen together.

- Each family member's ambivalent feelings toward the other;
- A lack of honesty in expressing emotions; and
- A poor role model for handling drugs.

Much of the evidence about the efficacy of family therapy consists of case studies, done without regard for representativeness of the clients or control groups (Hendin et al., 1981; Noone and Reddig, 1976; Reilly, 1975). Experimental studies have been rare, have involved small numbers of clients, but have shown promising results. Steinglass (1979; Steinglass, Davis, and Berenson, 1977) conducted a pilot experiment in which the spouse of an alcoholic was hospitalized along with the alcoholic as part of treatment. Ten couples were each hospitalized for a seven-to-ten-day treatment. The program was demonstrated to have an impact on marital interaction patterns, which in some but not all cases led to a change in drinking patterns. Large effects were associated with particular therapists, leading to the conclusion that experienced clinicians should be sought for this treatment.

Cadogan (1973) compared 20 marital groups with 20 waiting-list controls in a study of alcoholics, and found that 45 percent of clients in the group treatment remained abstinent, but only 10 percent of those in the control group. This study suggests that for alcoholics, at least, marital group therapy is better than no therapy at all.

Stanton, Todd, and Associates (1982) provide the single most carefully performed study of the effectiveness of family therapy for drug abusers. They randomly assigned young male heroin abusers to family therapy, to individual therapy, or to a program where the family came to the treatment center to watch movies. Treatment was brief, lasting from three to five months (in keeping with the tenets of the family therapy model). A considerable effort was expended to bring the families into treatment. The study demonstrated that short-term family therapy was superior to the other treatments across a variety of outcome measures of drug taking, societal productivity, and interpersonal familial relations. Gains from the treatment program were better than those claimed for treatment with heroin addicts in virtually any previous systematic study of outcomes.

Stanton (1979a), in a comprehensive review of family treatment approaches to drug abuse problems, concludes that this treatment is as beneficial as any other presently available. Kaufman (1980) largely agrees, but cautions that the unknowns in the family genesis of drug and alcohol abuse are still greater than the knowns, and that family treatment, although promising, remains unproven in any scientific sense. We concur with this assessment; the only demonstrated treatment effects of family therapy have been for alcohol and opiate abuse;

other findings are only suggestive. Furthermore, family therapy is an expensive undertaking, involving a large investment of professional time per client and considerable skill and expense in overcoming the family's psychological and economic disincentives to enter treatment as a unit. Before any large-scale treatment program could be recommended, research must ascertain what family factors are predictive of drug abuse and under what conditions family treatment is demonstrably effective.

FUTURE PROSPECTS FOR TREATMENT

Thus far, treatment practice has not been based on good empirical evidence about program effectiveness. As Einstein (1983, p. iii) says:

> Continuing discussions and arguments about the treatability of the drug user . . . have not ended in any clear decisions on the part of treatment agents, policy makers, the community at large, or for that matter, many drug users. . . . Recent efforts to evaluate the outcome of the types of treatment empirically have not added much light to this blurry issue. Neither have they been systematically used to change ongoing programs or to influence the creation, scope, or direction of new ones.

Despite the problems, several general conclusions with regard to treatment may be drawn from our survey. Adolescent drug abusers are typically not addicted to opiates, and have less physical dependence on drugs than adult abusers. There are fewer high-rate users among adolescents, the extent of impairment of function is less, and adolescents are more likely to be detected as abusers by family or school than adults, who generally come to the attention of treatment providers only when they get into trouble. Moreover, the behavioral, family, and "lifestyle" problems of the adolescent drug abuser are as likely to be the cause as the effect of his drug abuse; it is critical, therefore, that a drug treatment for adolescents be oriented towards those problems.

These factors lead to an optimistic conclusion that, given proper treatment, the prognosis for youth *might* be better than that for adults. Differences between youthful and adult abusers are generally those differences that predict treatment success. The qualification is important, however, because we do not yet know what constitutes a good treatment for either youth or adults.

This uncertainty underscores the need for more carefully conducted treatment research, especially in the face of the great numbers of adolescent drug abusers who do require some treatment. We acknowledge practical problems in random assignment of clients to treatment, constructing adequate and appropriate control groups, and having well-defined, meaningful outcome measures. Nonetheless, better and more standardized evaluation of adolescent treatment facilities is required to ascertain which, if any, of them are effective, and what factors lead to effectiveness. As theoretical concepts of drug abuse lead to implications for treatment, these should be tested, as has been done with family therapy for the addicts in the study by Stanton, Todd and Associates (1982).

All of this research is expensive, and does not directly provide treatment. But the alternative is to continue spending money on treatment programs without knowing whether they are doing any good. It may be that the only treatments that are effective are complex and expensive, in which case careful decisions must be made whether and when to implement them. But if any treatment proves effective, then at least a door is opened for consideration of less costly versions that may be nearly as effective. Therefore, at least for the present, treatment research should be as broad-based as possible.

SUMMARY

Treatment for drug abuse is a multifaceted phenomenon that appears in many varieties, depending on the definition of drug abuse and the theoretical view of its etiology taken by the treatment practitioner. Many different services, ranging from chemotherapy and psychotherapy to social assistance and residential care, are provided under the name of drug treatment. Often there is no coherence to the collection of services provided, and even less frequently is the treatment protocol tailored to the needs of the individual client.

Complicating the picture is the fact that adolescents entering drug abuse treatment differ from the general population of drug abusers. In particular,

- Many youth are in treatment involuntarily, having been brought in by parents or by authorities as a substitute for criminal sanctions. Their motivation is consequently suspect.
- Youth are often treated in unsuitable programs—usually, programs designed primarily for heroin addicts—whereas youth are rarely physically addicted to the drugs they abuse.
- While the consensus of researchers is that drug abuse in youth is best viewed as a problem of interpersonal relationships, the traditional treatments for drug abuse are based on theories that ascribe the problem to biological or psychological malfunctions.

During 1982, treatment for drug abuse consumed over one half billion dollars, in an attempt to aid frequent and heavy users of drugs who suffered dysfunctional consequences. These funds came from varied sources, including the federal government (24 percent), state and local governments (39 percent), and third-party insurance expenditures (20 percent). The population treated is largely adult; only 12 percent of all persons treated are under 18 years of age.

The lion's share of treatment, both in terms of expenditures and persons treated, is devoted to users of heroin and other opiates. But this finding does not apply to youthful drug abusers; 62 percent of all youth in treatment for drug abuse had marijuana recorded as their primary drug. Only 1.5 percent of all youth in treatment were primary abusers of opiates. For all other types of drugs, the percentages were similarly low. It appears, then, that in treatment of adults, opiates are the drug of primary concern; but in treatment of youth, marijuana presents the major problem. The drug treatment literature on opiate addiction, which accounts for the majority of the literature on nonalcohol substance abuse, is therefore of little use in understanding treatment of youth.

Drug treatment facilities may be generally classified into one of four types: detoxification, methadone maintenance, therapeutic communities, and (mostly outpatient) drug-free programs. Most of the treatment in the first three types of programs has been for opiate abuse. Of all youth in treatment, however, 79 percent are in drug-free programs, with most of the remainder in some form of therapeutic community.

The scientific evidence on the efficacy of treatment is scant; virtually all of the reported studies suffer from one or more serious defects in design. Nonetheless, several conclusions may be drawn. The DARP study of long-term treatment effects showed that methadone maintenance, therapeutic communities, and drug-free treatments were all superior to no treatment and to detoxification unaccompanied by other services. For nonopiate clients, where most adolescents would fall, drug-free programs were the treatment of choice, although therapeutic communities serving only adolescents were not included in the DARP study as a separate category.

DARP and other data indicate that the longer a client remains in treatment, the more likely the treatment is to be successful. However, the reasons why this is so are not well established. At present, it seems just as reasonable to assume that people who stay in treatment do so because of a predisposition to improve as it is to assume that staying longer increases the likelihood of improvement. In any event, a major problem with all drug treatment programs is the high dropout rate; any research leading to greater client retention would be a welcome development.

The research on program control over clients and behavior modification techniques is inconclusive; there is so little research, and its results are so mixed, that at present one cannot recommend how to structure a program or when to use behavior modification techniques.

With respect to treatment specifically aimed at adolescents, the research evidence is scarcely better than that for treatment in general. Programs for early intervention treatment, although popular, have not been proven effective by scientific standards. Family therapy, which is an increasingly popular form of treatment for adolescents, has been shown effective in some contexts, but because of its particular problems of implementation, needs better scientific support before it could be broadly recommended as a treatment of choice.

In conclusion, we recommend that the differences between adult and adolescent drug abusers be acknowledged in the planning of treatment. There is reason for guarded optimism that an effective treatment for adolescent drug abusers is possible, but more research is needed to lead to its formulation.

Chapter 5

PREVENTION OF DRUG USE

This chapter deals with the last, and most promising, of the three main drug control measures: prevention. We consider prevention programs aimed at the general adolescent population, rather than those addressed specifically to regular drug users, heavy users, or adults. We conclude that, although drug education has earned a rather disappointing reputation in the past, recent innovative approaches offer greater hope for reducing drug use among young people. The new methods focus on social influence and peer group norms as the primary factors motivating young people to start smoking or using drugs. Their success in preventing cigarette use, coupled with their grounding in a more accurate understanding of adolescent behavior, suggests they might well be adapted for programs to prevent drug use.

We begin by outlining the main types of prevention and the principal issues involved in designing prevention programs. We then review the scientific literature that documents how adolescents begin using drugs and suggests ways to interrupt that process. Finally, we describe and evaluate the main models for drug prevention, showing why earlier approaches proved unsatisfactory while the newer approaches hold promise.

WHAT IS PREVENTION?

The major distinction among interventions aimed at potential or actual drug users is between prevention and treatment. As we noted in Chap. 4, treatment programs seek to reduce or eliminate drug use among people for whom it has become so dominant that it interferes with their lives. Prevention programs aim at the reduction, delay, or prevention of drug use *before* it has become habitual or clearly dysfunctional.

This association between level of drug involvement and type of intervention also provides a context for relating categories of prevention to the successive stages of drug use through which an adolescent might pass over time. Figure 5.1 depicts four such stages based on frequency of use: (1) *non-use*, or never having tried the specific drug at issue; (2) *experimental* or episodic use; (3) *regular* or frequent use; and

118

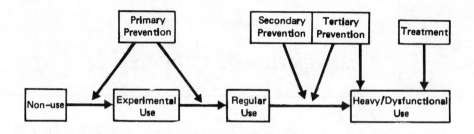

Fig. 5.1—Types of intervention associated with drug use stages

(4) *heavy use,* a stage reached by only a minority of users.[1] The definitions of these terms vary among researchers, but we define experimental use roughly as fewer than twelve times a year, and regular use as occurring at least monthly but not more than once or twice a week. Daily or near daily dosages would constitute heavy use.[2] In the latter stage, which may also signal physical, cognitive, or psychological impairment or dysfunction, drug taking has usually become an integral part of the young person's life and cannot easily be discontinued at will.

Within this scheme, we view *primary* prevention as focused on the early stages—trying to keep young people from ever starting at all or, if they have experimented, from shifting into regular use (see Fig. 5.1).

---

[1]Some authors insert a fifth stage between experimental or regular use, which they variously label "recreational" or "social" use (Ungerleider and Beigel, 1980). However, this category describes the context of use, not its frequency—distinguishing use that occurs as a by-product of a social occasion from situations in which the user deliberately seeks out the drug. We have followed the dominant practice of research on the prevalence and correlates of adolescent drug behavior, most of which uses indices of involvement based on frequency of use (Jessor and Jessor, 1977; Kandel, 1978a; Johnston, Bachman, and O'Malley, 1982).

[2]This scheme seeks to encompass the widely varying definitions of regular use among prevention researchers. For example, some define regular cigarette smoking for adolescents as at least weekly (Perry et al., 1980; Telch et al., 1982; Flay et al., 1983), while others define regular smoking as at least monthly or twice a month (Hurd et al., 1980; Luepker et al., 1983). Similarly, regular marijuana use has been variously defined as at least weekly (McAlister et al., 1980) or monthly. These variations appear to reflect a lack of consensus about the likely short- and long-term consequences of different drug-use levels for adolescents, different views of what constitutes potentially harmful or inappropriate behavior for adolescents as opposed to adults, and different (e.g., lower) levels of drug use among youthful populations and a consequent variation in what constitutes detectable variations in use.

Primary prevention programs can also be distinguished by their target audience: Most of them serve a *general* population or group of adolescents that has not been identified as having a problem resulting from drug use and "is in no imminent danger of developing a problem" (Goodstadt, 1981). Accordingly, primary prevention activities seek to alter the environment or the individual so that a drug-related condition or problem will not develop or exist (Newman, Martin, and Weppner, 1982).

Secondary and *tertiary* prevention programs seek to prevent regular users from getting into serious trouble, e.g., from becoming habitual users who are psychologically or physically dependent on the drug or mired in other maladaptive behavior such as frequent school absenteeism or delinquent activities. Secondary prevention programs target youths who have not yet exhibited ill effects from drug use, but who are identified as "at risk" of becoming problem users. Tertiary prevention programs focus on groups that have already manifested some problems resulting from or associated with drug use (absenteeism, learning difficulties, delinquency, health problems, etc.), but have not yet become psychologically or physically dependent on the drug. Both secondary and tertiary prevention programs serve specific target populations that have had prior drug experiences (Goodstadt, 1981; Bukoski, 1981).[3] As discussed in Chap. 4, the dividing line between tertiary prevention and treatment is indistinct, though treatment programs typically focus on people whose drug use is more habitual, extensive, or clearly dysfunctional.

These intervention labels correspond with the different stages of drug use, but the relationship is not precise. For example, regular users could fall into either of two groups: people at risk of becoming problem users, or those who have already exhibited drug-related problems. Thus Fig. 5.1 shows both secondary and tertiary prevention as aimed at the transition between regular and heavy use. Tertiary prevention may also focus on heavy users, particularly those who have exhibited initial signs of drug-related problems.

This chapter focuses on *primary* prevention programs aimed at preventing or delaying the onset of drug use and the transition from

---

[3]Some authors omit the tertiary prevention category, using the term "secondary prevention" to refer to all activities aimed at early detection of a "disease" (Newman, Martin, and Weppner, 1982) or for handling situations that are "seen as deteriorating but not yet to the point of irreversible damage" (Sugarman, 1977-78). In this latter sense, secondary prevention would cover efforts aimed at individuals with a high risk of becoming problem users and efforts aimed at those who have already exhibited some drug-related problems.

experimental to regular use. We have chosen to stress primary prevention because it targets a larger proportion of young people than the other drug intervention modes and has a higher prima facie likelihood of success. Like treatment, secondary and tertiary prevention programs face more difficult odds than primary prevention; in addition, they are rarely, if ever, subjected to rigorous evaluation and, therefore, lack adequate evidence to support claims of success (or failure).[4]

We have also chosen this focus because of the potential benefits to be gained from delaying the onset of regular use. During the teenage years, adolescents undergo profound physical, cognitive, and emotional changes. But we do not yet understand the long-term consequences of drug use during puberty on these maturational processes. We do know, however, that the longer a person engages in addictive behavior, like cigarette smoking, the more difficult it becomes to break the habit (Leventhal and Cleary, 1980). We also know that the longer a person delays taking up drugs, the less likely he is to become a habitual user and the more likely he is to stop using in the future (Brill and Christie, 1974; Davidson, Mellinger, and Manheimer, 1977; Kandel, 1978b). Preventing an adolescent from becoming an experimental or regular user may not ensure abstinence as an adult, but it may decrease both the likelihood and the effects of any future dependence. Similarly, persuading young people to at least delay using drugs may prevent long-term effects on their future health and physical functioning.[5]

PREVENTION ISSUES: WHICH SUBSTANCES TO TARGET, WHEN, AND HOW

Historically, most prevention programs for adolescents have focused on a single substance such as alcohol, marijuana, or cigarettes (Schaps et al., 1981). Some, however, have targeted a more or less undifferentiated category of drugs in general or several substances at once. The

---

[4]Some people argue that primary prevention programs merely prevent experimentation among those adolescents who would never go on to become regular or heavy users—in other words, that they reduce the number of young people in the experimental stage but have no significant effect on the number in later stages. For this argument to hold, there would have to be at least two distinct processes by which different adolescent "types" became initiated into drugs, one for those who are "preordained" to become addicted or dependent on drugs (and who are thus immune to the prevention program) and one for those who are not. That does not appear to be the case for at least one highly addictive drug (nicotine); as we show below, primary prevention programs have successfully reduced regular, as well as experimental, smoking among junior high students.

[5]Certainly, delaying the onset of smoking significantly reduces subsequent smoking-related morbidity and mortality (O'Rourke and Stone, 1971).

lack of coordination among specific drug, alcohol, and tobacco abuse programs largely reflects their different sources of funding (Nowlis, 1981) and different societal perceptions of which substances constitute serious problems when. But it also implies a belief that each substance has different antecedents and therefore requires a different solution. In contrast, the amalgamated, but undifferentiated, approach implies that all substances should have equal priority and that their use can be traced to similar causes and prevented by similar strategies. Which approach corresponds more closely with the actual patterns and antecedents of adolescent drug use?

We have suggested that not all substances should have equal priority. Since adolescent drug use typically does not fit an addictive model (see Chap. 2), an index of harm based on probability of use seems an appropriate yardstick for identifying which drugs should receive greater prevention resources. Using such an index, those substances that pose risks to the greatest numbers of adolescents are alcohol, marijuana, and cigarettes, followed by stimulants. Thus, we would argue that prevention programs aimed at one or more of these four substances offer the greatest potential benefits to adolescents.[6]

The next issue for prevention programming is that of commonality vs. differentiation: Can these four drugs be handled by a single strategy or do they require different approaches? Much of this section considers the research pertinent to this question. Here we focus on the inferences to be drawn from data showing the ages at which young people begin using the most prevalent drugs. These data support a differentiated approach for alcohol.

Figure 5.2 shows 1982 national household survey figures on monthly use for different age groups. By age 16 or 17, between 20 and 30 percent of high school students have become current users of cigarettes and marijuana. Clearly, a *prevention* program aimed at juniors or seniors in high school has little relevance for that group of users. While fewer 14- and 15-year-olds have become current users, the data suggest that the ideal age for primary prevention is even younger. Among 12- and 13-year-olds, very few (between 2 and 3 percent) have used cigarettes or marijuana in the past month. At this age, therefore, we face the theoretical possibility of being able to prevent regular use of these substances for over 95 percent of the junior high school cohort.[7]

---

[6]As we shall see below, research that identifies which substances young people use earliest also supports this conclusion.

[7]Focusing on this age group has other positive features. As we shall see below, peer pressure acts as a key stimulant to experimental drug use. Therefore, targeting prevention activities on younger adolescents takes advantage of the more positive group climate that exists when few of a child's friends and acquaintances take drugs and most of them also do not approve of it.

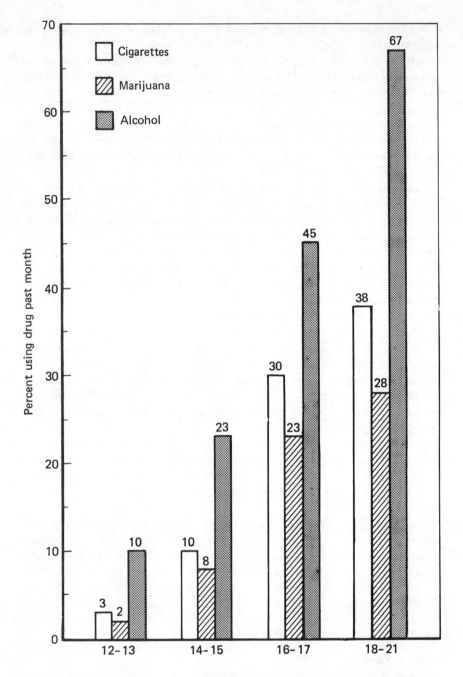

Fig. 5.2—Drug use rates by age (from NIDA household survey, 1982, presented in Miller et al., 1983)

The situation for alcohol is different: 10 percent of all 12- and 13-year-olds have used alcohol in the past month, a pattern that more closely resembles cigarette and marijuana use among their older peers, the 14- and 15-year-olds. These figures suggest that *alcohol* programs aimed at seventh graders may be inappropriately timed.[8]

This difference in patterns of early alcohol use is further underlined by the trend figures discussed in Chap. 2. Since 1978, alcohol use has remained fairly stable among high school seniors, whereas both cigarette and marijuana use have declined substantially. Even cocaine and stimulants, which had shown a consistent rise in the proportion of current users between 1977 and 1981, experienced small but significant drops in 1982.

Thus, alcohol alone has maintained a persistent and stable pattern of high use levels over the past several years. Not only is alcohol more commonly used among young people and adults than any other drug, but it also seems more firmly entrenched—unlike cigarettes and marijuana, whose popularity is declining. Thus, prevention programs aimed at adolescent alcohol use may require different timing *and* face less favorable odds of success than those aimed at cigarettes, marijuana, and most other drugs.

Additional insights about appropriate substances and strategies for prevention come from research on the etiology of drug use. Since the 1970s, longitudinal research based on samples of the secondary school or college age population has enlarged our understanding of the sequences and antecedents of drug use.[9] These studies provide information pertinent to three issues: (1) the most appropriate substances on which to target prevention activities; (2) the degree to which different drugs may require different intervention strategies; and (3) factors leading to drug use that prevention programs might seek to modify.

---

[8]Moreover, alcohol use at this age may be substantially higher than the 1982 figures indicate. In the four preceding measurement periods (1974, 1976, 1977, and 1979), the corresponding percentage of 12- and 13-year-olds who had used alcohol in the past month was as follows: 19, 19, 13, and 20. The degree to which the estimates for seventh graders have fluctuated from one survey to the next, coupled with the comparative stability of alcohol prevalence estimates for older teenagers, suggests that the 1982 figures may be low.

[9]See, for example, studies by Britt and Campbell (1977); Brook, Lukoff, and Whiteman (1978, 1980); Kandel (1973, 1978b); Kandel et al. (1976); Kandel, Kessler, and Margulies (1978); Smith and Fogg (1978, 1979); Brunswick (1976, 1979); Jessor, Jessor, and Finney, (1973); Jessor and Jessor (1973, 1977, 1978); Johnston, O'Malley, and Eveland (1978); Dunnette and Peterson (1977); Margulies, Kessler, and Kandel (1977); Huba, Wingard, and Bentler, (1979, 1980a,b, 1981); Igra and Moos (1977, 1979); Kaplan (1978b, 1980); Sadava (1973a,b); Sadava and Forsyth (1977a,b); Kellam, Ensminger, and Simon (1980); and Kellam, Simon, and Ensminger (1983).

Drug Use Sequences

In a review of several longitudinal studies, Kandel concluded that "there are clear-cut developmental steps and sequences in drug behavior, so that use of one of the legal drugs almost always precedes use of illegal drugs" (Kandel, 1978b, p. 14). Related follow-up studies of New York State adolescents identified a three-stage sequencing of drug use as follows: (1) legal drugs (beer, wine, cigarettes, and hard liquor); (2) marijuana; and (3) other illicit drugs (Kandel and Faust, 1975).[10] These findings do not imply that everyone who uses cigarettes, for example, will become a marijuana user. Nevertheless, Kandel clearly sees legal drugs as "necessary intermediates between complete nonuse and marijuana" and marijuana use as a "crucial step on the way to other illicit drugs" (1978b, p. 14). Most researchers now accept the propositions that there are typical sequential patterns to drug use behavior; that they begin with the legal drugs (cigarettes and alcohol); and that some portion of marijuana users will go on to experiment with or become occasional users of other illicit drugs (Richards, 1980).

Less clear-cut results apply to the ordering of illicit drugs after marijuana. Kandel's adolescent sample yielded the following sequence: pills (stimulants, depressants, tranquilizers), psychedelics, cocaine, and heroin. In contrast, an analysis of young black ghetto adults produced a different sequencing: cocaine, heroin, barbiturates, amphetamines, and psychedelics (Jessop, Kandel, and Lukoff, 1976). Thus patterns of use after marijuana may vary among cultural or ethnic groupings or from one historical period or another.

This research on drug use sequences parallels current prevalence rates among adolescents. Since the most commonly used substances also come earliest in the sequence, it is wise to target prevention efforts on them. These findings also suggest that prevention programs might profitably focus on *both* legal and illegal substances—that preventing or delaying cigarette smoking might have spillover effects on marijuana use, and that retarding the latter might also reduce experimentation with other illicit drugs.[11]

---

[10]This sequence has since been documented in countries as diverse as France, with the second highest rate of alcohol consumption in the world; and Israel, with one of the lowest rates (Kandel, 1981).

[11]This latter implication raises an important question for prevention research: To what degree do programs aimed at one substance have mitigating or spillover effects on other substances? For example, how much "extra" marijuana prevention does one buy with a direct program focused on marijuana as opposed to an indirect strategy aimed at cigarettes alone? Some recent articles have hinted at such spillover effects (Perry et al., 1980), but no one has systematically examined this issue.

Drug Use Antecedents

While the literature on drug use sequences points toward an emphasis on the legal and illegal substances that dominate early adolescent use, the antecedents literature helps clarify the degree to which similar or different factors lead to the use of different drugs. These findings, in turn, have implications for the content of specific prevention programs. Two programs of research dominate this literature: the work conducted by Kandel and her colleagues in New York, France, and Israel, and that carried out by the Jessors in Colorado. Each subscribes to a different theoretical perspective and each implies somewhat different strategies for prevention programs.

As described above, Kandel's model posits three progressive stages of drug use. Participation at the legal stage of drug use "puts the adolescent at risk for progression to the next stage;" each prior stage is a necessary, but not sufficient, condition for movement to the next level (Kandel and Adler, 1982, p. 306). Of particular importance to prevention program strategy is Kandel's proposition that different antecedent variables are associated with different stages of drug use. Since each stage is defined by different substances, this proposition implies that prevention programs aimed at the early substances might target different "precipitating factors" and, therefore, have different components than programs aimed at the other drugs.

In contrast, the theory of "problem behavior," as expounded by Jessor and Jessor (1977), implies that similar antecedent variables foster a wide range of adolescent problem behaviors (including delinquency, early sexual experience, and drug use).[12] This complex theory posits three broad categories of precipitating factors that together foster problem behavior "proneness": the perceived environment system, the behavior system, and the personality system. For example, perceived environment variables include peer approval and models for drug use; behavior system variables include engaging in problem and/or conventional behaviors (delinquency, cutting school, attending church); and personality system factors include attitudes, values, and expectations "that constitute instigations to engage in ˙problem behavior or attenuated controls against such behavior" (Jessor, Chase, and Donovan, 1980, p. 604). The greater the degree of problem-behavior proneness in these three systems, the greater the likelihood of drug use.

Jessor and Jessor also distinguish between factors that are closely related or proximal to drug use (such as parental use or approval of drugs) and those that are more remote in the causal chain (such as the

---

[12]In the Jessors' terminology, adolescent problem behaviors are those likely to elicit negative sanctions from society.

relationship between parent and child). They postulate that proximal variables will play a more dominant role in the onset of drug use than distal variables. The emphasis, however, is on the generality of the theory—that adolescents can be classified along a dimension of deviance proneness, which in turn will predict their use of drugs.

Which model is more relevant to prevention—that which implies different strategies for different substances or that which implies similar strategies for all substances? We have already argued that programs aimed at adolescent alcohol use may require a different age focus than programs aimed at cigarettes or marijuana.[13] But should they address the same or different precipitating factors? Our review of the research findings suggests that both models have merit.[14] Alcohol, cigarettes, marijuana, and other drugs do appear to share a similar set of psychosocial antecedents, but different variables within that overall set play more important roles for some substances than for others. The following discussion elaborates this view.

Sociodemographic Factors. Most of the research on drug use antecedents examines three broad classes of variables: (1) sociodemographic factors such as race and sex; (2) intrapersonal characteristics (variously labeled as personality attributes; attitudes, beliefs, or values; and actual problem behaviors); and (3) environmental or situational variables. The latter category typically refers to interpersonal influences such as parental and peer approval or use of the substance, but some researchers also focus on the drug's availability and additional factors such as the quality of the adolescent's relationship with his parents.

Most researchers agree that sociodemographic variables add little explanatory power to models of drug use initiation, especially marijuana (Kandel, 1978b; Jessor and Jessor, 1978; Gersick et al., 1981; Igra and Moos, 1979). Differences in drug use rates between adolescent males and females have been declining over time (Johnston, Bachman,

---

[13]However, we have not discussed the most appropriate age for alcohol prevention. One approach would be to focus on adolescents at an age when very few have tried it (before 12 or 13); another involves recognizing the widespread use and acceptance of alcohol use in American society and changing the focus from prevention of any use to prevention of irresponsible use. Such a strategy would suggest aiming the program at high school adolescents close to driving age.

[14]Our discussion of drug use antecedents rests largely on the findings from longitudinal studies buttressed, where appropriate, with cross-sectional results. Although there are innumerable cross-sectional studies identifying factors associated with drug use, cross-sectional data do not help clarify whether these factors came before or after drug use. Prospective longitudinal studies come closer to suggesting a causal ordering, although they do not definitely establish it. For reviews of cross-sectional studies, see Gorsuch and Butler (1976); Kandel (1975a); Sadava (1975); Stanton (1979b); and Radosevich et al. (1979).

and O'Malley, 1982) and now appear "too small and subtle to justify differential interpretations or program design" (Gersick et al., 1981, p. 43). Both Kandel (1978a) and Brunswick (1979) have documented racial differences in the sequencing of drug use *after* marijuana, and several cross-sectional studies show that ethnic minorities are over-represented among users of the less prevalent illicit drugs (Galchus and Galchus, 1977–78; Curtis and Simpson, 1977; Padilla et al., 1979; Iiyama, Nishi, and Johnson, 1976). Nevertheless, ethnic differences tend not to show up for junior-high age adolescents (Dembo et al., 1979).[15] Perhaps the low prevalence of such drug use in this age group obscures the relationship. In any event, other factors, such as the social context in which the adolescent lives, appear to offer more important levers for prevention strategy than ethnic differences per se.

Intrapersonal Characteristics. Among the attributes frequently labeled as personality traits, one factor consistently stands out as a drug use precursor: a predisposition toward rebellion, independence, and nonconformity. This predisposition, measured in different ways, has shown up in several studies.

Jessor and Jessor (1977, 1978) found that a stress on independence relative to achievement, a low value on academic achievement, tolerance of deviance, and low religiosity predicted onset of marijuana use; the same variables also correlated with adolescent problem drinking (Jessor, Chase, and Donovan, 1980). O'Malley (1975) reported that drug users, especially those who experimented with hallucinogens, had previously received high scores on several scales measuring independence. Smith (1973) found that the higher the rebelliousness score, the more likely the subsequent transition to more frequent use and use of less prevalent drugs. Conversely, a low score on a scale measuring obedience and law-abidance was the single most important predictor of adolescent marijuana use in a five-year longitudinal study of 7th and 8th graders, while lower academic aspirations and motivations also discriminated those who subsequently became marijuana users by the 11th and 12th grade (Smith and Fogg, 1978). Low scores on an index of conformity to adult expectations predicted the onset of marijuana and other illicit drug use in research by Kandel, Kessler, and Margulies (1978).

This constellation of values, motivations, and attitudes appears to reflect a rebellion against conventional adult norms and traditional authority coupled with the desire to appear more "adult," tendencies frequently associated with the adolescent's transitional status between

---

[15]Main effects are generally absent, but ethnic differences do interact with home environment variables for this age group (Dembo et al., 1979).

childhood and adult maturity. It does not imply a lack of conformity to the norms of other significant groups (particularly peers) and may in fact be correlated with greater susceptibility to peer values and models (Wingard, Huba, and Bentler, 1979). As we shall see below, its relevance to prevention strategy is further highlighted by the wealth of data indicating that peer influences rank among the most important precursors of drug use onset.

In contrast, there is only weak or conflicting evidence supporting the importance of personality traits such as low self-esteem, external locus of control, alienation, anomie, and other (usually) negatively valued characteristics (Kandel, 1978b; Gersick et al., 1981; Goldstein and Sappington, 1977; O'Malley, 1975; Orive and Gerard, 1980).[16] Perhaps these traits lack stability during adolescence; or perhaps they are too remote from drug use itself to attain significant explanatory power.

Considerably less remote are the individual's own *norms and beliefs* about using drugs and the *behaviors* that indicate rebellion against traditional norms or a desire to appear more mature. Several studies suggest that adolescents who will subsequently start using drugs develop favorable attitudes toward them *before* drug use onset (Kandel, Kessler, and Margulies, 1978; Jessor and Jessor, 1977, 1978; Sadava, 1973a, 1973b; Mittelmark et al., 1983; Sherman et al., 1983; Smith and Fogg, 1978).[17] Such attitudes may include beliefs about the consequences of using drugs (Kandel, Kessler, and Margulies, 1978), the functional uses of drugs (Jessor and Jessor, 1978), or the appropriateness of adolescent use (Rooney and Wright, 1982).

Thus Kandel and her colleagues (1978) found that adolescents were more likely to start using hard liquor, marijuana, or other illicit drugs when they had previously believed that casual use of the *specific* drug was not harmful; such beliefs were particularly important predictors of marijuana onset. Similarly, Jessor and Jessor (1977) reported that adolescents who started using marijuana had previously been more likely to espouse positive as opposed to negative reasons for or against using drugs, while those who started drinking had reported a preponderance of positive over negative reasons for using alcohol. In a cross-sectional study, Rooney and Wright (1982) found that

---

[16]Two exceptions are the relationship between feelings of depression and use of illicit drugs other than marijuana (Paton, Kessler, and Kandel, 1977) and between anxiety and hallucinogen use (Orive and Gerard, 1980). Since initiation into these drugs appears to represent a later stage in adolescent drug use, this finding supports the greater reliance on counseling and therapy found among secondary and tertiary prevention programs targeted at adolescents who are at risk of becoming problem drug users.

[17]However, Sherman and his colleagues (1983) stress that attitudes and beliefs about smoking are more important predictors of the transition from experimental to habitual smoking than of the initial experience.

adolescents' specific standards for cigarette or marijuana use (e.g., the belief that regular or occasional use is okay, okay only if one is careful or on certain occasions, not okay at all) accounted for the most variance in predicting actual use.

Behavior that indicates rebellion also predicts future drug use. As we have already seen, use of legal drugs precedes marijuana use and marijuana use precedes other illicit drug use. Similarly, several investigators have found that delinquency and poor school performance are related to subsequent drug use.

Jessor and Jessor (1977) report a positive relationship between general deviant behavior (lying, stealing, and aggression) and subsequent marijuana use. Johnston and his colleagues (1978) single out criminal activities involving property (vandalism, theft) as precursors of college and young adult use of marijuana, pills, and heroin. In Kandel's (1978b) study of adolescents, minor delinquent acts (cheating, minor theft, driving too fast) predicted marijuana and hard liquor initiation, while drug dealing and major delinquency (car theft, robbery, major stealing) predicted marijuana use and especially initiation into other illicit drugs.

Poor school performance (low grades, frequent class-cutting, absenteeism) shows up in several studies, especially those that focus on cigarette and marijuana use among younger students (Jessor and Jessor, 1977; Jessor, Jessor, and Finney, 1973; Johnston, 1973; Kandel, Kessler, and Margulies, 1978; Mellinger et al., 1976; Smith and Fogg, 1978). However, such relationships are less likely to appear for college students, suggesting that these behaviors are more normative in college populations or that poor school performance reflects lower interest and motivation rather than less intellectual aptitude or intelligence (Kandel, 1978b).[18]

Environmental Factors. By now, most authorities agree that social factors play a major role in the spread of drug use among adolescents. Initiation into drugs appears to be a group phenomenon: Most adolescents first try licit or illicit drugs with someone else—typically a friend, although relatives play a central role for alcohol (Orive and Gerard, 1980). Thus peer approval and drug use patterns rank among the most potent predictors of initiation into drug use, while parental drug use and norms also exert a strong influence (Andrews and Kandel, 1979; Ginsberg and Greenley, 1978; Kandel, 1978b; Kandel, Kessler,

---

[18]The Jessors (1977) have found direct relationships between lower achievement *motivation* and expectations and subsequent substance use (marijuana and alcohol) among secondary school students, while Sherman et al. (1983) found a similar relationship between cigarette use and academic expectations among the same age group.

and Margulies, 1978; Jessor and Jessor, 1978; Huba and Bentler, 1980; Lucas, Grupp, and Schmitt, 1975).

The importance of peer and adult influence varies across substances. Young people whose parents and friends drink are more likely to use hard liquor and certain illicit drugs, but *not* marijuana; for both cigarettes and marijuana, the major interpersonal influence is friends' use of the *specific* substance (Huba, Wingard, and Bentler, 1979, 1980b; Jessor, Jessor, and Finney, 1973; Kandel, 1978a; Rooney and Wright, 1982). Nevertheless, adolescents do appear to generalize from some drug-specific behaviors or attitudes to other substances: Initiation into illicit drugs *other than marijuana* is retarded by peer beliefs that casual marijuana use is harmful; it is also predicted by peer use of marijuana *and* by peer and adult use of hard liquor (Kandel, 1978b).

Certainly, peer influences are more important for some drugs than for others. Marijuana use, in particular, is a peer group phenomenon. Peer marijuana use and attitudes rank as the most important predictors of future marijuana use (accounting for 50 percent of the total variance explained in Kandel's research), whereas parental influences appear stronger for liquor (Kandel, Kessler, and Margulies, 1978). Nevertheless, peer influences are also among the three most important predictors of initiation into hard liquor and into illicit drugs other than marijuana (Kandel, 1978b). While the data are not longitudinal, Rooney and Wright's (1982) analysis of factors associated with cigarette smoking ranks close friends' smoking as the second most important factor, and their use of marijuana as the fourth. They also conclude that marijuana use is even more strongly related to peer influences than is cigarette smoking.

Parental and peer *attitudes* about drug use also affect an adolescent's decision to try drugs. However, in the studies cited above, the attitudes of such persons were not as powerful as their actual use patterns in predicting the adolescent's drug use.[19] Specific parental rules against drugs fail to prevent their offspring's use, but parental tolerance of marijuana use or belief in the harmlessness of various drugs supports later experimentation (Kandel, 1978b; Jessor, 1976). Moreover, the quality of the parent-child relationship affects onset of marijuana use (Jessor and Jessor, 1977; Brook, Lukoff, and Whiteman, 1980) and is an especially strong predictor of initiation into other illicit drugs (Kandel, Kessler, and Margulies, 1978).

---

[19]It should be noted that measures of peer or parental drug use are frequently based on the adolescent's *perceptions* of others' behavior as opposed to the friends' or parents' own reports. As Kandel (1980) has noted, correlations based on perceptions are consistently higher than those based on self-reports, a result that may reflect an upward bias in the perceptions of others' use by adolescents who have tried drugs themselves.

Finally, the availability of drugs in the social setting clearly reinforces and increases individual predispositions to use them. Drugs were readily available in Vietnam, an environment that also posed fewer restrictions on their use than existed in the United States at the time. Accordingly, many soldiers in Vietnam experimented with several classes of drugs, and substantially more of them tried narcotics than would have been expected under pre-Vietnam conditions (Robins, 1973). While the data are correlational only, high school seniors report that the widely used illicit drugs are more readily available than the less common drugs (Johnston, Bachman, and O'Malley, 1982).

Similarities and Differences Amongs Drugs. In sum, a common set of factors predisposes adolescents to try drugs, but different factors play more important roles for some drugs than for others. Among the more important antecedents of alcohol, marijuana, and other illicit drug use are the following:

- Peer drug use and approval;
- Parental drug use and approval;
- The adolescent's own beliefs and norms about drug use and its harmfulness;
- A predisposition toward nonconformity, rebellion, and independence;
- Low academic performance and motivation; and
- Engaging in "problem behaviors" that reflect deviance from traditional adult norms about appropriate adolescent activities.

Correlational and recent longitudinal studies indicate that similar psychosocial factors are associated with the onset of cigarette smoking (Chassin et al., 1981a; Evans et al., 1979; Levitt and Edwards, 1970; Mittelmark et al., 1983; Rooney and Wright, 1982; Sherman et al., 1983; Thompson, 1978; Wong-McCarthy and Gritz, 1982).

Within this overall cluster of antecedents, different factors play lesser or greater precipitating roles for different substances. Peer influences promote initial use of all drugs, especially marijuana. For both marijuana and cigarettes, the most important precursors are associating with peers who use the *specific* substance plus having favorable beliefs about it. Prior problem behaviors (use of cigarettes, beer, and wine; engaging in minor delinquent acts) constitute the most important predictors of drinking hard liquor, while depression, lack of closeness to parents, and exposure to drug-using peers and adults bear the strongest relationship with initiation into illicit drugs other than marijuana (Kandel, Kessler, and Margulies, 1978). Parental use of the *specific* substance predicts use of alcohol, cigarettes, and other psychoactive drugs; parental disapproval or belief that casual use is harmful helps to prevent adolescent involvement with hard liquor and marijuana.

While a general predisposition toward nonconformity is associated with earlier stages of drug use, its explanatory power is weak (Wingard, Huba, and Bentler, 1979). Deep-seated personality factors or family context variables that indicate maladjustment do not appear to play a decisive role in the onset of licit drug use but do enter in as important determinants of more advanced drug use (moving on to pills, cocaine, heroin, etc.).

Implications For Prevention

What do these findings imply for prevention program strategies? The consistent impact of peer (and adult) influences on initiation into drug use of all kinds suggests an overall program theme that targets these environmental and situational antecedents of drug use. The central role of those who use drugs or approve of doing so emphasizes the importance of teaching adolescents how to identify and resist social influences to use drugs—particularly those emanating from their friends and acquaintances, but also those linked to parental drug use or tolerance.[20] Since the actual behavior of parents and peers is more influential than their attitudes about drugs (Kandel, 1978b), we would also argue for providing adolescents with successful role models who do not use drugs. The dominance of peer influences suggests that these role models should be young people rather than adults.

Taken together, the findings also suggest that drug-taking behaviors represent a claim on a more mature status for those adolescents who initially try drugs (Jessor, Chase, and Donovan, 1980). For most adolescents, the transition toward adulthood is associated with the need to develop an autonomous self-image. As they move from elementary to secondary school, most also enter a more heterogeneous environment that offers varied opportunities for trying out different self-concepts (Simmons, Rosenberg, and Rosenberg, 1973). For many adolescents, this period also marks a rebellion against traditional adult norms about what constitutes appropriate behavior for young people. Drug-taking behaviors represent activities that are frequently forbidden to adolescents, but more acceptable for adults; therefore, they often symbolize a more mature, independent, and sophisticated status.

---

[20]The influence of drug-using peers on subsequent initiation into drugs could reflect a socialization process (whereby adolescents learn these behaviors from young people who have already engaged in them) or a selection process (wherein adolescents with similar attitudes select one another as friends). Kandel (1978c) suggests that socialization and selection are approximately equal in importance.

As the data indicate, adolescents with a predisposition toward non-conformity may be especially vulnerable to the influence of nonconforming peers. But the limited explanatory power of this predispositional tendency (Wingard, Huba, and Bentler, 1979) suggests that many adolescents who experiment with drugs may view themselves as conforming to their own social environment or to societal prescriptions to "act more mature." The task, then, is to influence the social norms surrounding young people and their images of what constitutes mature, independent behavior. This implies that prevention programs might profitably focus on changing or reinforcing adolescent *group* norms about the desirability and status implications of taking drugs.[21]

The literature also implies the need for preventive techniques tailored to specific drugs. The most influential beliefs and norms preceding drug use are those specific to a particular substance. For example, the belief that regular marijuana use is not harmful increases the probability of marijuana onset, and the belief that cigarettes promote an image of toughness, precocity, or sociability encourages initial smoking. Similarly, an individual's drug use is affected more by other persons' use of the specific substance than by their use of other drugs or drugs in general, while parental role models are more important for the onset of alcohol and cigarette use than for marijuana.[22] These findings argue for differentiating specific prevention techniques by drug—trying to modify, for example, *specific* beliefs about the prevalence of marijuana and its positive and negative consequences; combating both parental *and* peer influences for alcohol and cigarettes, while concentrating more on peer influence situations with marijuana.

Finally, the lack of strong evidence associating deep-seated personality problems or psychopathology with the *onset* of drug use suggests giving a lower priority to the promotion of "healthier" or better adjusted adolescent personality traits. There is no clear consensus that initial drug use is associated with such characteristics as self-esteem, locus of control, anxiety, anomie, and so on. Kandel (1978b) did find that depression was associated with later stages of drug use

[21]This implication is buttressed by research indicating that adolescents perceive increasing numbers of peer and adult models for drug use as they move from seventh to ninth grade and that these changes in perceptions are accompanied by stronger correlations between self-use and perceived peer use than between self-use and perceived adult use (Huba and Bentler, 1980).

[22]This finding should, however, be qualified by two caveats: (1) most studies of adolescent drug use fail to ask about parental use of illegal substances and, therefore, offer no data on the relationship between parental use of marijuana and the child's behavior; and (2) most studies have not included children of the 1960s generation of marijuana users (the generation that is most likely to include marijuana users among the parents of adolescents).

(particularly the less prevalent illicit drugs), but this result suggests that the motivations to *begin* using drugs are not necessarily the same as those to *continue* using them.[23]

While personal maladjustment may well be associated with progressing to heavier drug use (either more frequent use of the same drug or use of other substances), it appears to be less important for initial use. Secondary or tertiary prevention programs (for adolescents who have tried drugs and appear at risk of becoming problem users) should take these differences into account. However, primary prevention programs, which aim to prevent adolescents from experimenting or becoming regular users, should put greater emphasis on social influences—how these environmental factors directly affect drug use and how they interact with individual desires to achieve group or adult status, as well as individual beliefs about drug use.

PRIMARY PREVENTION PROGRAM MODELS

What, in fact, do drug prevention programs seek to accomplish and how successful have they been? The rest of this section addresses these questions, beginning with a brief description of the prevention movement, its history, and dominant approaches.

While the first half of the 20th century was marked by extensive efforts against drug use (the temperance movement of the first two decades and the campaigns against marijuana and heroin in the 1930s), concerted efforts to reduce youthful drug use did not arise until the late 1960s. By then it had become clear that drug use was widespread and growing among young people from all segments of society. In 1970, President Nixon called for preventive drug education at all levels of schooling from kindergarten through the 12th grade; subsequently, federal expenditures for drug prevention programs rose dramatically (Einstein et al., 1971).

School-based programs have continued as the dominant prevention mode for adolescents. Employing the mass media to inform adolescents about the dangers of drugs is another possibility. However, there is little persuasive evidence that mass media campaigns aimed at reducing or curbing drug use have positive results. Indeed, the general literature on media effects is inconsistent. While product advertising may affect consumer behavior to some extent, few public service campaigns have been able to show that they produced significant changes in individual behavior (Wallack, 1981; Liebert and Schwartzberg, 1977).

---

[23]See Kohn (1974) and Steffenhagen (1974) for a similar interpretation.

In the specific case of health risks, sustained dissemination of information may lead to changes in social norms and, ultimately, changes in behavior. Trends in cigarette smoking are an example. Between 1950 and 1975, major changes in public attitudes and significant reductions in aggregate cigarette consumption occurred in the wake of prolonged publicity about the hazards of smoking (Warner, 1977). Studies in both the U.S. and Britain have suggested that antismoking information campaigns played an important role in these processes (Warner, 1979; Russell, 1973).

Nonetheless, the weight of available data suggests that supplemental person-to-person communication *and* a long and sustained campaign may be required if the mass media are to succeed in altering habitual behavior. In contrast, school-based programs have two important advantages. First, schools have direct access to all children in the appropriate age range. Second, as we shall explain below, there is experimental evidence that school programs can prevent cigarette smoking. For these reasons, we have concentrated our review on prevention models that have been tested in school environments.[24]

Today there are thousands of drug prevention programs in schools and communities across the United States, but comparatively fewer federal dollars for financing them (see Fig. 1.3). Whether funded privately or publicly, however, most are based on one or more of four prevention models. As we show below, each model has a different diagnosis of why adolescents start using drugs and a correspondingly different solution.

The Information Model

The information model constituted the dominant prevention mode for many years. It assumes that adolescents use drugs because they lack information about their negative effects and therefore have neutral or even positive attitudes toward trying them. This model sees providing information about drugs—their properties, their methods of use, and their consequences—as the solution. Such information is expected to produce less positive attitudes toward drugs; those attitudes should, in turn, inhibit drug use (Goodstadt, 1978).

Several states require drug education in the schools, but the specific content and amount of time devoted to the subject are usually left up to the school district or even the individual school. Instruction therefore varies widely from one school to another;[25] and examples of

---

[24]Variants of these models have also been tried in other community settings. We briefly describe some of these efforts, but as they have not been adequately evaluated, we do not assess their effectiveness outside of schools.

[25]A notable exception is Nebraska's effort to develop a comprehensive drug education curriculum for use across the state public school system.

programs based on the information approach may vary from two pages in a school textbook to a highly structured multiple-session health curriculum with audiovisual materials.

Typically, these programs provide information about the physical and psychological effects of specific drugs, their pharmacology, and the legal implications of using illicit drugs. Most school-based information programs are presented by teachers using a didactic delivery style; some use outside experts such as a doctor, nurse, or narcotics officer, and some provide for class discussion.[26] While the questionable "scare" tactics of early drug-education programs have largely been abandoned in favor of a more balanced presentation of the facts (Kinder, Pape, and Walfish, 1980), the emphasis is usually on the harmful consequences of drugs, particularly the long-term effects of continued and heavy use. The content frequently goes beyond a "just the facts" approach to include an exhortation not to use drugs.

The Individual Deficiency Model

The individual deficiency model emerged as an important approach in the early 1970s. This model assumes that the problem lies within the child himself—that children use drugs to compensate for a lack of self-esteem, or because they lack adequate tools for making rational decisions. Programs based on this model seek to provide general skills that will enhance the youngster's self-esteem or decisionmaking skills. They also frequently seek to encourage a school or home climate that emphasizes each child's special qualities and value.

Because these programs are highly variable, it is difficult to provide a single overall description of them. Instead, we describe three examples, each of which seeks to foster one or more of the following: an improved self-image, the ability to communicate in a group, or improved skills in problem-solving or values clarification. As the examples indicate, many of these programs provide little or no information about drugs per se.

The first program, called Tribes, targets elementary school children in the 4th, 5th, or 6th grades. Its goal is to improve the child's self-image and academic achievement motivation (Altschuler, Carl, and Jackson, 1981). In a Tribes classroom, children are brought together in groups of four, five, or six. Each group prepares the same overall assignment, for example, writing a biography of Pulitzer. The individual child's assignment focuses on part of the overall task, such as learning about Pulitzer's early years. After doing his or her own research, the pupil meets with the other groups' "experts" on Pulitzer's

---

[26]Information programs presented by community organizations such as the Boy Scouts typically rely on outside experts and constitute one-shot (or single-session) efforts.

youth to pool information, subsequently returning to the original group with a revised and improved product that becomes part of the overall report. The expectation is that this experience will help children develop general skills, such as communicating with each other and working cooperatively at solving a problem, skills which will translate into improved self-confidence and academic motivation bolstered by the experience of having made a special contribution to the project.

The Ombudsman program, developed by the Charlotte Drug Education Center in North Carolina, is available to 5th grade, 6th grade, junior high, and senior high students (Kim, 1981, 1982). Its three-phase curriculum is designed to counteract low self-esteem, negative social attitudes, and low valuation of school. The first phase includes a series of exercises focused on enhancing self-awareness and the student's appreciation of his or her unique value; the second promotes group relationships and communication skills through mutual problem-solving and group discussion; and the third phase centers on student-developed community service projects.

The third program, values clarification, assumes that supplying facts about drugs is not sufficient to discourage their use, that children need to learn how to use those facts in making decisions, and that personal values affect choices made among two or more alternatives. According to this model, therefore, drug prevention efforts should focus on helping students clarify their values. As implemented in several Calfornia and Arizona schools (Carney, 1971, 1972), one such program emphasized clarifying the risks associated with various drug and non-drug behaviors, the child's attitudes toward taking risks, and the degree to which the child's risk-taking values were congruent with those behaviors.[27] Variants of this approach have since been implemented in schools across the country. Labeled "process" or "affective" education, they often contain other components aimed at enhancing self-esteem or improving problem-solving skills as in the above examples.

The Social Pressures Model

The social pressures model is the most recent approach to drug prevention. This approach emphasizes the external influences that push adolescents toward drug use, particularly the subtle pressures of the media and the actual behavior and attitudes of key people in the

---

[27]From the available descriptions, however, it is not clear precisely how the "values" training was implemented; it does appear that the program did not stop at merely clarifying the young person's attitudes towards risk but also sought to modify them. This blurring of the distinction between values-clarification and values-teaching is not uncommon. In theory, clarification implies maintaining a neutral posture when the individual's values support undesirable behavior; in practice, most programs adopt an advocacy position favoring values consonant with those of the program developers, administrators, or teachers.

adolescent's life: adults who drink, smoke, or use pills and, most important of all, friends and other peers who use drugs. The social pressures model also recognizes the special vulnerability of adolescents who are in a transitional status between childhood and adulthood: their general desire to appear grown up and to emulate what they perceive to be adult behavior. Accordingly, social pressures programs seek to provide adolescents with specific skills and support for saying "no."

Many of the parents' groups that have recently sprung up across the nation implicitly adhere to this approach, particularly in their emphasis on providing support for resisting drugs.[28] One example, the Parents Who Care group that originated in Palo Alto, California, does this by helping teenagers give drug-free parties and by providing firm, clear guidelines for curfews, party-going, and other activities. It also encourages young people to make antidrug presentations to junior and senior high schools, other parent groups, and civic organizations.

Another example is a Maricopa County (Arizona) program called Teen Involvement For Drug Abuse Prevention. This program, which uses high school students as role models for elementary pupils, combines elements of the social pressures and values clarification models. In eight lessons, the program examines why people become drug dependent, helps children clarify their values regarding drugs, and assists them in resisting the pressures they might face when confronted with peer drug use (Resnik and Gibbs, 1981).[29]

The Alternatives Model

Closely related to both the individual deficiency and the social pressures approaches, the alternatives model assumes that adolescents may start using drugs for a variety of reasons, including both internal and external pressures, but emphasizes providing alternative activities to keep them busy and productive as the solution. Channel One, a widespread example of this type of program, brings youth and private industry sponsors together in developing youth-initiated projects such

---

[28]Between one thousand and three thousand parent groups are reported to exist in the United States, most of which have arisen spontaneously in the past four or five years (Turner, 1982; Durell, 1982). In general, they focus on one or more of three goals: (1) changes at home (parent information, improved family communication, establishing individual family rules and guidelines regarding curfews, party-going, and drug use); (2) the development and support of drug-free group norms (typically through parent/peer groups that enforce and/or sponsor drug-free parties and parent skills training); and (3) social action aimed at advocating stronger and more strictly enforced school policies, political action (to ban the manufacture or sale of drug paraphernalia, reinstitute paraquat spraying, etc.), and community awareness campaigns.

[29]Several antismoking programs have also been based on this model. As we shall see, they constitute the most promising approaches to drug prevention identified by the research literature. We provide greater detail about these particular efforts in the section on prevention program effects.

as manufacturing and selling products, arranging festivals, or assisting the elderly (Resnik and Gibbs, 1981). Recently it has emphasized youth employment and career development.

Central to the Channel One concept is the requirement that adolescents select the project and participate in its planning, staffing, and operation, a posture that bears marked similarity to the underlying concepts of many programs run by the Scouts, the YMCA, and church groups. Channel One began as a secondary prevention program for youngsters already exhibiting problems, but now stresses primary prevention as well. By the spring of 1982, 153 Channel One programs had been started in 44 states and territories. However, none of them have been rigorously evaluated, nor have other programs based on the alternatives approach. For this reason, our discussion of prevention program effects omits detail on this model.

PREVENTION PROGRAM EFFECTS

While thousands of prevention programs have come and gone over the years, we know very little about their effectiveness. Few have been subjected to any evaluation of their impact; thus most claims of success lack adequate evidence. Moreover, many evaluations fail to measure program effects on whether or not people actually *use* drugs. As we shall see, demonstrating increased knowledge or disapproval of drugs does not necessarily imply forgoing them.

Among those programs that have been evaluated in some way, few have been subjected to rigorous scientific study: A recent review of 127 evaluations carried out since the late 1960s concluded that the majority of these studies fail to meet minimal canons for valid evidence (Schaps et al., 1981). To know whether a program has been effective, one must know what would have happened in its absence. Generally, this requires evidence that program participants showed lower drug use rates than nonparticipants *after* the intervention, and that the differences cannot easily be explained by preexisting group characteristics. Very few studies provide the experimental design features that meet this test.[30]

Most studies lack randomized assignment of participant groups to the experimental conditions, and many also fail to provide evidence indicating whether post-program rates of drug use were higher, lower, or the same as before the intervention. In these circumstances, even if

---

[30]For reviews of the results and limitations of drug prevention programs, see Blum, Blum, and Garfield (1976); Bry (1978); Dembo (1979); Goodstadt (1974, 1978); Hanson (1980); Janvier, Guthman, and Catalano (1980); Kinder, Pape, and Walfish (1980); and Schaps et al. (1981).

the treatment group shows lower post-program drug use rates than the control group, it is possible that the treatment group also began with lower rates. Thus, the differences between those exposed to the program and those who did not receive special treatment might be attributed to preexisting differences in the two groups. In a similar vein, other studies fail to compare program participants and nonparticipants at all, leaving open the possibility that an observed downward shift in participant drug use rates merely reflects a concomitant downward trend among all adolescents.

Evaluations that report ineffective programs have not been much more useful. When the research concludes that a program has failed, it is often difficult to tell why. Programs can fail for one of two reasons: (1) because the original diagnosis of the problem and its solution is wrong, or (2) because the diagnosis is correct but the treatment has been improperly carried out. Numerous studies have shown that social programs in education, criminal justice, housing, and other fields have failed because they were never put into place or resulted in activities only distantly related to the original design (Berman and McLaughlin, 1978; Derthick, 1972; Ellickson et al., 1983; Pressman and Wildavsky, 1973; Sumner and Zellman, 1977). Because so few drug prevention studies offer documentation of program activities, it is frequently impossible to judge whether failure is attributable to a faulty model or to faulty implementation.

Nevertheless, we do know that most of the *early* primary prevention programs that have been subjected to a reasonably valid analysis have had little success. In 1973, the National Commission on Marihuana and Drug Abuse concluded that "no drug education program in this country, or elsewhere, has proven sufficiently successful to warrant our recommending it." In 1980, the situation was little different: A review of more than 100 programs (largely of the information, values clarification, or affective modes) reported that "by far the largest number of studies have found no effects of drug education upon use" (Hanson, 1980, p. 263).

Information Program Effects

Information-only programs frequently do increase children's knowledge about drugs. But they less often lead to antidrug attitudes and even more rarely affect actual behavior (whether adolescents use drugs or how often).[31] In fact, information programs have sometimes appeared to increase drug use (Stuart, 1974; Blum, Blum, and Garfield,

---

[31]See Blum, Blum, and Garfield (1976); Goodstadt (1978); Swisher (1974); Hanson (1980); and Kinder, Pape, and Walfish (1980) for similar conclusions.

1976; Tennant, Weaver, and Lewis, 1973; Williams, DiCicco, and Unterberger, 1968). Results like these caused a flurry of adverse publicity in the 1970s, an unofficial moratorium on the production and distribution of new materials, and a reduction in drug education budgets.

However, it is not clear that the results justified the alarmed reaction. One study reporting increased drug use lacked an acceptable scientific evaluation; three others reported complex results. Although Stuart (1974) suggested that higher use occurred in the combined presence of increased knowledge and low "worry," his results could have been an artifact of greater attrition among the experimental subjects or could have been attributable to a greater tendency for experimental subjects to use and sell drugs more before the program intervention. Moreover, the drug use measures were taken only four months after the intervention and were not repeated. Since subsequent studies of smoking prevention programs have shown an immediate post-program increase in cigarette use that was eventually replaced by a significant decline (Evans et al., 1981), it is possible that Stuart's increased-use effects were also short-lived.

Blum, Blum, and Garfield (1976) and Williams, DiCicco, and Unterberger (1968) reported negative effects that were also balanced by positive results. In the latter study, more experimental subjects became intoxicated during the year after the intervention, but among those experimental and control subjects who did get intoxicated, the experimental subjects did so less often. Blum's teacher-led information program increased the *frequency* of shifts from lower to higher drug use levels among 6th graders, but also dampened the *extremity* of the shift for those who made the transition to a higher level of drug use.

While information programs may stimulate increased curiosity about drugs and a corresponding rise in short-term experimentation, the evidence is not conclusive. Even if conclusive evidence were available, that alone would not justify trying to shelter adolescents from such information, particularly in a world where informal sources of drug information are plentiful. It might suggest, however, that providing information without also providing some useful tools for resisting incentives to try drugs is a doubtful strategy.

Why have information programs had so little effect? At least three explanations are plausible. First, such programs frequently assumed that more information about drugs would automatically decrease their use. However, many people use damaging substances even when aware of their harmful consequences. Years after the 1964 Surgeon General's report, millions of adults have continued to smoke and millions of adolescents have begun to.

Second, these programs postulated a complex causal sequence of events, assuming that increased knowledge would lead to antidrug attitudes and that changes in drug attitudes would foster changes in drug use. However, many programs that enhanced knowledge about drugs had little effect on people's attitudes one way or the other. Moreover, a considerable body of research suggests that changes in attitudes seldom lead to behavior change (Abelson, Aronson, and McGuire, 1968; Kiesler, Collins, and Miller, 1969; McGuire, 1969). Indeed, the more typical causal relationship is frequently just the opposite: A person changes his behavior first and his attitudes later. When attitudes *do* affect behavior, special conditions must also be present: (1) The attitude should be highly specific to the behavior at issue (attitudes about *taking* specific drugs vs. drugs in general); and (2) other social and situational factors (social norms, situational barriers to drug use, and incentives for taking drugs) should support the attitude-behavior relationship (Fishbein, 1973; Goodstadt, 1978; Ostram, 1969; Rokeach and Kliejunas, 1972; Wicker, 1971).

Third, the weakness of the knowledge —> attitude —> behavior model was frequently compounded by implementation errors. Many of the earlier programs exaggerated the negative consequences of drug use (Kinder, 1975). Not surprisingly, adolescents frequently recognized these tactics and responded by dismissing both the inaccurate appeals *and* those who articulated them as lacking credibility. In addition, many information programs overemphasized the long-term effects of drug use—for example, the possibility of becoming an alcoholic or dependent on barbiturates as an adult. Since many adolescents saw their own parents drinking or taking pills without showing signs of alcoholism or addiction, these arguments were frequently ignored.[32]

Affective Education Effects

Programs based on the individual deficiency or affective model have had inconclusive results. Among those that have been adequately evaluated, a minority claim positive effects (Carney, 1975; D'Augelli, 1975), while most report conflicting, ambiguous, or zero effects (Blum, Blum, and Garfield, 1976; Branca, d'Augelli, and Evans, 1975; Carney, 1971; D'Augelli, Swisher, and Evans, 1975; Gerbasi, 1976; Jackson and

---

[32]Furthermore, adolescents tend to be present-oriented: Rather than consider possibilities in the distant future, they worry about their immediate problems—making friends, getting invitations to the "right" parties, or succeeding in school. Arguments about the likelihood of getting cancer from habitual smoking have less weight with many young people than those stressing immediate consequences (such as unpleasant breath, increased blood pressure, or peer disapproval).

Calsyn, 1977; Kim, 1981, 1982; McClelland, 1975; Ryan, 1974; Sine, 1976; Swisher and Piniuk, 1973). None of those that focus on values clarification have demonstrated a link between value change (or change in value priorities) and drug-related behavior change (Goodstadt, 1978).

As we have seen, these programs vary considerably in their approach to improving a child's self-esteem or decisionmaking capacity, but they share a common problem: They are very difficult to implement. Teachers frequently have problems learning the new classroom styles associated with the program, or they may simply resist changing their own behavior. Consequently, programs that seek to teach general skills in the classroom and to provide an accepting school climate may show no results simply because the program was never put into place as the original designers intended.

However, the National Institute on Drug Abuse commissioned a study in Napa, California, that tested several variations of the individual deficiency model, with some information components as well. Carefully designed and implemented, this evaluation both met the canons of valid scientific evidence and invested substantial resources in facilitating and monitoring the implementation process. Despite these efforts, the programs failed. Not only did they fail to inhibit drug use, but they also failed to produce the expected intervening effects of improved self-esteem and more positive attitudes toward school (Schaeffer et al., 1981, 1982a,b; Malvin et al., 1982). Why was this so?

The drawbacks of this model differ from those associated with the information approach. First, many of these programs set an ambitious agenda of trying to affect a central self-concept that is the product of the child's entire life experience. Evidence that short-term programs can raise self-esteem is limited; moreover, most research does not support a strong relationship between low self-esteem and the onset of drug use (Kandel, 1978a; Gersick et al., 1981).

Second, we know little about the relationship between values and drug use—which values are associated with specific drug behaviors, or under what conditions value changes might lead to behavior change (Goodstadt, 1978). Nor do we have anything approaching consensus on how values should be defined (Bond, 1971). Thus questions about the validity of the value-behavior model have as much, if not more, force as those about the attitude-behavior model.

Third, most of these programs failed to link general skills in communication or decisionmaking with specific drug situations—such as what an adolescent should do when a friend offers him marijuana, or how to counter the argument that taking drugs gives one a more adult status. Learning to break decisions into distinct choices and their associated positive and negative consequences does not necessarily help a young person decide what to do in a specific situation.

Finally, *both* the information and the affective education approaches failed to counter the single most important reason for beginning drug use, peer influence. In contrast, programs that do counter such peer pressure have had more positive results. We turn now to these more recent efforts, programs based on the social pressures model.

Effects of Programs Based on the Social Pressures Model

Until the late 1970s, drug education programs had largely ignored the environmental or social precursors of adolescent drug use. NIDA has recently begun to encourage research efforts that target social influences, but the programs are too recent to show results. However, results are available from several antismoking programs that treat smoking as a social behavior; they reveal a promising record of success in reducing the rate of smoking among adolescents.

Figure 5.3 shows the impact of one program tested by researchers at Stanford University (Telch et al., 1982). They provided special training to 7th graders in one school, while students in the control school continued to receive the normal drug education curriculum. Two and a half years after that training, 15 percent of the students who did not receive the special program had smoked in the past week, compared with only 5 percent of those who did receive it—a two-thirds reduction in the proportion of adolescents engaged in regular smoking.

These results take on added significance because several researchers have reported similar findings. Similar programs have been evaluated in Texas, New York, Minnesota, and Ontario, Canada (Arkin et al., 1981; Botvin and Eng, 1980, 1981, 1982; Evans et al., 1978, 1981; Flay et al., 1983; Luepker et al., 1983).[33] In general, they have had scientifically acceptable evaluations and have reduced the proportion of adolescents engaged in experimental or regular smoking by one- to two-thirds. Because of their promise, we now present a detailed description of the antismoking programs and the components that appear to have made them successful.

---

[33]The Oregon Research Institute has also begun testing a conceptually similar antismoking program in three Oregon school districts, but has not yet reported results. See Severson et al. (1981) for additional details.

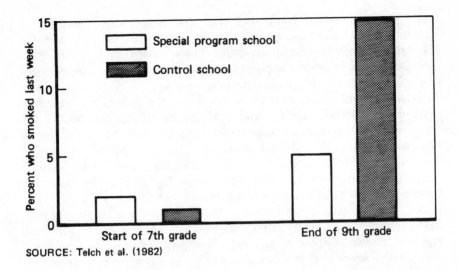

SOURCE: Telch et al. (1982)

Fig. 5.3— Effect of 7th-grade antismoking program
(Stanford Heart Disease Prevention Program)

FEATURES OF THE ANTISMOKING PROGRAMS

Despite individual variations, these programs share similar intellectual traditions. In particular, they stress developing deterrence strategies that are rooted in an understanding of four basic issues: (1) the factors that lead adolescents to start using cigarettes; (2) the mechanisms by which young people learn; (3) the best methods for communicating effectively; and (4) the specific concerns and developmental idiosyncrasies of adolescents.

Key Program Components

All of these programs focus on the social influences that promote cigarette smoking, familiarizing adolescents with the pressures to smoke and teaching them techniques for dealing with those pressures. In so doing, they also seek to reinforce group norms against smoking and to undermine beliefs that it is a desirable and harmless behavior. Based on social inoculation theory, which argues that exposure to persuasive arguments reduces susceptibility to subsequent persuasion (McGuire, 1969), many programs also help adolescents identify and refute the arguments for smoking. For example, a widely used set of Virginia Slims advertisements links smoking with being a mature, glamorous, and independent woman. These advertisements are typically countered by encouraging young people to question the independence of someone who is addicted to cigarettes.

Teaching adolescents how to "say no" gracefully rests on principles derived from social learning theory (Bandura, 1977), specifically the use of role playing to learn resistance techniques and the reinforcement of newly learned skills through practice. This teaching is neither general nor vague, but involves specific situations in which adolescents might find themselves: the girl who wants the "cool" motorcycle type to like her and is afraid he will never ask her out if she isn't "cool" also, or the boy who doesn't want to look different at a party. By having children act out likely situations in which they might be offered a cigarette or feel tempted to try one, these programs also seek to avoid the "passive spectator" problem and to lock in a repertoire of responses for dealing with real situations. Some add a reinforcement component, asking adolescents to make a public decision against smoking.

Most of the antismoking programs have stressed using peers to facilitate or model the resistance training.[34] When carefully chosen as role models for different adolescent groups (the studious, the athletes, the socially adept), peer leaders help accomplish two important aims: (1) showing young people that it is possible to be independent and more mature without smoking, and (2) strengthening the arguments against smoking by using credible communicators. These methods rest on the notion that adolescents believe other adolescents (particularly those who are a little older) more readily than they believe teachers or parents.[35]

Finally, these programs do not ignore the informational or cognitive elements of persuading adolescents not to smoke, but they place that information in a context that is immediately accessible and understandable to young people. In particular, they emphasize the short-

---

[34]At least one program in each of the sites listed above has used same-age or older peers, either as role models in films or teacher/facilitators in the classroom, or both. Where the effectiveness of peer as opposed to adult "trainers" has been tested, peers appear to be more effective (Luepker et al., 1983).

[35]This strategy derives from both social learning and communications theory. Social learning theory posits that adolescents learn from significant others in two ways: (1) direct modeling (imitation) of the behavior of peers or adults who use drugs; (2) reinforcement of adolescent beliefs, attitudes, and use of drugs through social approval or disapproval (Bandura, 1977). The use of peer role models who do not smoke and disapprove of doing so is relevant to both ways of learning. Communications theory stresses the greater persuasive effectiveness of credible communicators (McGuire, 1969; Hovland, Janis, and Kelley, 1953; Kiesler, Collins, and Miller, 1969). Factors that increase credibility include expertise and familiarity (perceived similarity to the audience). Using peer communicators emphasizes the latter characteristic.

term effects of smoking, graphically showing students how much nicotine is in the saliva of smokers and nonsmokers or the level of carbon monoxide in the breath of a smoker. Recognizing that many adolescents fail to believe serious harm will befall them, they place less stress on long-term harmful consequences such as developing cancer in later life.

Specific Program Examples

The first such antismoking program, developed by Evans and his colleagues (1978), used nonsmoking peers on film. These peers provided 7th graders with information about social influences and modeled resistance techniques. The program also emphasized the short-term (immediate) consequences of smoking and collected saliva samples as a strategy for improving the validity of self-reports.[36] At the end of the 7th grade, the mean proportion of smokers was actually higher in the treatment group, but a reduction in smoking showed up by the 8th grade (Evans et al., 1981). However, a group exposed only to the saliva monitoring condition also showed a reduction, thereby raising the possibility that monitoring alone, as opposed to the curriculum, had produced the effect.

The Stanford Counselling Leadership Against Smoking Project (CLASP) added "live" high school peer leaders, role-playing practice in the classroom, and a public commitment session to Evans's program (McAlister, Perry, and Maccoby, 1979; McAlister et al., 1980; Perry et al., 1980; Telch et al., 1982). As we have noted, with three consecutive sessions followed by four additional sessions spread out over the 7th grade school year, they reported a two-thirds reduction in regular smoking 33 months later.

Two different program series were tested in Minnesota. The Robbinsdale Anti-Smoking Project (RASP) incorporated Evans's method of using same-age peers demonstrating resistance techniques on videotapes (unknown peers were used in one experimental condition and classroom opinion leaders in another) and added a public commitment component that also included videotaping students as they stated why they were not going to smoke. It also focused on the immediate harmful consequences of smoking and used inoculation, role playing, and rehearsal strategies (Hurd et al., 1980; Luepker et al., 1983). Two years after treatment, students exposed to the intensive program using known peer leaders and public commitment smoked significantly fewer

---

[36]Known as the "bogus pipeline" technique, the saliva-collection strategy is thought to motivate more honest reports of smoking behavior by convincing students that smoking can be detected by analyzing their saliva (Evans, Hansen, and Mittlemark, 1977; Luepker et al., 1981).

cigarettes per week, and fewer of them had become regular smokers (20 percent vs. 30 percent in the control school). In the school where the program was taught by young adults, smoking rates differed little from the control school (Luepker et al., 1983).[37]

The Minnesota Prevention of Cigarette Smoking in Children Project (PCSC) compared three variants of the resistance to social pressures program used in RASP[38] with an information program that focused on the long-term consequences of smoking. One year later, the two peer-led programs showed significantly better results than the adult-led conditions in retarding the transition from nonsmoking to smoking. However, no effects were found for those who had already started experimental smoking at baseline.

In Waterloo, Ontario, Flay and his colleagues tested a resistance program targeted at 6th graders with one booster session each in grades 7 and 8 (Flay et al., 1983). The Waterloo program followed the basic principles of social resistance training but added a component on decisionmaking that was tailored to the smoking decision. With a sample of 11 matched pairs of schools, most of which were randomly assigned to the experimental or control conditions, this program sought to minimize pretest differences between treatment and control groups. Results at the end of grade 7 indicated that the program held down the proportion of experimental smokers, reduced the average number of cigarettes smoked by regular smokers (but did not affect the proportion of regular or nonsmokers), induced experimenters to quit smoking, and deterred smoking onset for high-risk students.

The Life Skills Training (LST) program, developed by Botvin and his colleagues at Cornell University, took a somewhat different approach. It incorporated strategies designed to improve general personal competence (autonomy, self-esteem, and self-confidence) as well as the capacity to identify and resist social pressures to smoke (Botvin and Eng, 1980, 1982; Botvin, Renick, and Baker, in press). Botvin has tested three programs that include more general communication, social decisionmaking, and assertiveness skills in addition to the familiar resistance training, modeling, and behavior rehearsal techniques. Reporting only on those 7th grade students who were nonsmokers at baseline, Botvin and his colleagues found significant treatment effects one year later: a reduction in new regular smoking in one 12-session program led by older peers (Botvin and Eng, 1982); and a one-third to 50 percent reduction in the proportion of new, regular, monthly, and

---

[37]The treatment did not, however, have a significant impact on the proportion of quitters or experimental smokers.

[38]One was led by adults with three videotapes using peer actors; one was led by peers with the same videotapes, and one used peer leaders but no media.

daily smokers in a 15-session teacher-led program (Botvin, Renick, and Baker, in press). However, his reported effects on personality variables are neither consistent nor stable over time; thus it is unclear whether the addition of components aimed at general personal competence adds to the program's effectiveness.

All of these programs were school-based, were targeted at the age of onset (6th or 7th grade), and used concepts and techniques that have, until recently, been relatively foreign to the world of drug prevention. All had quasi-experimental designs (pre- and post-tests, comparisons of treatment and control groups), although only a few randomly assigned schools to the experimental conditions, and fewer can claim to have eliminated group pre-test differences that might explain their results. All except Botvin's first program conducted saliva or breath tests in an effort to improve the validity of self-reports, but they did not always compare physiological test results for treatment vs. control groups.

As a group, these studies provide cumulative evidence that programs based on the social pressures model help reduce the smoking onset rate among adolescents. Their very success raises a question: Can these techniques be adapted for substances other than cigarettes and, if so, will they be successful?

Transferring Smoking Prevention Concepts to Drug Prevention

While the prognosis appears favorable, there are reasonable arguments on both sides. On the positive side, we know that many of the factors that precipitate smoking also apply to marijuana, the most commonly used illicit drug among adolescents. The primary factors associated with smoking onset include the influence of friends and parents; attitudes and beliefs about smoking; rebelliousness and independence; low academic performance and motivation; and prior manifestation of problem behavior (Hansen, Johnson, and Collins, 1983). As we have seen, each of these factors plays a role in adolescent experimentation with other drugs.

On the other hand, it can be argued that antismoking programs work because the general social climate has changed so radically over the past twenty years. As compared with 20 or 30 years ago, today most people (both adults and adolescents) do not smoke; the great majority believe it is harmful to their health; and increasing numbers not only disapprove of smoking but feel much freer to ask others to refrain from smoking in their presence. One might argue that these are preconditions for an effective antismoking program, and that these preconditions do not exist for other drugs.

However, recent data provide evidence that beliefs about marijuana and cigarettes, at least, are converging. Figure 5.4 shows the proportion of high school seniors who believe that regular marijuana use and daily cigarette use pose great risks of personal harm. As recently as 1978, one might have concluded that marijuana and cigarettes were indeed different: So few adolescents thought marijuana was harmful that any program aimed at preventing its use would have faced very difficult odds. In the past five years, however, high school seniors have become increasingly concerned about the dangers of regular marijuana use, so much so that the difference in risk perceptions between smoking and marijuana has disappeared.

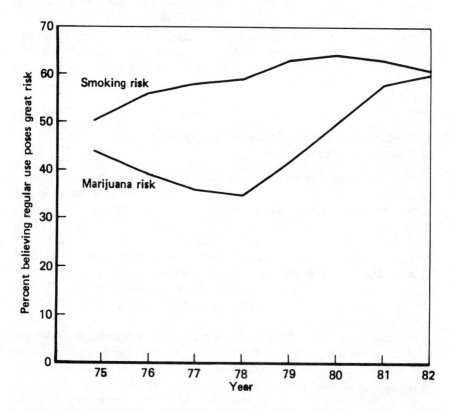

Fig. 5.4—High school seniors' beliefs about harm from cigarettes
and marijuana (from annual high school senior surveys,
Johnston, Backman, and O'Malley, 1982)

Disapproval of marijuana use is even more prevalent. By 1982, 80 percent of high school seniors disapproved of regular marijuana use. While fewer (59 percent) disapproved of occasional use, that proportion still represents a majority (Johnston, Bachman, and O'Malley, 1982). Thus it seems likely that adolescents do not make insurmountably sharp distinctions between being a regular marijuana user and merely smoking it occasionally.

That is not the case for alcohol. Only 22 percent of high school seniors think having one or two drinks daily poses "great risks" of harm. Moreover, only 18 percent disapprove of trying one or two drinks, compared with 46 percent who disapprove of trying marijuana once or twice. The figures shown earlier on the prevalence of alcohol use in the past month appear to reflect these beliefs.

Further evidence that smoking prevention concepts might also work for other substances comes from a Stanford pilot study in which peer leaders pointed out that the sources of pressures to use alcohol and marijuana were similar to those for tobacco (Perry et al., 1980). Although no pre-test data were collected, there were substantial differences between treatment and control groups in the proportions who indicated they had ever smoked marijuana (14 vs. 20 percent) or used alcohol (37 vs. 49 percent). These results could be attributable to pre-test differences in treatment and control group prevalence rates or to the program itself. If the latter, they may reflect a spillover effect from the cigarette program to other substances.

These statistics suggest the desirability of testing a drug prevention program based on principles derived from the successful antismoking programs—adapted, where appropriate, to the specific conditions surrounding adolescent use of other drugs. Because casual use of alcohol is so much more acceptable among both adolescents and adults, we suspect such a program would have more success inhibiting marijuana use than preventing the onset of drinking. Finally, the data also suggest the relevance of testing for spillover effects, e.g., the possibility that drug use might be inhibited by a smoking-only program even if it were not specifically targeted at other drugs.

SUMMARY

Thus we conclude that drug prevention offers the most promising arena for efforts aimed at controlling adolescent drug use. While past prevention programs have not had encouraging results, the newest smoking prevention programs have been more successful. We believe their success derives from their understanding of how adolescents start smoking cigarettes, how young people learn and develop, and how they respond to different persuasive techniques.

Three key principles underlie the smoking prevention programs. First, the main influences on adolescent drug use are *social*. Adolescents typically start using drugs in a group setting, among friends or relatives. The principal factors affecting whether and when young people begin using drugs are peer use and approval of drugs plus the behavior and norms of adult "role models" at home or in other settings. Second, adolescents have a strong desire to appear mature and independent. If they perceive drug use as an adult activity and see admired peers and adults doing it, they are more likely to emulate that behavior. Third, adolescent beliefs about the harmfulness or desirability of drugs affect the likelihood of early use, but the long-term consequences of drug use are less salient to adolescents than the immediate physical and social effects.

The smoking programs build on these principles by stressing the adverse short-term physical and social consequences of smoking, helping adolescents identify and counter pro-smoking influences, and teaching them graceful methods of "saying no."

Because the same factors that lead adolescents to smoking also lead to use of other drugs, we have suggested that this approach could well be adapted to drug use. In recent years, high school seniors' skepticism about the wisdom of using marijuana has first approached and then exceeded that for cigarettes, indicating that a solid majority view these two substances as harmful. If this base exists for other drugs, a social-influence-based prevention program may well be able to reduce use of marijuana and other substances.

We believe that prevention programs should be aimed at specific drugs rather than drugs in general. Each drug differs from others in its effects, patterns of use, and the stage of life where its use is initiated. However, targeting one or two of the substances most likely to pose risks for adolescents—cigarettes and marijuana—may help prevent use of other drugs. Longitudinal studies of drug use suggest that going through a given stage (e.g., using legal drugs) may be a necessary condition for transition into successive stages (e.g., using marijuana). Thus, a program that reduces cigarette smoking may well have "spillover" effects on marijuana use, while one targeted on marijuana may also delay initiation into later-stage drugs.

Chapter 6

CONCLUSIONS AND RECOMMENDATIONS

What to do about illicit drug use has been a topic of vigorous debate for almost a century. Even before 1900, there was public concern about use and over-the-counter sale of opium and cocaine. At that time, the debate was over whether, and how, to restrain the uncontrolled sale of such substances. The eventual outcome, a policy of prohibition and law enforcement combined with programs to treat drug addicts, is the basic approach that still guides U.S. drug policy.

Although much has changed in the meantime, the basic question-- how to control drug use--remains as vital now as ever. In many ways the question is more urgent today, because (1) there are more drugs subject to abuse now than before; (2) the user population is much larger and younger; and (3) the nation is spending a much larger amount of money for drug control. Those considerations prompted this study, the purpose being to review current knowledge and to plot a course for future efforts at reducing adolescent drug use.

Earlier chapters of this report have reviewed studies that describe the characteristics of drug use and consider methods of controlling it. In this chapter we draw our major conclusions from that information and offer recommendations for the future.

CHARACTERISTICS OF ADOLESCENT DRUG USE

Drug use is a mass phenomenon in the United States, among both adults and adolescents. We estimate that 20 million people in the U.S. use marijuana at least once a month, and 4 million use cocaine. Several million others take stimulants, sedatives, and tranquilizers without medical supervision. Although it is difficult to obtain accurate figures for the extent of the illegal drug trade, available estimates indicate that the total retail value of marijuana, cocaine, and heroin--the three drugs that receive the most attention--is at least $27 billion per year, and perhaps as high as $53 billion.

Young adults and adolescents account for a disproportionate share of this mass market. According to national survey estimates, 29 percent of high school seniors use marijuana at least once a month. The other leading psychoactive drugs are alcohol (used by 70 percent of high school seniors) and cigarettes (used by 30 percent). Smaller but still significant numbers of seniors use amphetamines and cocaine (11 and 5 percent, respectively). The other drugs, including heroin, lag far behind.

Drug use is widespread, then, and trade in drugs is a big business. But does that constitute a drug problem for the nation? In a legal sense it does, because users, buyers, and sellers of drugs face arrest and prosecution, and the illicit drug trade creates large criminal incomes. It also inspires violence, fraud, corruption of public officials, and other crime. Furthermore, heroin addicts often commit large numbers of property crimes to support their addiction.

Nonetheless, those considerations are much less relevant to adolescents than to adults. Heroin, for instance, is little used by adolescents. Moreover, according to commonly accepted indicators such as rates of hospital emergencies and deaths, heroin affects adolescents much less often than other drugs do. In fact, addiction or physical dependence on any drug appears to be rather uncommon among young people, only a small minority of whom use drugs frequently enough to cause physical dependence; most of them take drugs occasionally, and only in social situations. The principal problem with adolescent drug use lies elsewhere, in the risks that it may pose.

In the judgment of numerous professionals (Institute of Medicine, 1982), these risks warrant serious concern. The risks vary greatly by type of drug, but can include toxic effects, temporary impairment of function, and potential for physical or psychic dependence. All of the drugs that we have reviewed can have damaging psychological and physical effects, if taken frequently in large doses. Marijuana, for example, is implicated by existing scientific evidence as a potential cause of memory impairment, lung disease, immune system disorders, and reproductive dysfunctions.

Furthermore, even if one does not observe overt effects of a drug in the short term, toxic effects may appear after chronic use. It took years of accumulated experience to document the ill effects of cigarette smoking, and the same may be true of marijuana, cocaine, and other drugs. Similarly, the effects of alcohol--the other major socially approved drug--have only recently been fully documented, and even so the threshold dose for many adverse effects is uncertain. There may be threshold doses for illicit drugs as well, but no one knows what they are.

There are several additional reasons for special concern about drug use by children and adolescents. First, all psychoactive drugs have acute effects on mood, concentration, and cognitive functioning, including memory. Such effects are very likely to interfere with learning.

Hence psychoactive drug use may impair school performance, reduce the amount learned in school, and retard educational development.

Second, if drugs do have ill effects, it is advisable to postpone the onset of use as long as possible. Many toxic substances require a long period of exposure to produce an effect, or a long incubation period for the effect to become manifest. Thus the older the point at which use is begun, the less likely are adverse effects. In addition, postponing the age of first use may reduce the likelihood that the individual will become a habitual user, as in the case of cigarette smoking.

Finally, a conservative course of action is especially appropriate when dealing with children and adolescents. During adolescence young people undergo major changes in physical, cognitive, emotional, and social functioning. Drugs administered during this period could have subtle effects on physical maturation, and could delay or impair psychological and social development. In general, medical practice is guided by the basic tenet that a drug should not be administered when it is not known to be safe. When safety is in doubt--for example, during pregnancy or immaturity--restrictions are often imposed to avoid harm. In the case of illicit drugs, none has been sufficiently studied to warrant a claim of safety. Thus on balance, we conclude that self-administration of these drugs by young people is not advisable, and reducing adolescent drug use is a goal worthy of considerable national attention.

EFFECTIVENESS OF DRUG CONTROL STRATEGIES

If controlling adolescent drug use is a desirable goal, what is the best approach? We have noted that real federal expenditures for law enforcement have recently increased, while expenditures on treatment and prevention have declined. Our conclusions suggest that these priorities may not be the most appropriate ones.

Law Enforcement

U.S. policy has always relied heavily on law enforcement to control the illicit drug market, particularly for marijuana, cocaine, and heroin. In one sense this strategy has already accomplished much: Illegal drugs, particularly heroin, are more difficult to obtain than other substances, and they are very expensive relative to their production cost. Nonetheless, we conclude that further increases in law enforcement effort are not likely to substantially reduce drug use.

There are some enforcement policies that we have not been able to examine. For example, police and school authorities in several cities have attempted "crackdowns" on drug use and trading on high school campuses, but we have found no systematic data that could be used to evaluate such efforts. Similarly, we have not attempted to estimate the effects of reduced law enforcement or of drug legalization. Some observers argue that legalization would benefit society because it would reduce the cost of law enforcement, eliminate the illegal incomes and official corruption associated with drug dealing, and avoid stigmatizing users who otherwise abide by the law (National Academy of Sciences, 1982).[1] However, there are scant data to suggest the magnitude of other, negative, effects of legalization. We presume that even if sales were regulated, the greater availability under legalization would lead to increased consumption. The risks of greater consumption would then have to be weighed against the reductions in social and economic costs of law enforcement. Probably the best evidence would come from a policy experiment in a restricted geographic area; however, given the high current demand for drugs and the openness of state borders, we see no feasible method for controlling such an experiment. Because of the virtual absence of data on the effects of different legal control mechanisms, we have not attempted an analysis of that issue.

From the analysis we have conducted, the most basic point is that the supply of drugs can never be eliminated. Most of the illegal drug supply originates overseas, in regions where drug crops are the farmers' most profitable products. The central governments in these regions are often weak, and some are not sympathetic with U.S. concerns. Perhaps most important, every illicit drug is exported by several source countries; when one source is shut down, other producers fill the vacuum. Accordingly, past efforts to reduce drug crops have had little lasting effect on the U.S. market, and we cannot expect more in the foreseeable future.

Nor is it likely that supply can be much reduced by stopping drugs "at the border." Although the federal government has greatly expanded its interdiction efforts, most drug shipments still get through and prices have not risen (GAO, 1983). We concluded that even a doubling of interdiction would have little effect on retail prices. The

---

[1]For heroin, it is also argued that legal dispensing through medical channels would reduce addict crime and would prevent deaths due to drug overdose or adulteration (Brecher, 1972). However, adolescents are much more likely to use other drugs, to which those arguments do not apply; marijuana smoking, for instance, does not drive users to crime, and rarely causes serious toxic reactions. Moreover, legalization might not achieve what is expected; in Britain, a policy of medical heroin maintenance failed to prevent the growth of a substantial illicit market alongside the legal dispensing clinics (Trebach, 1982).

key reason is that a drug's import cost is only a small fraction of its retail price. The price for a given quantity rises very steeply as it passes down the chain from producer to consumer. Hence, intervening at the top levels of the market can exert very limited effect on the final price. Other factors also work against interdiction, such as smugglers' ability to adapt to enforcement pressure, and their capacity to recruit large numbers of foreign boat crewmen at low wages.

Within the U.S., we see poor prospects for increasing pressure against retail drug dealers. Local police make many arrests, but retailers number probably over half a million. Therefore, only a small fraction are arrested, and a tiny proportion are imprisoned—by our estimates, far less than 1 percent. With state prisons currently over-crowded and local courts backlogged, it is not feasible to raise those risks significantly. Even if it were feasible to arrest and incarcerate many more, we have concluded that the effect would be only a small price rise. The trade has simply become so vast that any reasonable increase in police pressure could deliver only a small impact on a very large market.

Undercover investigations of high-level dealers may offer better prospects, but even here the costs would be great and the results uncertain. Most of the innovative techniques that law enforcement agencies have developed can be evaded by dealer adaptations. Possibly, federal agencies could incarcerate more high-level dealers if their investigative budgets were greatly increased. However, such investigations are time-consuming and expensive. We have concluded that to increase the price of all illicit drugs by as much as 15 percent, investigative outlays might have to be tripled--which would mean spending $800 million more per year than in 1983. Even so, the results might not be seen for several years, and drug dealers might find effective methods of countering the increased law enforcement pressure.

We conclude, then, that more intense law enforcement is not likely to substantially affect either the availability or the retail price of drugs in this country. We do not thereby mean to imply that enforcement against drug dealers should be abandoned. Past enforcement has certainly increased the price of drugs beyond what it otherwise would have been. In addition, enforcement may make it more difficult for novices to find dealers. Nevertheless, the answer to adolescent drug use does not seem to lie with increased law enforcement.

Treatment

Treatment of drug abuse is an extensive and multifaceted industry in the United States, accounting for over $500 million in annual expenditures. Originally, federal authorities conceived of treatment and law enforcement as complementary methods of containing the heroin problem: Law enforcement would deter addicts and dry up drug supplies, so users would be forced into treatment centers where they could be withdrawn from the drug. Thus, treatment was, and still is, largely oriented to heroin users.

That model is clearly inappropriate for adolescent drug abusers. Most adolescents admitted to treatment are not heroin addicts, but abusers of marijuana, stimulants, or hallucinogens. Few of them are physically dependent, and their drug abuse often seems to grow out of other underlying conditions, such as family disorganization, problems with interpersonal relationships, or difficulty in school.

According to several recent studies, existing programs are not well adapted to help such clients. Many adolescents still receive treatment in programs whose primary goal is to overcome physical dependence. In addition, many practitioners are unfamiliar with treatments for nonopiate drug abuse, and adolescent clients often find the institution's philosophy at odds with their own values and expectations. Treatment programs for adolescents need to be better designed.

Does this mean that present treatment is not effective? We do not have the scientific evidence to answer that question. Nearly all studies suffer from design defects such as inadequate outcome measures, absence of appropriate control groups, or lack of randomized assignment to treatments. Overcoming those methodological problems is difficult, but unless they are addressed we cannot be confident about the effects of treatment.

Obviously, a critical issue is the relative effectiveness of the various treatment approaches. For instance, many observers recommend "early intervention" with young people, before their drug abuse has become severe, but no such program has been evaluated systematically. Another promising approach, family therapy, is based on the premise that adolescent drug abuse often originates in family dysfunctions; accordingly, the therapy brings the family together into treatment in an attempt to resolve the underlying problem. However, even though family therapy has achieved demonstrated positive effects in a randomized experiment with young adult heroin users, it has not been systematically tested with adolescent drug abusers, and the costs could be quite high.

Some evidence suggests that it should be possible to develop effective treatment for adolescent drug abusers. First, evaluation studies indicate that certain forms of treatment--drug-free therapy, methadone maintenance, and residential "therapeutic communities"--work better than no treatment at all. Second, the longer a patient remains in treatment, the better is his or her chance of improvement, and patients who complete treatment have better outcomes than those who drop out. Although we cannot say with certainty whether this means that patients would benefit from longer treatment (because dropouts could differ from graduates in other ways), the relationship lends some credence to the belief that treatment, in general, produces positive effects. Third, many adolescents possess attributes associated with a good prognosis; compared with adult patients, fewer of them are high-rate users, fewer are dependent, and they exhibit less functional impairment.

Against these positive signs must be arrayed some less promising factors. Because young people are often required to undergo treatment, their motivation is sometimes low. If their drug abuse in fact stems from underlying psychosocial problems, those problems may prove refractory to treatment. And even if theoretically possible, treatment might prove very costly, particularly if it attempts to alter basic individual characteristics or social relationships.

These limitations in knowledge of treatment effectiveness prevent us from recommending specific treatment program initiatives. We conclude that at present a major expansion of treatment resources for adolescents would lack a sound basis. In the future, more emphasis should be placed on developing and evaluating drug abuse treatment programs specifically designed for youth.

Prevention

Prevention programs offer brighter prospects for reducing adolescent drug use than any other method. There is now a considerable base of knowledge about how young people begin using drugs, plus some experimental evidence that prevention programs can keep adolescents from starting to smoke cigarettes. Consequently, our conclusions about prevention are more optimistic.

Preventing a phenomenon can best be done with a clear understanding of the processes that cause it. In the case of drug use, there is now abundant evidence that the primary cause of initial drug use is *social influence*. Most people first begin using drugs because their friends do. This carries several implications for prevention programs. First, such programs should be designed to help individuals learn effective methods of resisting social pressure. Second, the programs should also try to reinforce and cement social norms against drug use. Third, the most effective appeals are likely to come from other adolescents, rather than from teachers, parents, or adult authorities.

Peer influence, of course, interacts with the individual's beliefs and orientations. Two aspects of adolescents' orientations are particularly important: (1) their desire to appear mature; and (2) their orientation toward the present rather than the future. Adolescents are vulnerable to pro-drug appeals because they wish to appear mature and free of the restrictions of childhood. Smoking, drinking, and using illicit drugs are all methods of demonstrating a new-found independence. Furthermore, young people are not likely to be deterred by warnings about adverse effects far in the future; most adolescents are much more concerned about their immediate circumstances, friendships, and activities than about future health problems. Therefore, prevention programs need to counteract the belief that drug use shows maturity, and to indict drugs for their short-term rather than long-term consequences.

The effectiveness of such an approach is illustrated by the contrast between older antidrug programs and the newer antismoking programs. In the past, many prevention efforts assumed that drug use resulted directly from adolescents' lack of information or from their personal problems such as lack of self-esteem. Early drug education programs based on these concepts produced disappointing results.

The more recent antismoking programs, based on a social influence model of initial use, have accumulated a more positive record. Such programs help children identify the pressures to smoke, particularly peer influences, and arm them with arguments against smoking. To tap into the adolescent's present orientation, these programs base their counterarguments on the immediate undesirable effects of smoking, especially those that harm one's appearance. And to counter the claim that smoking represents maturity, they often use nonsmoking older peers who can testify that smoking does not confer independence or adult status. These programs have been tested in several locations and evaluated by independent research teams, and they generally have shown significant effects in preventing cigarette smoking.

How should such a prevention program be structured? First, we conclude that the optimal method is to approach adolescents through the schools, as the antismoking programs do. Schools are promising because they offer direct access to the great majority of the youth population, rather than to a self-selected subset such as might be reached through voluntary organizations or mass media. Moreover, schools contain natural social groups that can reinforce the program message. Finally, we have encouraging empirical evidence that smoking, at least, can be prevented using school-based programs. In contrast, there is little convincing evidence about the short-term effects of media messages on individual drug-taking behavior. We have noted some evidence that since the 1950s, publicity about the dangers of cigarette smoking has gradually reduced cigarette consumption. However, the effects are likely to take a long time to gather force.

National survey data suggest that for most drugs, prevention programs can be appropriately targeted at junior high school students. By age 12, about the beginning of the 7th grade, fewer than 5 percent of children use cigarettes or illicit drugs at least once a month. Thus, at that age the great majority of drug use can still be prevented, and the program can take advantage of the antidrug social norms that exist in a group of nonusers. After age 12, the percentage of users increases rapidly--reaching 20 to 30 percent by age 17.

Unfortunately, these arguments do not hold for alcohol. Alcohol is so common in American society that a substantial number of 7th grade students have already become regular users. Moreover, unlike cigarette smoking and illicit drug use, adults' use of alcohol is broadly accepted, and a "primary" prevention program suggesting that young people never start drinking is likely be ineffective. Thus we conclude that prevention approaches that appear workable for cigarettes and drugs are not well suited for preventing adolescent drinking.

However, we believe there is a reasonable chance of adapting the antismoking model to other drugs. Marijuana is likely to be the best immediate target. Adolescent beliefs about marijuana and cigarettes have recently been converging; in 1982, about equal proportions of high school seniors believed that regular marijuana use and regular cigarette smoking posed great risks of harm. Furthermore, longitudinal studies of adolescents have shown that drug use develops in a series of successive stages, beginning with use of alcohol or cigarettes; some of those users subsequently go on to marijuana, and some of the latter then proceed to other illicit drugs. This offers hope that a program starting early and targeting marijuana and cigarettes may not only prevent use of those substances, but may also "spill over" to prevent use of later-stage illicit drugs.

FUTURE DIRECTIONS FOR PROGRAMS TO REDUCE DRUG USE

Our findings lead to several implications about the future directions for programs to reduce adolescent drug use. We suggest that prevention programs can be implemented and tested now. We recommend initiatives in law enforcement and treatment to improve the information base we now possess, because current knowledge is too limited to indicate immediate policy or program actions. Some activities that we suggest stem directly from our research findings; others we propose have less certain outlooks based on current knowledge, but in our judgement have promising possibilities. We begin with the most immediate action-oriented possibilities and then go on to more long-term programs.

Implementing Prevention Programs

Drug Prevention in Junior High Schools. Our highest-priority recommendation is for programs to counter the social influences that encourage young adolescents to begin drug use. Given the evidence on effectiveness of antismoking programs, we believe it is now appropriate to design and test a similar antidrug program. Such a program could effectively target cigarettes, marijuana, and, possibly, "pills" in a junior high school classroom setting. As we have argued earlier, the 7th grade (age 12 to 13) is approximately the right point to begin, since at that age students are beginning to come into contact with pro-drug influences but fewer than 5 percent of them use drugs. Thus an antidrug program based on the social-pressures model of drug use can take advantage of junior high school students' beliefs and attitudes about drugs at a time where there are still very few drug users among their peers.

We caution that designing such a program entails a major effort, both in time and resources. Innovative programs of this type are best developed and initially implemented on a modest scale, where abstract research knowledge can be translated into concrete program materials and tested under controlled conditions. Such a program could encounter significant differences in adolescent attitudes or perceptions of risks for illicit drugs as compared with cigarettes. Therefore, we recommend that the program contain components emphasizing different substances, and that each component be tested at a matched set of sites. Ideally, the results should be evaluated by detailed monitoring of student drug use at program and control sites from a pre-intervention point until well after the program's completion. To provide the best evidence about program effectiveness, a given cohort of students should be followed, preferably using physiological measures as well as self-reports, and statistical comparisons should be made to assess how well the intervention worked.

High School Alcohol Prevention Programs. At this point, we cannot recommend that a similar program related to cigarettes and illicit drugs be implemented for high school students. We have found no evidence of successful prevention programs at the high school level, and we infer that by the time students enter high school, the social pressures to use drugs have already had their maximum effect. However, there may be other approaches that merit development for high school students. In particular, the problems associated with drinking alcoholic beverages may be best addressed at the senior high school level, when young people must actually confront concrete situations, such as automobile driving, in which drinking can pose an immediate risk. It seems worthwhile to undertake further research and development on alternative programs for high schools.

Information Programs. We have argued that direct informational appeals to adolescents are unlikely to produce immediate changes in drug-related behavior. Nevertheless, general community norms can be affected, in the long run, by dissemination of scientific information. The recent history of public attitudes toward cigarette smoking illustrates that process. Throughout the past three decades the population has been increasingly subjected to publicity about the hazards of smoking, and social norms governing smoking have become gradually less permissive. Scientific evidence about the adverse health effects of smoking played an influential role in these changes, which led to declines in cigarette consumption. However, the process is slow at best, and the immediate results are difficult to measure.

No scientific data base establishes the effects of information campaigns about illicit drugs. Nevertheless, public demand for information about drugs is intense and is likely to continue (U.S. Senate, Subcommittee on Alcoholism and Drug Abuse, 1982). That demand should be satisfied by balanced and accurate information from scientifically credible sources. Ultimately, such information may be able to play a role like that of the Surgeon General's report (1979). We therefore suggest greater production and dissemination of informational materials, including brochures, pamphlets, and print and broadcast announcements aimed at the general public, as well as prepackaged information and teaching kits for professionals who may influence children (such as physicians, teachers, and media personnel). Such information about drugs may ultimately prove valuable in establishing a base of concern upon which direct initiatives can build. If such a program is undertaken, the informational materials should be tested in selected media markets at the outset and the resulting changes in target group knowledge and attitudes should be tracked.

Setting Law Enforcement Policy

Law Enforcement Data Collection. Law enforcement presently accounts for a substantial majority of the federal antidrug effort. Nevertheless, as we argued in Chap. 3, the available data base for managing that enforcement is deficient. Basic parameters of the drug market, including prices at various levels of distribution, are estimated by informal and unsystematic methods. To set strategy, law enforcement agencies must make estimates, as we did, about such parameters as prices, numbers of dealers, extent of competition among dealers, interdiction rates, and total consumption rates. The effects of law enforcement actions depend intimately on such variables--yet the necessary data are not regularly reported, some data are not carefully or systematically collected, and the methods used to make projections are insufficiently documented (NNICC, 1983a).

These problems make it difficult to assess law enforcement effects quantitatively. Therefore, we recommend that the federal government regularly collect and publish more complete information about drug prices, consumption, and the conditions of drug distribution at all levels of the drug market. Only when such data are available will it be possible to determine the most effective strategies and to target them at the correct market levels to achieve the maximum effect.

School Enforcement. We have found no convincing evidence on the effectiveness of enforcement within schools. Nevertheless, it seems plausible that many students are first introduced to drugs at school, that drugs are often taken during school hours, and that numerous transactions take place in school because sellers and buyers can meet there conveniently.

We can see arguments both for and against increased school enforcement. On the one hand, it is possible that the main effect would be simply to displace drug-related activity to other locales. On the other hand, announcement and enforcement of such rules could deter some use, prevent some transactions by making them impossible or inconvenient, and reinforce society's general norms against adolescent drug use. Inhibiting drug use during school hours seems an especially important goal, in view of drug effects on learning, memory, and concentration. Thus, we suggest a research effort to compare various current school enforcement strategies and to evaluate the effect of each on the rate of drug use and in-school drug sales.

Drug Market Analysis. Both federal and local law enforcement agencies measure their efforts by the numbers of arrests, seizures, and cases they make. However, our analysis suggests that these intermediate measures may fail to indicate the ultimate effects of law enforcement actions. It is quite possible to change the intermediate factors without affecting the overall drug market appreciably. Instead, law enforcement effort should be evaluated in relation to specific indicators of drug price and availability.

Analysis of these indicators should include evaluation of various possible combinations of law enforcement strategies. Although we have concluded that intensifying any particular type of law enforcement would increase retail prices by no more than 15 percent, perhaps some combination of efforts might achieve more. If budgets cannot be increased, greater impact might still be achieved by redistributing existing resources--say, increasing investigative effort against high-level dealers while reducing interdiction. Specific evaluation of each alternative, coupled with cost estimates, would permit better informed choices about the best mix of enforcement activities.

Finally, a better understanding of the structure and operation of the illicit drug market could help formulate more efficient policies. We have speculated, for example, that national or regional high-level dealers, when incarcerated, may be easily replaced by their counterparts one level below; if so, enforcement might gain more impact by targeting several levels of the market simultaneously in one locality, rather than focusing on the national level. To address such issues, more information is needed about how dealers relate to each other, how many suppliers and customers they have, and how they adapt to changes in law enforcement pressure. Such information could be acquired through analysis of intelligence data, examination of court records, and direct interviews with incarcerated drug dealers.

Improving Treatment of Drug Abusers

Treatment Evaluation. Informed management of treatment for adolescent drug abusers is currently very difficult. Treatment facilities are confronted with large numbers of young people who experience problems related to drug use, but practitioners have few useful guidelines for choosing the best therapy. There are no standard forms of treatment for drug abusers, and there is little reliable evidence about what kinds of treatment work best, either in a global sense or for special groups such as youthful nonopiate abusers. Treatment programs themselves lack the technical resources to provide scientific evidence of their effects. The best evidence would be provided by experimental studies that compare patients receiving different treatment regimens, based on quantitative baseline and outcome data. Since a large amount of effort is now being invested in the provision of treatment, a sensible allocation of resources should include more funding for treatment research, with the emphasis on well-controlled experiments, randomized if possible, to compare the efficacy of various treatment approaches.

Evaluation of Early Intervention. Treatment need not be delayed until a drug abuser has reached the point of serious health or behavioral problems. Recognizing this, numerous programs of "early intervention" exist to help adolescents who are regular drug users or who seem at risk of developing a chronic drug problem. As promising as this concept sounds in principle, we located few evaluations of the effectiveness of early intervention programs, and found no credible scientific evidence on their success or failure. Given the popularity of early intervention and the public concern that something be done about it, we urge that treatment research give higher priority to evaluating programs of this kind.

Research on Development of Serious Drug Problems. Ultimately, better understanding of the etiology of drug problems would help treatment efforts. However, we lack any systematic knowledge about the process by which people develop dysfunctional patterns of drug use. Although there is a literature on the *onset* of drug use, published studies of the successive stages of drug use (other than heroin) are few and far between. It may be that while social factors largely determine the onset of drug use, biological factors, family characteristics, or deep-seated psychological characteristics play a larger role in the transition from regular use to heavy or dysfunctional use. Such research is difficult to conduct because the incidence rates of serious drug abuse are low. Other methodological problems, such as the need to use retrospective designs rather than prospective designs, complicate the task. However, the best basis for designing treatment for drug-related disorders will be a clear understanding of their causes, and hence more etiological research is needed.

Risk Assessment

Scientific research has not yet adequately explored the possible risks of most psychoactive drugs. The two most popular illicit drugs--marijuana and cocaine--have only recently become prevalent enough to stimulate research into the effects of their recreational use. For example, cocaine "freebasing," a method of administration developed in the past ten years, is thought to carry significantly more risk than sniffing, but reliable experimental and clinical data are lacking (Siegel, 1982). Similarly, the National Academy of Sciences' Institute of Medicine (1982), responding to a request to assess the risks of marijuana use, found existing studies inadequate to resolve most issues and called for more research into the biological and behavioral consequences of current marijuana use patterns.

We presently lack basic information about several important issues: (1) the extent of functional impairment caused by various doses and frequencies of administration; (2) the risks of short-term or intermittent use vs. chronic use; (3) the probability of becoming dependent given various use patterns; and (4) the ease or difficulty of discontinuing drug administration once dependence has been established.

Research into these issues should receive a higher priority than it now gets. Although such effort will not directly contribute to controlling drug use, a better understanding of the risks would help to set program priorities among drugs. And, in the long term, any successful program to reduce drug use will depend on public perceptions of risk. Those perceptions, we believe, are most likely to be influenced by credible scientific data.

Overall Priorities

Our results suggest a need for a somewhat different balance in national priorities on the control of drug use. At least as expressed in the federal budget, those priorities favor the traditional enforcement-plus-treatment approach. Within that framework, the relative emphasis given to law enforcement and treatment has varied (more emphasis on treatment in the 1970s, less in the 1980s), but together they have received the lion's share of the money and attention.

Through all of this, prevention seems to have been neglected. In Fiscal Year 1983, for example, the National Institute on Drug Abuse spent $5.9 million for prevention efforts.[2] That was less than 10 percent of NIDA's budget, and it was an even smaller fraction of total federal expenditures for all drug abuse programs (Drug Abuse Policy Office, 1982). Perhaps those priorities were appropriate in the past, but today the scientific evidence is, if anything, in favor of prevention approaches over the others. It seems, therefore, that prevention should receive greater credence in the future, and that a higher priority should be placed on developing and testing prevention methods that may ultimately reduce the demand for drugs. This strategy may take some time to produce visible effects, and it will require substantial

---

[2]The prevention total is expected to rise to $7 million in 1984 (NIDA, personal communication), but it will still represent a small proportion of the agency's direct expenditures. In addition, the federal block grants to states for alcohol, drug abuse, and mental health contain a provision requiring that 20 percent of substance abuse funds be set aside for prevention activity; however, since the prevention category is defined to include early intervention, it seems likely that much less than 20 percent goes into primary prevention.

168

investments, but in the end we believe that it has the best chance to counter adolescent drug use.

REFERENCES

Abelson, R. et al. (eds), *Theories of Cognitive Consistency: A Sourcebook,* Rand McNally, Chicago, 1968.

Addiction Research Foundation, *Report of an ARF/WHO Scientific Meeting on Adverse Health and Behavioral Consequences of Cannabis Use,* Addiction Research Foundation, Toronto, 1981.

Advisory Council on the Misuse of Drugs, *Report of the Expert Group on the Effects of Cannabis Use,* U.K. Home Office, London, 1982.

Ajzen, I., and M. Fishbein, "Attitudinal and Normative Variables as Predictors of Specific Behaviors," *J. Personality and Social Psychol.,* 27:41–57, 1973.

Altschuler, A., J. Carl, and B. W. Jackson, *State of the Art: Occasional Paper 1: Does Alcohol and Drug Abuse Education Work?,* National Data Base and Program Support Project, University of Massachusetts, Amherst, 1981.

Amini, F., and S. Salasnek, "Adolescent Drug Abuse: Search for a Treatment Model," *Comprehensive Psychiatry,* 16:379–389, 1975.

Amini, F., S. Salasnek, and E. L. Burke, "Adolescent Drug Abuse: Etiological and Treatment Considerations," *Adolescence,* 11:281–299, 1976.

Andrews, K. H., and D. B. Kandel, "Attitude and Behavior: A Specification of the Contingent Consistency Hypothesis," *Am. Sociol. Rev.,* 44:298–310, 1979.

Anker, A. L., and T. J. Crowley, "Use of Contingency Contracts in Specialty Clinics for Cocaine Abuse," in L. S. Harris (ed.), *Problems of Drug Dependence, 1981,* Proceedings of the 43rd Annual Scientific Meeting of the Committee on Problems of Drug Dependence, Research Monograph 41, National Institute on Drug Abuse, Rockville, Maryland, 1982.

Arkin, R. M., et al., "The Minnesota Smoking Prevention Program: A Seventh Grade Health Curriculum Supplement," *J. of School Health,* 51:611–616, 1981.

Bachman, J. G., L. D. Johnston, and P. M. O'Malley, *Monitoring the Future,* Vols. 1–6, Institute for Social Research, University of Michigan, Ann Arbor, 1981.

Baither, R. C., "Family Therapy with Adolescent Drug Abusers: A Review," *J. Drug Ed.,* 8:337–343, 1978.

Ball, J. C., et al., "Lifetime Criminality of Heroin Addicts in the United States," *J. Drug Issues,* 12:225–239, 1982.

Bandura, A., *Social Learning Theory,* Prentice-Hall, Englewood Cliffs, New Jersey, 1977.

Bennett, G., "Youthful Substance Abuse," in G. Bennett, C. Vourakis, and D. S. Woolf (eds.), *Substance Abuse: Pharmacologic, Developmental, and Clinical Perspectives,* John Wiley and Sons, New York, 1983.

Berman, P., and M. W. McLaughlin, *Federal Programs Supporting Educational Change:* Vol. VIII, *Implementing and Sustaining Innovations,* The Rand Corporation, Santa Monica, Calif., R-1589/8-HEW, 1978.

Beschner, G. M., and A. S. Friedman, *Youth Drug Abuse,* Lexington Books, Lexington, Mass., 1979.

Blasinsky, M., and G. K. Russell (eds.), *Urine Testing for Marijuana Use: Implications for a Variety of Settings,* American Council on Marijuana and Other Psychoactive Drugs, Inc., New York, 1981.

Blum, R., E. Blum, and E. Garfield, *Drug Education: Results and Recommendations,* Lexington Books, Lexington, Mass., 1976.

Blum, R., and L. Richards, "Youthful Drug Use," in R. I. DuPont et al. (eds.), *Handbook on Drug Abuse,* National Institute on Drug Abuse, Rockville, Maryland, 1979.

Blum, R., et al., "Drug Education: Further Results and Recommendations," *J. of Drug Issues,* 8:379–426, 1978.

Blumstein, A., "Prison: Population, Capacity and Alternatives," in J. Q. Wilson (ed.), *Crime and Public Policy,* Institute for Contemporary Studies Press, San Francisco, 1983.

Bond, D. J., "An Analysis of Valuation Strategies in Social Science Education Materials," Ed.B. dissertation, University of California, Berkeley, 1971.

Botvin, G., and A. Eng, "A Comprehensive School-Based Smoking Prevention Program," *J. School Health,* 50:209–213, 1980.

——, "The Efficacy of a Multicomponent Peer-Leadership Approach to the Prevention of Cigarette Smoking," *Preventive Med.,* 11:199–211, 1982.

——, *Life Skill Training and Smoking Prevention: A One Year Follow-Up,* presented at American Public Health Association meeting, Los Angeles, November 1981.

Botvin, G., A. Eng, and C. L. Williams, "Preventing the Onset of Cigarette Smoking through Life Skills Training," *Preventive Med.,* 9:135–143, 1980.

Botvin, G., N. Renick, and E. Baker, "The Effects of Scheduling Format and Booster Sessions on a Broad-Spectrum Psychosocial Approach to Smoking Prevention," *J. Behavioral Med.,* in press.

Bourne, P., L. Hunt, and J. Vogt, *A Study of Heroin Use in the State of Wyoming*, Foundation for International Resources, Washington, D.C., 1975.

Branca, M. D., J. F. d'Augelli, and K. L. Evans, *Development of a Decision-Making Skills Education Program, Study 1*, Addictions Prevention Laboratory, Pennsylvania State University, State College, Pennsylvania, 1975.

Bray, R. M., et al., *Client Characteristics, Behaviors, and Intreatment Outcomes: 1979 TOPS Admission Cohort*, Report RTI/1500/04/04F, Research Triangle Institute, Research Triangle Park, North Carolina, 1981.

Brecher, E. M., *Licit and Illicit Drugs*, Little, Brown and Company, Boston, 1972.

Brill, L., *The Clinical Treatment of Substance Abusers*, Free Press, New York, 1981.

Brill, N. W., and R. L. Christie, "Marihuana Use and Psychosocial Adaptation," *Arch. of Gen. Psychiat.* 31:713–719, 1974.

Britt, D. W., and E. Q. Campbell, "Assessing the Linkage of Norms, Environments, and Deviance," *Social Forces*, 56:532–550, 1977.

Brook, J. S., I. F. Lukoff, and M. Whiteman, "Correlates of Adolescent Marihuana Use as Related to Age, Sex, and Ethnicity," *Yale J. Biol. Med.*, 50:383–390, 1977a.

——, "Peer, Family, and Personality Domains as Related to Adolescents' Drug Behavior," *Psychol. Reports*, 41:1095–1102, 1977b.

——, "Family Socialization and Adolescent Personality and Their Association with Adolescent Use of Marihuana," *J. Genetic Psychol.*, 133:261–271, 1978.

——, "Initiation into Adolescent Marihuana Use," *J. Genetic Psychol.*, 37:133–142, 1980.

Brunswick, A. F., "Black Youth and Drug Use Behavior," in G. Beschner and A. Friedman (eds.), *Youth Drug Abuse*, Lexington Books, Lexington, Mass., 1979.

——, *Predicting Drug Use by Harlem Youth: A Feasibility Study*, Final report to the National Institute on Drug Abuse, Columbia University, New York, 1976.

Bry, B., "Research Design in Drug Abuse Prevention: Review and Recommendations," *Intern. J. Addictions*, 13:1157–1168, 1978.

Bukoski, W. J., *A Review of Drug Abuse Prevention Research*, National Institute on Drug Abuse, Rockville, Maryland, 1981.

Cadogan, D. A., "Marital Group Therapy in the Treatment of Alcoholism," *Quart. J. Studies on Alcohol*, 34:1187–1194, 1973.

Califano, J., *The 1982 Report on Drug Abuse and Alcoholism: A Report to Hugh L. Carey, Governor, State of New York*, Albany, New York, 1982.

Carde, M. D., "An Interpersonal Perception Study of Twenty Alcoholic Families," Ph.D. dissertation, University of Southern California, Los Angeles, 1977.

Carlson, K., et al., *Unreported Taxable Income from Selected Illegal Activities*, Abt Associates Inc., Cambridge, Mass., 1983.

Carney, R. E., *An Evaluation of the Effect of a Values-Oriented Drug Abuse Education Program Using the Risk Taking Attitude Questionnaire*, Coronado Unified School District, Coronado, California, 1971.

——, *An Evaluation of the Tempe, Arizona 1970–71 Drug Abuse Prevention Education Program Using the RTAQ and B-VI: Final Report*, Tempe School District, Tempe, Arizona, 1972.

——, *An Evaluation of the Effects of a Program to Enhance Responsible Behavior (Especially Drug Abuse Prevention) in Grades 4 through 6 in Representative Schools in Five Orange County, California, School Districts: 1973–75*, California School of Professional Psychology, Santa Ana, California, 1975.

Chaiken, J. M., and M. R. Chaiken, *Varieties of Criminal Behavior*, The Rand Corporation, Santa Monica, Calif., R-2814-NIJ, August 1982.

Chasanoff, E., and C. Schrader, "A Behaviorally-Oriented Activities Therapy Program for Adolescents," *Adolescence*, 14:569–577, 1979.

Chassin, L., et al., "Predicting Adolescents' Intentions to Smoke Cigarettes," *J. Health and Social Behavior*, 22:445–455, 1981a.

——, "Self-Images and Cigarette Smoking in Adolescents," *Personality and Social Psychol. Bull.*, 7:670–676, 1981b.

Chitwood, D. D., K. S. Wells, and B. R. Russe, "Medical and Treatment Definitions of Drug Use: The Case of the Adolescent User," *Adolescence*, 64:817–830, 1981.

Clayton, R. R., "The Family and Federal Drug Abuse Policies Programs: Toward Making the Invisible Family Visible," *J. Marriage and the Family*, 41:637–647, 1979.

Coleman, S. B., *The Use of Family Therapy in Drug Abuse Treatment: A National Survey*, Services Research Report, National Institute on Drug Abuse, Rockville, Maryland, 1977.

——, "Sib Group Therapy: A Prevention Program for Siblings from Drug-Addicted Families," *Intern. J. Addictions*, 13:115–127, 1978.

Coombs, R. H., "Back on the Streets: Therapeutic Communities' Impact Upon Drug Users," *Am. J. Drug and Alcohol Abuse*, 8:185–201, 1981.

Cooper, J. R. (ed.), *Sedative-Hypnotic Drugs: Risks and Benefits*, National Institute on Drug Abuse, Rockville, Maryland, 1977.

Coupey, S. M., and S. K. Schonberg, "Evaluation and Management of Drug Problems in Adolescents," *Pediatric Ann.*, 11:653–658, 1982.

Cox, T. C., et al., *Drugs and Drug Abuse: A Reference Text,* Addiction Research Foundation, Toronto, 1983.

Craddock, S. G., et al., *Summary and Implications: Client Characteristics, Behaviors and Intreatment Outcomes: 1980 TOPS Admission Cohort,* Research Triangle Institute, Research Triangle Park, North Carolina, 1982.

Cross, H. J., and R. R. Kleinbessilink, "Psychological Perspectives on Drugs and Youth," in J. F. Adams (ed.) *Understanding Adolescents,* Allyn and Bacon, Boston, 1980.

Curtis, B., and D. Simpson, "Differences in Background and Drug Use History Among Three Types of Drug Users Entering Drug Therapy Programs," *J. Drug Ed.,* 4:369–376, 1977.

D'Augelli, J. F., *Brief Report: Initial Evaluation of a Televised Effective Education Program as a Primary Prevention Strategy,* Addictions Prevention Laboratory, Pennsylvania State University, State College, Pennsylvania, 1975.

D'Augelli, J. F., J. D. Swisher, and K. L. Evans, *Initial Assessment of the Manchester Plan: An Affective Drug Abuse Curriculum,* Addictions Prevention Laboratory, Pennsylvania State University, State College, Pennsylvania, 1975.

Davidson, S. T., G. D. Mellinger, and D. I. Manheimer, "Changing Patterns of Drug Use Among University Males," *Addictive Diseases,* 3:215–233, 1977.

Davis, B. L., "The PCP Epidemic: A Critical Review," *Intern. J. Addictions,* 17:1137–1155, 1982.

DeAngelis, G. G., and E. Goldstein, "Treatment of Adolescent Phencyclidine (PCP) Abusers," *Am. J. Drug and Alcohol Abuse,* 5:399–414, 1978.

DeLeon, G., H. K. Wexler, and N. Jainchill, "The Therapeutic Community: Success and Improvement Rates 5 Years After Treatment," *Intern. J. Addictions,* 17:703–747, 1982.

Demaree, R., R. Hudiburg, and B. Fletcher, *Estimates of the Prevalence of Heroin Use Nationwide and in 24 Metropolitan Areas,* Texas Christian University, Fort Worth, Texas, 1980.

Dembo, R., "Substance Abuse Prevention Programming and Research: A Partnership in Need of Improvement," *J. Drug Ed.,* 9:189–208, 1979.

——, "Critical Issues and Experiences in Drug Treatment and Prevention Evaluation," *Intern. J. Addictions,* 16:1399–1414, 1981.

Dembo, R., et al., "Neighborhood Relationships and Drug Involvement Among Inner City Junior High School Youths: Implications for Drug Education," *J. Drug Ed.,* 8:235–252, 1978.

——, "Ethnicity and Drug Use Among Urban Junior High School Youths," *Intern. J. Addictions,* 14:557–568, 1979.

Dembo, R., J. Schneidler, and W. Burgos, "Life-Style and Drug Involvement Among Youths in an Inner City Junior High School," *Intern. J. Addictions,* 15:171–188, 1980.

Derthick, M., *New Towns In-Town,* The Urban Institute, Washington, D.C., 1972.

DiPalma, J. R., "Cocaine Abuse and Toxicity," *Am. Family Physician,* 24:236–238. 1981.

Domestic Council Drug Abuse Task Force, *White Paper on Drug Abuse,* The White House, Washington, D.C., 1975.

Drug Abuse Council, *The Facts About "Drug Abuse,"* Free Press, New York, 1980.

Drug Abuse Policy Office, *Federal Strategy for Prevention of Drug Abuse and Drug Trafficking, 1982,* The White House, Washington, D.C., 1982.

Dunnette, M. D., and N. G. Peterson, *Causes and Consequences of Adolescent Drug Experiences: A Progress Report and Research Perspective,* Personnel Decisions Research Institute, Minneapolis, 1977.

DuQuesne, T., and J. Reeves, *A Handbook of Psychoactive Medicines,* Quartet Books, London, 1982.

Durell, Jack, "Statement of the Deputy Director, National Institute on Drug Abuse," *Hearing before the U.S. Senate Subcommittee on Juvenile Justice, Committee on the Judiciary: Juveniles and Dangerous Drugs,* January 28, 1982, U.S. Government Printing Office, Washington, D.C., 1982.

Einstein, S., "Understanding Drug User Treatment Evaluation: Some Unresolved Issues," *Intern. J. Addictions,* 16:381–400, 1981.

——, "Treating the Drug User: Built-in Conceptual Problems," *Intern. J. Addictions,* 18(5):iii-vii, 1983.

Einstein, S., et al., "The Training of Teachers for Drug Abuse Education Programs: Preliminary Considerations," *J. Drug Ed.,* 1:323–345, 1971.

Elinson, J., and D. N. Nurco, *Operational Definitions in Socio-Behavioral Drug Use Research, 1975,* Research Monograph Series 2, National Institute on Drug Abuse, U.S. Government Printing Office, Washington, D.C., 1975.

Ellickson, P. L., et al., *Implementing New Ideas in Criminal Justice,* The Rand Corporation, Santa Monica, Calif., R-2929-NIJ, 1983.

Ellis, B. G. (ed.), *Drug Abuse from the Family Perspective,* National Institute on Drug Abuse, Rockville, Maryland, 1980.

Epstein, E. J., *Agency of Fear*, G. P. Putnam, New York, 1977.

Evans, R. I., W. B. Hansen, and M. B. Mittlemark, "Increasing the Validity of Self-Reports of Behavior in a Smoking in Children Investigation," *J. Applied Psychol.*, 62:521–523, 1977.

Evans, R. I., et al., "Deterring the Onset of Smoking in Children: Knowledge of Immediate Physiological Effects and Coping with Peer Pressure, Media Pressure and Parent Modelling," *J. Appl. Social Psychol.*, 8:126–135, 1978.

——, "Current Psychological, Social, and Educational Programs in Control and Prevention of Smoking: A Critical Methodological Review," in A. Gotto and R. Paoletti (eds.), *Atherosclerosis Reviews*, Vol. 6, Raven Press, New York, 1979.

——, "Social Modelling Films to Deter Smoking in Adolescents: Results of a Three Year Field Investigation," *J. Appl. Psychol.*, 66:339–414, 1981.

Ewing, J. A., V. Long, and G. G. Wenzel, "Concurrent Group Psychotherapy of Alcoholic Patients and their Wives," *Intern. J. Group Psychotherapy*, 11:329–338, 1961.

Farley, E. C., Y. Santo, and D. W. Speck, "Multiple Drug-Abuse Patterns of Youths in Treatment," in G. M. Beschner and A. S. Friedman (eds.), *Youth Drug Abuse*, Lexington Books, Lexington, Mass., 1979.

Federal Bureau of Investigation, *Uniform Crime Reports*, Washington, D.C. (various dates).

Ferguson, P., T. Lennox, and D. J. Lettieri (eds.), *Drugs and Family/Peer Influence: Family and Peer Influences on Adolescent Drug Use*, Research Issues Vol. 4, National Institute on Drug Abuse, Rockville, Maryland, 1974.

Fishbein, M., "Introduction: The Prediction of Behaviors from Attitudinal Variables," in C. D. Mortensen and K. K. Sereno (eds.), *Advances in Communication Research*, Harper and Row, New York, 1973.

Fishburne, P., H. Abelson, and I. Cisin, *National Survey on Drug Abuse: Main Findings, 1979*, National Institute on Drug Abuse, Rockville, Maryland, 1980.

Flanagan, T., and M. McLeod, *Sourcebook of Criminal Justice Statistics: 1982*, Bureau of Justice Statistics, U.S. Department of Justice, Washington, D.C., 1983.

Flay, B., et al., "Cigarette Smoking: Why Young People Do It and Ways of Preventing It," in P. Firestone and P. McGrath (eds.), *Pediatric Behavioral Medicine*, Springer-Verlag, New York, 1983.

Galchus, D., and K. Galchus, "Drug Use: Some Comparisons of Black and White College Students," *Drug Forum*, 6:65–76, 1977–1978.

General Accounting Office [GAO], *Action Needed to Improve Management and Effectiveness of Drug Abuse Treatment,* Report HRD-80–32, Washington, D.C., 1980a.

——, *Heroin Statistics Can Be Made More Reliable,* Report GGD-80–84, Washington, D.C., 1980b.

——, *Federal Drug Interdiction Efforts Need Strong Central Oversight,* Report GGD-83–52, Washington, D.C., 1983.

Gerald, M. C., *Pharmacology: An Introduction to Drugs,* Prentice-Hall, Englewood Cliffs, New Jersey, 1981.

Gerbasi, K. F., "Drug Education and Evaluation: An Application of Social Psychological Commitment Theory and an Examination of the Values Clarification Hypothesis," Ph.D. dissertation, University of Rochester, Rochester, N.Y., 1976.

Gersick, K. E., et al., "Personality and Sociodemographic Factors in Adolescent Drug Use," in D. J. Lettieri and J. P. Ludford (eds.), *Drug Abuse and the American Adolescent,* Research Monograph 38, National Institute on Drug Abuse, Rockville, Maryland, 1981.

Gibbs, J. T., "Psychosocial Factors Related to Substance Abuse Among Delinquent Females: Implications for Prevention and Treatment," *Am. J. Orthopsychiatry,* 52:261–271, 1982.

Ginsberg, I. J., and J. R. Greenley, "Competing Theories of Marihuana Use: A Longitudinal Study," *J. Health and Social Behavior,* 19:22–34, 1978.

Glynn, T. J. (ed.), *Drugs and the Family,* Research Issues Vol. 29, National Institute on Drug Abuse, Rockville, Maryland, 1981.

Goldstein, J. W., and J. T. Sappington, "Personality Characteristics of Students Who Became Heavy Drug Users: An MMPI Study of an Avant-Garde," *Am. J. Drug and Alcohol Abuse,* 4:401–402, 1977.

Goldstein, P., "Getting Over: Economic Alternatives to Predatory Crime Among Street Drug Users," in James Inciardi (ed.), *The Drugs-Crime Connection,* Sage Publications, Beverly Hills, California, 1981.

Goodstadt, M. S., "Myths and Methodology in Drug Education: A Critical Review of the Research Evidence," in M. S. Goodstadt (ed.), *Research on Methods and Programs of Drug Education,* Addiction Research Foundation, Toronto, 1974.

Goodstadt, M. S., "Alcohol and Drug Education: Models and Outcomes," *Health Education Monographs,* 6:263–279, 1978.

——, "Planning and Evaluation of Alcohol Education Programmes," *J. Alcohol and Drug Ed.,* 26:1–10, 1981.

Gorsuch, R. L., and M. C. Butler, "Initial Drug Abuse: A Review of Predisposing Social Psychological Factors," *Psychol. Bull.,* 83:120–137, 1976.

Gotestam, K. G., and L. Melin, "A Behavioral Approach to Drug Abuse," *Drug and Alcohol Dependence*, 5:5–25, 1980.

Gottesfeld, M. L., P. Caroff, and F. Lieberman, "Treatment of Adolescent Drug Abusers," *Psychoanalytic Rev.*, 59:527–538, 1973.

Gottheil, E., et al., "An Outpatient Drug Program for Adolescent Students: Preliminary Evaluation," *Am. J. Drug and Alcohol Abuse*, 4:31–41, 1977.

Gottschalk, L. A., et al., "The Laguna Beach Experiment as a Community Approach to Family Counseling for Drug Abuse Problems in Youth," *Comprehensive Psychiatry*, 11:226–234, 1970.

Greene, B. T., "Concurrent and Sequential Use of Drugs and Alcohol: Patterns, Characteristics of Users, and Implications for Treatment," *Am. J. Drug and Alcohol Abuse*, 6:447–462, 1979.

Gritz, E. R., and A. Brunswick, "Psychosocial and Behavioral Aspects of Smoking in Women: Initiation," in *The Health Consequences of Smoking for Women: A Report of the Surgeon General*, U.S. Public Health Service, Washington, D.C., 1980.

Guess, L. L., and B. S. Tuchfeld, *Manual for Drug Abuse Treatment Program Self-Evaluation, Supplement 1: DARP Tables*, Publication No. (ADM) 77–450, Department of Health, Education, and Welfare, Rockville, Maryland, 1977.

Gulas, I., and F. W. King, "On the Question of Pre-Existing Personality Differences Between Users and Nonusers of Drugs," *J. Psychol.*, 92:65–69, 1976.

Gurman, A. S., and D. P. Kniskern, "Research on Marital and Family Therapy: Progress, Perspective, and Prospect" in S. L. Garfield and A. E. Bergin (eds.), *Handbook of Psychotherapy and Behavior Change: An Empirical Analysis*, 2d ed., John Wiley and Sons, New York, 1978.

Hahn, J., and K. P. King, "Client and Environmental Correlates of Patient Attrition from an Inpatient Alcoholism Treatment Center," *J. Drug Ed.*, 23:75–86, 1982.

Hansen, W. B., C. A. Johnson, and L. M. Collins, "Cigarette Smoking Onset Among High School Students," Paper presented at the 91st Annual Convention of the American Psychological Association, August, 1983.

Hanson, D. J., "Drug Education: Does It Work?" in F. R. Scarpitti and S. K. Datesman (eds.), *Drugs and the Youth Culture*, Sage Publications, Beverly Hills, California, 1980.

Harbin, H. T., and H. M. Maziar, "The Families of Drug Abusers: A Literature Review," *Family Process*, 14:411–431, 1975.

Harris, L. S. (ed.), *Problems of Drug Dependence 1981: Proceedings of the 43rd Annual Scientific Meeting*, Research Monograph 41, National Institute on Drug Abuse, Rockville, Maryland, 1982.

Hartmann, D., "A Study of Drug-Taking Adolescents," *Psychoanalytic Study of the Child*, 24:384–398, 1969.

Hedberg, A. G., and L. Campbell III, "A Comparison of Four Behavioral Treatments of Alcoholism," *J. Behavior Therapy and Experimental Psychiatry*, 5:251–256, 1974.

Heilig, S. M., J. Diller, and F. L. Nelson, "A Study of 44 PCP-related Deaths," *Intern. J. Addictions*, 17:1175–1184, 1982.

Hendin, H., et al., *Adolescent Marijuana Abusers and their Families*, Research Monograph 40, National Institute on Drug Abuse, Rockville, Maryland, 1981.

Hendricks, W. J., "Use of Multifamily Counseling Groups in Treatment of Male Narcotic Addicts," *Intern. J. Group Psychotherapy*, 21:84–90, 1971.

Henry, G. M., "Treatment and Rehabilitation of Narcotic Addiction" in R. J. Gibbins et al. (eds.), *Research Advances in Alcohol and Drug Problems*, Vol. 1, John Wiley and Sons, New York, 1974.

Hoffman, L., *Foundations of Family Therapy*, Basic Books, New York, 1981.

Holland, S., *Evaluating Community-based Treatment Programs: A Model for Strengthening Inferences About Effectiveness*, Gateway Foundation, Chicago, 1981.

Holland, S., and A. Griffin, *Adolescent and Adult Drug Treatment Clients: Patterns and Consequences of Use*, Gateway Foundation, Chicago, 1983.

Hovland, C. I., I. L. Janis, and H. H. Kelley, *Communication and Persuasion*, Yale University Press, New Haven, 1953.

Huba, G. J., and P. M. Bentler, "The Role of Peer and Adult Models for Drug Taking at Different Stages in Adolescence," *J. Youth and Adolescence*, 9:449–465, 1980.

Huba, G. J., J. A. Wingard, and P. M. Bentler, "Beginning Adolescent Drug Use and Peer and Adult Interaction Patterns," *J. Consulting and Clin. Psychol.*, 47:265–276, 1979.

——, "A Longitudinal Analysis of the Role of Peer Support, Adult Models, and Peer Subcultures in Beginning Adolescent Substance Use," *Multivariate Behavioral Research*, 15:259–279, 1980a.

——, "Framework for an Interactive Theory of Drug Use," in D. J. Lettieri, M. Sayers, and H. W. Pearson (eds.), *Theories on Drug Abuse*, National Institute on Drug Abuse, Rockville, Maryland, 1980b.

——, "Intentions to Use Drugs Among Adolescents: A Longitudinal Analysis," *Intern. J. Addictions*, 16:331–339, 1981.

Huberty, D. J., "Treating the Adolescent Drug Abuser: A Family Affair," *Contemporary Drug Problems*, 4:179–194, 1975.

Hunt, L., and C. Chambers, *The Heroin Epidemics: A Study of Heroin Use in the U.S., 1965–1975*, Spectrum Publications, New York, 1976.

Hurd, P. D., et al., "Prevention of Cigarette Smoking in Seventh Grade Students," *J. Behavioral Med.*, 3:15–28, 1980.

Igra, A., and R. H. Moos, *Drinking Among College Students: A Longitudinal Study*, Social Ecology Laboratory Report, Department of Psychiatry, Stanford University, Stanford, Calif., 1977.

——, "Alcohol Use Among College Students: Some Competing Hypotheses," *J. Youth and Adolescence*, 8:393–406, 1979.

Iiyama, P., S. Nishi, and B. Johnson, *Drug Use and Abuse Among U.S. Minorities*, Praeger Publications, New York, 1976.

Inciardi, J., "Heroin Use and Street Crime," *Crime and Delinquency*, 25:335–346, 1979.

Institute of Medicine, National Academy of Sciences, *Marijuana and Health*, National Academy Press, Washington, D.C., 1982.

International Narcotics Control Board, *Report for 1982*, United Nations, New York, 1982.

Iverson, D. C., et al., "The Effects of an Education Intervention Program for Juvenile Drug Abusers and their Parents," *J. Drug Ed.*, 8:101–111, 1978.

Jackson, J., and R. J. Calsyn, "Evaluation of a Self-Development Approach to Drug Education: Some Mixed Results," *J. Drug Ed.*, 7:15–26, 1977.

Jaffe, J. H., "Drug Addiction and Drug Abuse," in A. G. Gilman, L. S. Goodman, and A. Gilman (eds.), *The Pharmacological Basis of Therapeutics*, 6th ed., Macmillan, New York, 1980.

Jaffe, J. H., and W. R. Martin, "Opioid Analgesics and Antagonists," in A. G. Gilman, L. S. Goodman, and A. Gilman (eds.), *The Pharmacological Basis of Therapeutics*, 6th ed., Macmillan, New York, 1980.

Janeczek, C. L., *Marijuana: Time for a Closer Look*, Healthstar, Columbus, Ohio, 1980.

Janvier, R., D. Guthman, and R. Catalano, *Reports of the National Juvenile Justice Assessment Centers: An Assessment of Evaluations of Drug Abuse Prevention Programs*, U.S. Department of Justice, Office of Juvenile Justice and Delinquency Prevention, U.S. Government Printing Office, Washington, D.C., 1980.

Jessop, D. J., D. B. Kandel, and I. F. Lukoff, *Comparative Analyses of Stages of Drug Use in Different Ethnic Groups*, Center Cross-Study 1, Bedford-Stuyvesant and New York State Center for Socio-Cultural Research on Drug Use, Columbia University, New York, 1976.

Jessor, R., "Predicting Time of Onset of Marijuana Use: A Developmental Study of High School Youth," *J. Consulting and Clin. Psychol.*, 44:125–134, 1976.

Jessor, R., and S. L. Jessor, "Problem Drinking in Youth: Personality, Social, and Behavioral Antecedents and Correlates," in M. E. Chafetz (ed.), *Psychological and Social Factors in Drinking: Proceedings of the Second Annual Alcoholism Conference*, National Institute on Alcohol Abuse and Alcoholism, U.S. Government Printing Office, Washington, D.C., 1973.

——, "Adolescent Development and the Onset of Drinking: A Longitudinal Study," *J. Studies on Alcohol*, 36:27–51, 1975.

——, "The Transition from Virginity to Nonvirginity Among Youth: A Social-Psychological Study Over Time," *Developmental* Psychology, 11:473–484, 1975.

——, *Problem Behavior and Psychosocial Development: A Longitudinal Study of Youth*, Academic Press, New York, 1977.

——, "Theory Testing in Longitudinal Research on Marihuana Use," in D. B. Kandel (ed.), *Longitudinal Research on Drug Use: Empirical Findings and Methodological Issues*, Hemisphere-Wiley, Washington, D.C., 1978.

Jessor, R., J. A. Chase, and J. E. Donovan, "Psychosocial Correlates of Marijuana Use and Problem Drinking in a National Sample of Adolescents," *Am. J. Public Health*, 70:604–613, 1980.

Jessor, R., M. I. Collins, and S. L. Jessor, "On Becoming a Drinker: Social-Psychological Aspects of an Adolescent Transition," in F. A. Seixas (ed.), *Nature and Nurture in Alcoholism*, Annals of the New York Academy of Sciences, Vol. 197, Scholastic Reprints, New York, 1972.

Jessor, R., J. Donovan, and K. Widmer, *Psychosocial Factors in Adolescent Alcohol and Drug Use: The 1978 National Sample Study, and the 1974–78 Panel Study*, Institute of Behavioral Sciences, University of Colorado, Boulder, 1980.

Jessor, R., S. L. Jessor, and J. A. Finney, "A Social Psychology of Marijuana Use: Longitudinal Studies of High School and College Youth," *J. Personality and Social Psychol.*, 26:1–15, 1973.

Johnson, C. A., "Untested and Erroneous Assumptions Underlying Anti-Smoking Programs," in T. C. Coates, A. Peterson, and C. Perry (eds.), *Promotion of Health in Youth*, Academic Press, New York, in press.

Johnston, L. D., *Drugs and American Youth*, Institute for Social Research, University of Michigan, Ann Arbor, 1973.

Johnston, L. D., J. G. Bachman, and P. M. O'Malley, *Student Drug Use, Attitudes, and Beliefs: National Trends, 1975–1982*, National Institute on Drug Abuse, Rockville, Maryland, 1982.

Johnston, L. D., P. M. O'Malley, and L. Eveland, "Drugs and Delinquency: A Search for Causal Connections," in D. B. Kandel (ed.), *Longitudinal Research on Drug Use: Empirical Findings and Methodological Issues,* Hemisphere-Wiley, Washington, D.C., 1978.

Kalant, O. J., *The Amphetamines: Toxicity and Addiction,* Charles C. Thomas, Springfield, Ill., 1966.

Kandel, D. B., "Adolescent Marihuana Use: Role of Parents and Peers," *Science,* 181:1067–1070, 1973.

——, "Some Comments on the Relationship of Selected Criteria Variables to Adolescent Illicit Drug Use," in D. J. Lettieri (ed.), *Predicting Adolescent Drug Abuse: A Review of Issues, Methods and Correlates,* National Institute on Drug Abuse, U.S. Government Printing Office, Washington, D.C., 1975a.

——, "Stages in Adolescent Involvement in Drug Use," *Science,* 190:912–914, 1975b.

—— (ed.), *Longitudinal Research on Drug Use: Empirical Findings and Methodological Issues,* Hemisphere-Wiley, Washington, D.C., 1978a.

——, "Convergences in Prospective Longitudinal Surveys of Drug Use in Normal Populations," in D. B. Kandel (ed.), *Longitudinal Research on Drug Use: Empirical Findings and Methodological Issues,* Hemisphere-Wiley, Washington, D.C., 1978b.

——, "Homophily, Selection, and Socialization in Adolescent Friendships," *Am. J. Sociol.,* 84:427–436, 1978c.

——, "Drug and Drinking Behavior Among Youth," *Annual Rev. Sociology,* 6:235–285, 1980.

——, "Drug Use by Youth: An Overview," in D. J. Lettieri and J. P. Ludford (eds.), *Drug Abuse and the American Adolescent,* Research Monograph 38, National Institute on Drug Abuse, Rockville, Maryland, 1981.

Kandel, D. B., and I. Adler, "Socialization into Marijuana Use Among French Adolescents: A Cross-Cultural Comparison with the United States," *J. Health and Social Behavior,* 23:295–309, 1982.

Kandel, D. B., I. Adler, and M. Sudit, "The Epidemiology of Adolescent Drug Use in France and Israel," *Am. J. Public Health,* 71:256–265, 1981.

Kandel, D. B., and R. Faust, "Sequence and Stages in Patterns of Adolescent Drug Use," *Arch. Gen. Psychiat.,* 32:923–932, 1975.

Kandel, D. B., R. C. Kessler, and R. Z. Margulies, "Antecedents of Adolescent Initiation into Stages of Drug Use: A Developmental Analysis," in D. B. Kandel (ed.), *Longitudinal Research on Drug Use: Empirical Findings and Methodological Issues,* Hemisphere-Wiley, Washington D.C., 1978.

Kandel, D. B., et al., "Adolescent Involvement in Legal and Illegal Drug Use: A Multiple Classification Analysis," *Social Forces,* 55:438–458, 1976.

Kaplan, H. B., "Social Class, Self-Derogation and Deviant Response," *Social Psychiatry,* 13:19–28, 1978a.

——, "Deviant Behavior and Self-Enhancement in Adolescence," *J. Youth and Adolescence,* 7:253–277, 1978b.

——, *Deviant Behavior in Defense of Self,* Academic Press, New York, 1980.

Kaufman, E. , "Myth and Reality in the Family Patterns and Treatment of Substance Abusers," *Am. J. Drug and Alcohol Abuse,* 7:257–279, 1980.

——, "The Relationship of Alcoholism and Alcohol Abuse to the Abuse of other Drugs," *Am. J. Drug and Alcohol Abuse,* 9:1–18, 1982.

Kaufman, E., and P. Kaufmann (eds.), *Family Therapy of Drug and Alcohol Abuse,* Gardner Press, New York, 1979a.

——, "From a Psychodynamic Orientation to a Structural Family Therapy Approach in the Treatment of Drug Dependency," in E. Kaufman and P. Kaufmann (eds.), *Family Therapy of Drug and Alcohol Abuse,* Gardner Press, New York, 1979b.

——, "Multiple Family Therapy with Drug Abusers," in E. Kaufman and P. Kaufmann (eds.), *Family Therapy of Drug and Alcohol Abuse,* Gardner Press, New York, 1979c.

Kaufmann, P., "Family Therapy with Adolescent Substance Abusers," in E. Kaufman and P. Kaufmann (eds.), *Family Therapy of Drug and Alcohol Abuse,* Gardner Press, New York, 1979.

Kellam, S. G., M. E. Ensminger, and M. B. Simon, "Mental Health in First Grade and Teenage Drug, Alcohol and Cigarette Use," *J. Drug and Alcohol Dependence,* 5:273–304, 1980.

Kellam, S., M. Simon, and M. E. Ensminger, "Antecedents in First Grade of Teenage Drug Use and Psychological Well-Being. A Ten Year Community-Wide Prospective Study," in D. Ricks and B. Dohrenwend (eds.), *Origins of Psychopathology: Research and Public Policy,* Cambridge University Press, Cambridge, England, 1983.

Kenward, K., and J. Rissover, "A Family Systems Approach to the Treatment and Prevention of Alcoholism: A Review," *Family Therapy,* 7:97–106, 1980.

Kessler, R. C., D. B. Kandel, and R. Z. Margulies, "Predicting Changing Involvement in Marihuana Use: A Panel Analysis," Paper presented at the meetings of the Society for the Study of Social Problems, New York City, August 1976.

Khantzian, E. J., and G. J. McKenna, "Acute Toxic and Withdrawal Reactions Associated with Drug Use and Abuse," *Ann. Internal Med.,* 90:361–372, 1979.

Kiesler, C. A., B. E. Collins, and N. Miller, *Attitude Change: A Critical Analysis of Theoretical Approaches,* John Wiley and Sons, New York, 1969.

Kim, S., "An Evaluation of Ombudsman Primary Prevention Program on Student Drug Abuse," *J. Drug Ed.,* 11:27–36, 1981.

———, "Feeder Area Approach: An Impact Evaluation of a Prevention Project on Student Drug Abuse," *Intern. J. Addictions,* 17:305–313, 1982.

Kinder, B. N., "Attitudes Toward Alcohol and Drug Abuse. II. Experimental Data, Mass Media Research, and Methodological Considerations," *Intern. J. Addictions,* 6:1035–1054, 1975.

Kinder, B., N. Pape, and S. Walfish, "Drug and Alcohol Education Programs: A Review of Outcome Studies," *Intern. J. Addictions,* 7:1035–1054, 1980.

Klagsbrun, M., and D. I. Davis, "Substance Abuse and the Family," *Family Process,* 16:149–164, 1977.

Kleber, H. D., and F. Slobetz, "Outpatient Drug-free Treatment," in R. I. Dupont et al. (eds.), *Handbook on Drug Abuse,* National Institute on Drug Abuse, Rockville, Maryland, 1979.

Kohn, P., "Motivation for Drug and Alcohol Use," in M. S. Goodstadt (ed.), *Research on Methods and Programs of Drug Education,* Addiction Research Foundation, Toronto, 1974.

Lavenhar, M. A., "Methodology in Youth Drug-Abuse Research," in G. M. Beschner and A. S. Friedman (eds), *Youth Drug Abuse,* Lexington Books, Lexington, Mass., 1979.

Leclair, S. W., and R. R. Roberts, "Characteristics of Drug Abuse Counselors and their Relationship to Treatment Process and Outcome," *J. Drug Education,* 10:153–158, 1980.

Lettieri, D. J., M. Sayers, and H. W. Pearson (eds.), *Theories on Drug Abuse: Selected Contemporary Perspectives,* Research Monograph 30, National Institute on Drug Abuse, Rockville, Maryland, 1980.

Levenberg, S. B., "Outpatient Treatment of the Problem Drinker: Strategies for Attaining Abstinence," *Gen. Hosp. Psychiat.,* 3:219–225, 1981.

Leventhal, H., and P. Cleary, "The Smoking Problem: A Review of the Research and Theory in Behavioral Risk Modification," *Psychol. Bull.,* 88:370–405, 1980.

Levitt, E. E., and J. A. Edwards, "Multivariate Study of Correlative Factors in Youthful Cigarette Smoking," *Developmental Psychology,* 2:5–11, 1970.

Liebert, R. M., and N. S. Schwartzberg, "Effects of Mass Media," *Ann. Rev. Psychol.*, 28:141–173, 1977.

Lipton, D. S., and M. J. Maranda, "Detoxification from Heroin Dependency: An Overview of Method and Effectiveness," *Advances in Alcohol and Substance Abuse*, 2:31–55, 1982.

Los Angeles Times, "Students Held in Drug Sweep at 9 Schools," December 15, 1983.

Lucas, W. L., S. E. Grupp, and R. L. Schmitt, "Predicting Who Will Turn On: A Four-Year Follow-up," *Intern. J. Addictions,* 10:305–326, 1975.

Luepker, R. V., et al., "Saliva Thiocyanate: A Chemical Indicator of Smoking in Adolescents," *Am. J. Public Health,* 77:12, 1981.

———, "Prevention of Cigarette Smoking: Three Year Follow-Up of an Education Program for Youth," *J. Behavioral Med.,* 6:53–62, 1983.

Lukoff, I. F., and J. S. Brook, "A Sociocultural Exploration of Reported Heroin Use," in C. Winick (ed.), *Sociological Aspects of Drug Dependence,* CRC, Cleveland, 1974.

Macdonald, D. I., and M. Newton, "The Clinical Syndrome of Adolescent Drug Abuse," *Advances in Pediatrics,* 28:1–25, 1981.

Mackenzie, R. G., "The Adolescent as a Drug Abuser: A Paradigm for Intervention," *Pediatric Annals,* 11:659–668, 1982.

Malvin, J. H., et al., *Evaluation of Two Alternatives Programs for Junior High School Students,* Pacific Institute for Research and Evaluation, Napa, Calif., 1982.

Manatt, M., *Parents, Peers, and Pot,* Publication No. (ADM) 80–812, Department of Health and Human Services, Rockville, Maryland, 1979.

Mann, M. J., "A Model for Client/Program Evaluation in a Comprehensive Out-patient Drug Abuse Treatment Program," *J. Drug Ed.,* 7:305–310, 1977.

Manpower Demonstration Research Corporation, *Summary and Findings of the National Supported Work Demonstration,* Ballinger, Cambridge, Mass., 1980.

Margulies, R. Z., R. C. Kessler, and D. B. Kandel, "A Longitudinal Study of Onset of Drinking Among High School Students," *Quart. J. Studies on Alcohol,* 38:897–912, 1977.

Marquis, K. H., et al., *Response Errors in Sensitive Topic Surveys,* The Rand Corporation, Santa Monica, Calif., R-2710/2-HHS, April 1981.

Mayer, W., "Statement of the Administrator, Alcohol, Drug Abuse, and Mental Health Administration, *Hearing before the U.S. Senate Subcommittee on Alcoholism and Drug Abuse: Oversight on Prevention Activities of the National Institute on Alcohol Abuse and Alcoholism and the National Institute on Drug Abuse,* February 24, 1982, U.S. Government Printing Office, Washington, D.C., 1982.

McAlister, A., C. Perry, and N. Maccoby, "Adolescent Smoking: Onset and Prevention," *Pediatrics,* 63:650–658, 1979.

McAlister, A., et al., "Pilot Study of Smoking, Alcohol, and Drug Abuse Prevention," *Am. J. Public Health,* 70:719–721, 1980.

McBride, R., "Business as Usual: Heroin Distribution in the United States," *J. Drug Issues,* 13:147–166, 1983.

McClelland, P. P., "The Pulaski Project: An Innovative Drug Abuse Prevention Program in an Urban High School," *J. Psychedelic Drugs,* 7:355–362, 1975.

McGlothlin, W. H., "Marijuana Use, Distribution and Control," in Richard Blum (ed.), *Drug Dealers—Taking Action,* Jossey-Bass, San Francisco, 1973.

McGlothlin, W. H., M. D. Anglin, and B. D. Wilson, "A Followup of Admissions to the California Civil Addict Program," *Am. J. Drug and Alcohol Abuse,* 4:179–199, 1977.

McGuire, W. J., "The Nature of Attitudes and Attitude Change," in G. Lindzey and E. Aronson (eds.), *The Handbook of Social Psychology,* 2d ed., Addison-Wesley, Reading, Mass., 1969.

McLellan, A. T., et al., "Is Drug Abuse Treatment Effective?" in L. S. Harris (ed.), *Problems of Drug Dependence 1981: Proceedings of the 43rd Annual Scientific Meeting,* Research Monograph 41, National Institute on Drug Abuse, Rockville, Maryland, 1982.

Mellinger, G. D., et al., "The Amotivational Syndrome and the College Student," *Ann. New York Acad. Sci.,* 282:37–55, 1976.

Miami Herald, "U.S. Drug Enforcement: The Billion-Dollar Bust," October 11 and October 18, 1981.

Milby, J. B., et al., "Effectiveness of Urine Surveillance as an Adjunct to Outpatient Psychotherapy for Drug Abusers," *Intern. J. Addictions,* 15:993–1001, 1980.

Miller, D., "The Medical and Psychological Therapy of Adolescent Drug Abuse," *Intern. J. Child Psychotherapy,* 2:309–330, 1973.

Miller, J. D., et al., *National Survey on Drug Abuse: Main Findings 1982,* National Institute on Drug Abuse, U.S. Government Printing Office, Washington, D.C., 1983.

Mitchell, T., and R. Bell, *Drug Interdiction Operations by the Coast Guard,* Center for Naval Analysis, Alexandria, Virginia, 1980.

Mittlemark, M. B., et al., "Adolescent Smoking Transition States Over Two Years," presented as part of the symposium "Becoming a Cigarette Smoker: The Acquisition Process in Youth," American Psychological Association, Anaheim, Calif., August 1983.

Monopolis, S., and C. Savage, "Substance Abuse, Public Health, and the Pediatrician," *Paediatrician*, 11:176–196, 1982.

Moore, M., *Buy and Bust*, D. C. Heath, Lexington, Mass., 1977.

——, "Limiting Supplies of Drugs to Illicit Markets," *J. Drug Issues*, 9:291–308, 1979.

Moore, M., and D. Gerstein (eds.), *Alcohol and Public Policy: Beyond the Shadow of Prohibition*, National Academy Press, Washington, D.C., 1981.

Moos, R., B. Moos, and J. Kulik, "Behavioral and Self-Concept Antecedents and Correlates of College-Student Drinking Patterns," *Intern. J. Addictions*, 12:603–615, 1977.

Musgrave, R., *The Theory of Public Finance*, McGraw-Hill, New York, 1959.

Musto, D., *The American Disease*, Yale University Press, New Haven, 1973.

National Academy of Sciences, Committee on Substance Abuse and Habitual Behavior, *An Analysis of Marijuana Policy*, National Academy Press, Washington, D.C., 1982.

National Commission on Marihuana and Drug Abuse, *Marihuana: A Signal of Misunderstanding*, Appendix Vols. 1 and 2, U.S. Government Printing Office, Washington, D.C., 1972.

——, *Drug Use in America: Problem in Perspective*, U.S. Government Printing Office, Washington, D.C., 1973.

National Institute on Alcohol Abuse and Alcoholism, *Fourth Special Report to the U.S. Congress on Alcohol and Health*, Department of Health and Human Services, U.S. Government Printing Office, Washington, D.C., 1981.

National Institute on Drug Abuse [NIDA], *An Evaluation of the Teen Challenge Treatment Program*, Services Research Report, Publication No. (ADM) 81–425, Department of Health and Human Services, Rockville, Maryland, 1977.

National Institute on Drug Abuse, *Evaluation of Drug Abuse Treatments Based on First Year Followup*, Research Monograph Series, Publication No. (ADM) 78–701, Department of Health, Education, and Welfare, Rockville, Maryland, 1978.

National Institute on Drug Abuse, *A Comparison of Mental Health Treatment Center and Drug Abuse Treatment Center Approaches to Nonopiate Drug Abuse*, Services Research Report, Publication No. (ADM) 79–879, Department of Health, Education, and Welfare, Rockville, Maryland, 1979.

National Institute on Drug Abuse, *Effectiveness of Drug Abuse Treatment Programs*, Treatment Research Report, Publication No. (ADM) 81–1143, Department of Health and Human Services, Rockville, Maryland, 1981a.

National Institute on Drug Abuse, *Final Report, September 1980: Data from the National Drug and Alcoholism Treatment Utilization Survey,* Statistical Series F, Number 9, Publication No. (ADM) 81-1172, Department of Health and Human Services, Rockville, Maryland, 1981b.

National Institute on Drug Abuse, *Proceedings for the National Institute on Drug Abuse Prevention Research Symposium, October 26-27, 1981,* National Institute on Drug Abuse, Rockville, Maryland, 1981c.

National Institute on Drug Abuse, *Statistical Perspectives on Drug Abuse Treatment,* Publication No. (ADM) 81-1107, Department of Health and Human Services, Rockville, Maryland, 1981d.

National Institute on Drug Abuse, *Annual Data 1981: Data from the Client Oriented Data Acquisition Process (CODAP),* Statistical Series E, No. 25, Publication No. (ADM) 82-1223, Department of Health and Human Services, Rockville, Maryland, 1982a.

National Institute on Drug Abuse, *Annual Data 1981: Data from the Drug Abuse Warning Network (DAWN),* Statistical Series I, No. 1, Publication No. (ADM) 82-1227, Department of Health and Human Services, Rockville, Maryland, 1982b.

National Institute on Drug Abuse, *Data from the Drug Abuse Warning Network, Quarterly Report, July-September 1982,* Statistical Series G, No. 12, Department of Health and Human Services, Rockville, Maryland, 1983a.

National Institute on Drug Abuse, *Population Projections Based on the National Survey on Drug Abuse 1982,* Publication No. (ADM) 83-1303, Department of Health and Human Services, Rockville, Maryland, 1983b.

National Institute on Drug Abuse, *Main Findings for Drug Abuse Treatment Units, September 1982: Data from the National Drug and Alcoholism Treatment Utilization Survey,* Series F, Number 10, Publication No. (ADM) 83-1284, Department of Health and Human Services, Rockville, Maryland, 1983c.

National Narcotics Intelligence Consumers Committee [NNICC], "The Supply of Drugs to the U.S. Illicit Market From Foreign and Domestic Sources in 1980 (With Projections Through 1984)," *Narcotics Intelligence Estimate* series, Drug Enforcement Administration, Washington, D.C., 1982.

——, *An Evaluation of the Methodologies for Producing Narcotics Intelligence Estimates,* Drug Enforcement Administration, Washington, D.C., 1983a.

——, "The Supply of Drugs to the U.S. Illicit Market From Foreign and Domestic Sources in 1981 (With Projections Through 1985),"

Narcotics Intelligence Estimate series, Drug Enforcement Administration, Washington, D.C., 1983b.

New York Times, "Dropout Rate in Schools Rose Sharply Since `72," January 6, 1984, p. 10.

Newman, I. M., G. L. Martin, and R. Weppner, "A Conceptual Model for Developing Prevention Programs," *Intern. J. Addictions,* 17:493–504, 1982.

Nicholi, A. M., Jr., "The Nontherapeutic Use of Psychoactive Drugs," *New England J. Med.,* 308:925–933, 1983.

Noone, R. J., and R. L. Reddig, "Case Studies in the Family Treatment of Drug Abuse," *Family Process,* 15:325–332, 1976.

Nowlis, H. H., "Coordination of Prevention Programs for Children and Youth," *Public Health Reports,* 96:34–37, 1981.

O'Malley, P. M., *Correlates and Consequences of Illicit Drug Use,* Ph.D. dissertation, University of Michigan, Ann Arbor, 1975.

O'Rourke, T. W., and D. B. Stone, "A Prospective Study of Trends in Youth Smoking," *J. Drug Ed.,* 1:49–61, 1971.

Ogborne, A. C., "Patient Characteristics as Predictors of Treatment Outcomes for Alcohol and Drug Abusers," in Y. Israel et al. (eds.), *Research Advances in Alcohol and Drug Problems,* Vol. 4, Plenum Press, New York, 1978.

Olson, D. H., C. S. Russell, and D. H. Sprenkle, "Marital and Family Therapy: A Decade Review," *J. Marriage and the Family,* 42:973–994, 1980.

Orive, R. and H. B. Gerard, "Personality, Attitudinal, and Social Correlates of Drug Use," *Intern. J. Addictions,* 15:869–881, 1980.

Ostram, T. M., "The Relationship Between the Affective, Behavioral, and Cognitive Components of Attitude," *J. Experimental and Social Psychol.,* 5:12–30, 1969.

Padilla, E., et al., "Inhalant, Marijuana, and Alcohol Abuse among Barrio Children and Adolescents," *Intern. J. Addictions,* 14:945–964, 1979.

Paton, S., and D. B. Kandel, "Psychological Factors and Adolescent Illicit Drug Use: Ethnicity and Sex Differences," *Adolescence,* in press.

Paton, S., R. Kessler, and D. Kandel, "Depressive Mood and Adolescent Illegal Drug Use: A Longitudinal Analysis," *J. Genetics and Psychol.,* 131:267–289, 1977.

Pekkanen, J. R., "Drug-Law Enforcement Efforts," in Drug Abuse Council (ed.), *The Facts About "Drug Abuse,9* Free Press, New York, 1980.

Peng, S. S., "High School Dropouts: Descriptive Information from High School and Beyond," *National Center for Education*

189

Statistics Bulletin, Publication No. 83–221b, U.S. Department of
Education, Washington, D.C., November 1983.

Penning, M., and G. E. Barnes, "Adolescent Marijuana Use: A
Review," *Intern. J. Addictions,* 17:749–791, 1982.

Perry, C. L., et al., "Modifying Smoking Behavior of Teenagers: A
School-Based Intervention," *Am. J. Public Health,* 70:722–725,
1980.

Person, P., R. Retka, and J. A. Woodward, *Toward a Heroin Problem
Index,* National Institute on Drug Abuse, Rockville, Maryland,
1976.

———, *A Method for Estimating Heroin Use Prevalence,* National Institute on Drug Abuse, Rockville, Maryland, 1977.

Poklis, A., "Drug Abuse Trends in Metropolitan St. Louis," in *Assessment of Drug Abuse in North America and Europe,1981,* National
Institute on Drug Abuse, Rockville, Maryland, 1981.

Polakow, R. L., and R. M. Doctor, "Treatment of Marijuana and Barbiturate Dependency by Contingency Contracting," *J. Behavior
Therapy and Experimental Psychiat.,* 4:375–377, 1973.

Post, R. M., "Cocaine Psychoses: A Continuum Model," *Am. J.
Psychiat.,* 132:225–231, 1975.

Pressman, J., and A. Wildavsky, *Implementation,* University of California Press, Berkeley, 1973.

Radosevich, M., et al. "The Sociology of Adolescent Drug and Drinking Behavior: A Review of the State of the Field" (Part 1), *Deviant Behavior,* 1:15–35, 1979.

———, "The Sociology of Adolescent Drug and Drinking Behavior: A
Review of the State of the Field" (Part 2), *Deviant Behavior,*
2:145–169, 1980.

Raymond, J. S., and S. Hurwitz, "Client Preference-Treatment
Congruence as a Facilitator of Length of Stay: Supporting an Old
Truism," *Intern. J. Addictions,* 16:431–441, 1981.

Reilly, D. M., "Family Factors in the Etiology and Treatment of
Youthful Drug Abuse," *Family Therapy,* 11:149–171, 1975.

———, "Drug Abusing Families: Intrafamilial Dynamics and Brief Tri-
phasic Treatment," in E. Kaufman and P. Kaufmann (eds.), *Family Therapy of Drug and Alcohol Abuse,* Gardner Press, New York,
1979.

Resnik, H. S., and J. Gibbs, "Types of Peer Program Approaches," in
Adolescent Peer Pressure, National Institute of Drug Abuse, U.S.
Government Printing Office, Washington, D.C., 1981.

Reuter, Peter, *Disorganized Crime: The Economics of the Visible Hand,*
MIT Press, Cambridge, Mass., 1983.

190

———, "The (Continued) Vitality of Mythical Numbers," *The Public Interest,* in press.

Richards, L. G., "The Epidemiology of Youthful Drug Use," in F. R. Scarpitti and S. K. Datesman (eds.), *Drugs and the Youth Culture,* Sage Publications, Beverly Hills, Calif., 1980.

Robins, L. N., *A Follow-up of Vietnam Drug Users,* Interim Final Report, Special Action Office Monograph, Series A, No. 1, U.S. Government Printing Office, Washington, D.C., 1973.

———, *The Vietnam Drug User Returns,* Final Report, Special Action Office Monograph, Series A. No. 2, U.S. Government Printing Office, Washington, D.C., 1974.

Rokeach, M., "Attitude Change and Behavioral Change," *Public Opinion Quart.,* 30:529–550, 1966.

———, *The Nature of Human Values,* Free Press, New York, 1973.

Rokeach, M., and P. Kliejunas, "Behavior as a Function of Attitude-Toward-Object and Attitude-Toward-Situation," *J. Personality and Social Psychol.,* 22:194–201, 1972.

Room, R., "Survey vs. Sales Data for the U.S.," *Drinking and Drug Practices Surveyor,* 3:15–16, 1971.

Rooney, J. F., and T. L. Wright, "An Extension of Jessor and Jessor's Problem Behavior Theory from Marijuana to Cigarette Use," *Intern. J. Addictions,* 17:1273–1287, 1982.

Russell, M. A., "Changes in Cigarette Price and Consumption by Men in Britain, 1946–71: A Preliminary Analysis," *Brit. J. Preventive and Social Med.,* 27:1–7, 1973.

Ryan, W. P., "A School-Based Drug Abuse Prevention Program: An Evaluation," *J. Drug Ed.,* 4:61–67, 1974.

Sabbag, R., *Snowblind: A Brief Career in the Cocaine Trade,* Avon Books, New York, 1976.

Sadava, S. W., "Initiation to Cannabis Use: A Longitudinal Social Psychological Study of College Freshmen," *Canad. J. Behavioral Sci.,* 5:371–384, 1973a.

———, "Patterns of College Student Drug Use: A Longitudinal Social Learning Study," *Psychol. Reports,* 33:75–86, 1973b.

———, "Research Approaches in Illicit Drug Use: A Critical Review," *Genetic Psychol. Monographs,* 91:3–59, 1975.

Sadava, S. W., and R. Forsyth, "Drug Use and a Social Psychology of Change," *Brit. J. Addiction,* 71:335–342, 1976.

———, "Turning On, Turning Off and Relapse: Social Psychological Determinants of Status Change in Cannabis Use," *Intern. J. Addictions,* 12:509–528, 1977a.

———, "Person-Environment Interaction and College Student Drug Use: A Multivariate Longitudinal Study," *Genetic Psychol. Monographs,* 96:211–245, 1977b.

Sansone, J., "Retention Patterns in a Therapeutic Community for the Treatment of Drug Abuse," *Intern. J. Addictions,* 15:711–736, 1980.

Santo, Y., "The Methodology of the National Youth Polydrug Study (NYPS)," in G. M. Beschner and A. S. Friedman (eds.), *Youth Drug Abuse,* Lexington Books, Lexington, Mass., 1979.

Scarpitti, F. R., and S. K. Datesman (eds.), *Drugs and the Youth Culture,* Vol. 4, Annual Reviews of Drug and Alcohol Abuse, Sage Publications, Beverly Hills, 1980.

Schaeffer, G. A., et al., *A Process and Outcome Evaluation of Magic Circle: Second Year Results,* National Institute on Drug Abuse, Rockville, Maryland, 1981.

——, *The Effects of Three Years of Participation in a Primary Prevention Program on Elementary School Students,* National Institute on Drug Abuse, Rockville, Maryland, 1982a.

——, *The Effects of Jigsaw on 5th and 6th Grade Students at Follow-Up,* National Institute on Drug Abuse, Rockville, Maryland, 1982b.

Schaps, E., et al., "A Review of 127 Drug Abuse Prevention Program Evaluations," *J. Drug Issues,* 11:17–43, 1981.

Schlegel, R., C. A. Crawford, and M. D. Sanborn, "Correspondence and Mediational Properties of the Fishbein Model: An Application to Adolescent Alcohol Use," *J. Experimental Psychol.,* 13:421–430, 1977.

Secretary of Health and Human Services, *Third Annual Report: Drug Abuse Prevention, Treatment, and Rehabilitation in Fiscal Year 1980,* Department of Health and Human Services, Washington, D.C., 1980.

——, *Marijuana and Health: Ninth Annual Report,* National Institute on Drug Abuse, Rockville, Maryland, 1982.

Sells, S. B., "Treatment Effectiveness," in R. I. DuPont et al. (eds.), *Handbook on Drug Abuse,* National Institute on Drug Abuse, Rockville, Maryland, 1979.

——, "Matching Clients to Treatments: Problems, Preliminary Results, and Remaining Tasks," in E. Gottheil, A. T. McLellan, and K. A. Druley (eds.), *Matching Patient Needs and Treatment Methods in Alcoholism and Drug Abuse,* Charles C. Thomas, Springfield, Illinois, 1981.

Sells, S. B., R. G. Demaree, and C. W. Hornick, *Comparing Effectiveness of Drug Abuse Treatment Modalities,* Publication No. (ADM) 81–1067, Department of Health and Human Services, Rockville, Maryland, 1980.

192

Severson, H., et al., "Oregon Research Institute's Smoking Prevention Program: Helping Students Resist Peer Pressure," *OSSC Bull.*, Vol. 25, No. 4, December 1981.

Sheffet, A. M., et al., "Assessment of Treatment Outcomes in a Drug Abuse Rehabilitation Network: Newark, New Jersey," *Am. J. Drug and Alcohol Abuse*, 7:141–173, 1980.

Sherman, S. J., et al., *Becoming a Cigarette Smoker: A Social-Psychological Perspective*, Paper presented at the symposium "Becoming a Cigarette Smoker: The Acquisition Process in Youth," at the 91st Annual Convention of the American Psychological Association, Anaheim, California, August, 1983.

Siegel, Ronald K., "Part I: History of Cocaine Smoking," *J. Psychoactive Drugs*, 14:277–300, 1982.

Silverman, L., and N. Spruill, "Urban Crime and the Price of Heroin," *J. Urban Econ.*, 4:80–103, 1977.

Simmons, R. G., F. Rosenberg, and M. Rosenberg, "Disturbance in the Self-Image at Adolescence," *Am. Sociol. Rev.*, 38:553–568, 1973.

Simon, C., and A. Witte, *Beating the System*, Auburn House, Boston, 1982.

Simpson, D. D., "Treatment for Drug Abuse. Follow-up Outcomes and Length of Time Spent," *Arch. Gen. Psychiat.*, 38:875–880, 1981.

Simpson, D. D., and S. B. Sells, *Evaluation of Drug Abuse Treatment Effectiveness: Summary of the DARP Follow-up Research*, Department of Health and Human Services, Publication No. (ADM) 82–1209, National Institute on Drug Abuse, Rockville, Maryland, 1982.

Simpson, D. D., et al., *DARP Data Book: Statistics on Characteristics of Drug Users in Treatment During 1969–1974*, Institute of Behavioral Research, Texas Christian University, Report 76–14, Fort Worth, 1976.

Sine, R., "The Comparative Effect of a Values Approach with a Factual Approach on the Drug Abuse and Smoking Behavior of College Students," *J. Am. College Health Assoc.*, 25:113–116, 1976.

Singh, B. K., et al., "A Descriptive Overview of Treatment Modalities in Federally Funded Drug Abuse Treatment Programs," *Intern. J. Addictions*, 17:977–1000, 1982.

Skinner, H. A., "The Drug Abuse Screening Test," *Addictive Behaviors*, 7:363–371, 1982.

Sloane, R. B., et al., *Psychotherapy Versus Behavior Therapy*, Harvard University Press, Cambridge, Mass., 1975.

Smith, D. E., et al., *Amphetamine Use, Misuse, and Abuse*, G. K. Hall & Co., Boston, 1979.

Smith, D., S. J. Levy, and D. E. Striar, "Treatment Services for Youthful Drug Users," in G. M. Beschner and A. S. Friedman (eds.), *Youth Drug Abuse*, Lexington Books, Lexington, Mass., 1979.

Smith, G. M., "Antecedents of Teenage Drug Use," paper presented at the meeting of the Eastern Psychological Association, Washington, D.C., May 1973, and at the 35th Meeting of the Committee on Problems of Drug Dependence, National Academy of Sciences, National Research Council, Chapel Hill, N.C., May 22, 1973.

Smith, G. M., and C. P. Fogg, *Teenage Drug Use: A Search for Causes and Consequences,* paper presented at the 82d Annual Convention of the American Psychological Association, New Orleans, September 1974a.

——, "Early Precursors of Teenage Drug Use," paper presented at the 36th Meeting of the Committee on Problems of Drug Dependence, National Academy of Sciences, National Research Council, Mexico City, 1974b.

——, "Psychological Predictors of Early Use, Late Use, and Non-Use of Marihuana Among Teenage Students," in D. B. Kandel (ed.), *Longitudinal Research on Drug Use: Empirical Findings and Methodological Issues,,* Hemisphere-Wiley, Washington, D.C., 1978.

——, "Psychological Antecedents of Teenage Drug Use," in R. G. Simmons (ed.), *Research in Community and Mental Health: An Annual Compilation of Research,* Vol. I, JAI Press, Greenwich, Conn., 1979.

Smith, M., and J. Thompson, "Employment, Youth and Violent Crime," in K. Feinberg (ed.), *Violent Crime in America*, National Policy Exchange, Washington, D.C., 1983.

Sobell, L. C., "Alcohol Treatment Outcome Evaluation: Contributions from Behavioral Research," in P. E. Nathan, G. A. Marlatt, and T. Loberg (eds.), *Alcoholism: New Directions in Behavioral Research and Treatment*, Plenum Press, New York, 1978.

Stanton, M. D., "Family Treatment Approaches to Drug Abuse Problems: A Review," *Family Process*, 18:251–280, 1979a.

——, "Drugs and the Family," *Marriage and Family Review*, 2:1–10, 1979b.

Stanton, M. D., T. C. Todd, and Associates, *The Family Therapy of Drug Abuse and Addiction,* Guilford Press, New York, 1982.

Steffenhagen, R. A., "Motivation for Drug and Alcohol Use: A Social Perspective," in M. Goodstadt (ed.), *Research on Methods and Programs of Drug Education,* Addiction Research Foundation, Toronto, 1974.

Stein, M. D., and J. K. Davis, *Therapies for Adolescents,* Jossey-Bass, San Francisco, 1982.

Steinglass, P., "Experimenting with Family Treatment Approaches to Alcoholism, 1950–1975: A Review," *Family Process,* 15:97–123, 1976.

———, "Family Therapy in Alcoholism," in B. Kissin and H. Begleiter (eds.), *The Biology of Alcoholism: Vol. V, Treatment and Rehabilitation of the Chronic Alcoholic,* Plenum Press, New York, 1977.

———, "An Experimental Treatment Program for Alcoholic Couples," *J. Studies on Alcohol,* 40:159–182, 1979.

Steinglass, P., D. I. Davis, and D. Berenson, "Observations of Conjointly Hospitalized 'Alcoholic Couples' During Sobriety and Intoxication: Implications for Theory and Therapy," *Family Process,* 16:1–16, 1977.

Stimmel, B., "Treatment for Substance Abuse: Myths Versus Realities," *Advances in Alcohol and Substance Abuse,* 2:1–6, 1982.

Strug, D., "The Foreign Politics of Cocaine," *J. Drug Issues,* 13:135–145, 1983.

Stuart, R. B., "Teaching Facts About Drugs: Pushing or Preventing?" *J. Ed. Psychol.,* 66:189–201, 1974.

Sugarman, B., "Drug Abuse Prevention: A Human Development Model for Defining the Problem and Devising Solutions," *Drug Forum,* 6:387–397, 1977–78.

Sumner, G., and G. Zellman, *Federal Programs Supporting Educational Change: Vol. VI, Implementing and Sustaining Title VII Bilingual Projects,* The Rand Corporation, Santa Monica, Calif., R-1589/6-HEW, January 1977.

Surgeon General, *Smoking and Health: A Report of the Surgeon General,* Department of Health, Education, and Welfare, U.S. Government Printing Office, Washington, D.C., 1979.

Swisher, J. D., "The Effectiveness of Drug Education: Conclusions Based on Experimental Evaluation," in M. Goodstadt (ed.), *Research on Methods and Programs of Drug Education,* Addiction Research Foundation, Toronto, 1974.

Swisher, J. D., and A. J. Piniuk, *An Evaluation of Keystone Central School District's Drug Education Program,* Pennsylvania Governors Justice Commission, Harrisburg, 1973.

Telch, M. J., et al., "Long-Term Follow-up of a Pilot Project on Smoking Prevention with Adolescents," *J. Behavioral Med.,* 5:1–8, 1982.

Tennant, F. S., Jr., S. C. Weaver, and C. E. Lewis, "Outcomes of Drug Education: Four Case Studies," *Pediatrics,* 52:246–251, 1973.

Thompson, E. L., "Smoking Education Programs, 1960–1976," *Am. J. Public Health,* 68:250–257, 1978.

Tims, F. M., *Assessing Treatment: The Conduct of Evaluation in Drug Abuse Treatment Programs,* Treatment Research Report,

Department of Health and Human Services, Publication No. (ADM) 82–1218, National Institute on Drug Abuse, Rockville, Maryland, 1982.

Trebach, A., *The Heroin Solution*, Yale University Press, New Haven, 1982.

Turner, C. E., "Statement of the Senior Policy Adviser for Drug Policy, Office of Policy Development" [White House], *Hearing before the U.S. Senate Subcommittee on Alcoholism and Drug Abuse: Oversight on Prevention Activities of the National Institute on Alcohol Abuse and Alcoholism and the National Institute on Drug Abuse*, February 24, 1982, U.S. Government Printing Office, Washington, D.C., 1982.

U.S. Department of State, Bureau of International Narcotics Matters, *Narcotics Profile Papers*, Washington, D.C., 1983 (mimeograph).

U.S. House of Representatives, Select Committee on Narcotics Abuse and Control, *Annual Report for the Year 1982 of the Select Committee on Narcotics Abuse and Control*, U.S. Government Printing Office, Washington, D.C., 1982.

U.S. House of Representatives, Subcommittee on the Departments of Commerce, Justice, and State, the Judiciary, and Related Agencies of the Committee on Appropriations, *Hearings*, 1978–1982.

U.S. Senate, Committee on Appropriations, *Hearings on Foreign Assistance and Related Programs: Appropriations, Fiscal Year 1978*, U.S. Government Printing Office, Washington, D.C., 1977.

U.S. Senate, *International Narcotics Trafficking*, Hearings before the Permanent Subcommittee on Investigations of the Committee on Government Affairs, U.S. Government Printing Office, Washington, D.C., 1981.

U.S. Senate, Subcommittee of Alcoholism and Drug Abuse, *Oversight on Prevention Activities of the National Institute on Alcohol Abuse and Alcoholism and the National Institute on Drug Abuse, 1982*, Hearings, February 24, 1982, U.S. Government Printing Office, Washington, D.C., 1982.

Unger, R. A., "The Treatment of Adolescent Alcoholism," *Social Casework*, 59:27–35, 1978.

Ungerleider, J. T., and A. Beigel, "Drug Abuse: Crisis in the Treatment Arena," *J. Drug Ed.*, 10:279–288, 1980.

Usher, M. L., J. Jay, and D. R. Glass, "Family Therapy as a Treatment Modality for Alcoholism," *J. Studies on Alcohol*, 43:927–938, 1982.

Vaglum, P., and I. Fossheim, "Differential Treatment of Young Abusers: A Quasi-experimental Study of a 'Therapeutic Community' in a Psychiatric Hospital," *J. Drug Issues*, 10:505–515, 1980.

Van Ryswyk, C., et al., "Effectiveness of Halfway House Placement for Alcohol and Drug Abusers," *Am. J. Drug and Alcohol Abuse,* 8:499–512, 1981.

Wall Street Journal, "High Flyers: Use of Cocaine Grows Among Top Traders in Financial Centers," September 12, 1983.

Wallack, L. M., "Mass Media Campaigns: The Odds Against Finding Behavior Change," *Health Ed. Quart.,* 8: 209–260, 1981.

Warner, K. E., "The Effects of the Anti-Smoking Campaign on Cigarette Consumption," *Am. J. Public Health,* 67:645–650, 1977.

———, "Possible Increases in the Underreporting of Cigarette Consumption," *J. Am. Statist. Assoc.,* 73:314–318, 1978.

———, "Clearing the Airwaves: The Cigarette Ad Ban Revisited," *Policy Analysis,* 5:435–450, 1979.

Wicker, A. W., "An Examination of the 'Other Variables' Explanation of Attitude-Behavior Inconsistency," *J. Personality and Social Psychol.,* 19:18–30, 1971.

Wieder, H., and E. H. Kaplan, "Drug Use in Adolescents," *Psychoanalytic Study of the Child,* 24:399–431, 1969.

Williams, A. F., L. M. DiCicco, and H. Unterberger, "Philosophy and Evaluation of an Alcohol Education Program," *Quart. J. Studies on Alcohol,* 29:685–702, 1968.

Williams, S. G., and J. Baron, "Effects of Short-term Intensive Hospital Psychotherapy on Youthful Drug Abusers: I. Preliminary MMPI Data," *Psychological Reports,* 50:79–82, 1982.

Wingard, J. A., G. J. Huba, and P. M. Bentler, "The Relationship of Personality Structure to Patterns of Adolescent Substance Use," *Multivariate Behavioral Research,* 14:131–143, 1979.

Wolf, B. M., "The Struggling Adolescent: A Social-phenomenological Study of Adolescent Substance Abuse," *J. Alcohol and Drug Ed.,* 26:51–61, 1981.

Wong-McCarthy, W. J., and E. R. Gritz, "Preventing Regular Teenage Cigarette Smoking," *Pediatric Annals,* 11:683–689, 1982.

World Health Organization, *Report of the Second Session of the Alcoholism Subcommittee, Expert Committee on Mental Health,* Technical Report Series No. 48, Geneva, 1952.

———, *Expert Committee on Drug Dependence: Twentieth Report,* Technical Report No. 551, Geneva, 1974.

Young, L. A., et al., *Recreational Drugs,* Macmillan, New York, 1977.

Ziegler-Driscoll, G., "Family Research Study at Eagleville Hospital and Rehabilitation Center," *Family Process,* 16:175–189, 1977.

Ziegler-Driscoll, G., "The Similarities in Families of Drug Dependents and Alcoholics," in E. Kaufman and P. Kaufmann (eds.), *Family Therapy of Drug and Alcohol Abuse,* Gardner Press, New York, 1979.